PATHS OF AFRICAN THEOLOGY

£3

PATHS OF AFRICAN THEOLOGY

Edited by
Rosino Gibellini

SCM PRESS

Translated from the Italian *Percorsi di teologia africana*
published by Editrice Queriniana, Brescia
Italian copyright © Editrice Queriniana 1994
English translation copyright © Orbis Books 1994

This edition published by arrangement with Orbis Books, Maryknoll

0 334 02568 0

First published in Britain 1994
by SCM Press Ltd
26-30 Tottenham Road, London N1 4BZ

Manufactured in the United States

CONTENTS

INTRODUCTION

AFRICAN THEOLOGIANS WONDER . . . AND MAKE SOME PROPOSALS

Rosino Gibellini

The evangelization of Africa dates from earliest Christian times. Only in our own era, however, has Christianity penetrated sub-Saharan or black Africa. With Europe on the threshold of the third millennium of Christian history, black Africa is only entering its second century of evangelization.

In ancient times, the major centers of the Christian presence in Africa were Alexandria, in Egypt, and Carthage, in Proconsular Africa (today's Tunisia). The church of Alexandria, according to a tradition whose historical accuracy cannot be verified, traces its foundation to the preaching of St. Mark the Evangelist. It boasted illustrious theologians such as Clement of Alexandria and Origen (second to third centuries) and patriarchs such as Athanasius and Cyril (fourth to fifth centuries). It was the church of Alexandria that, about the middle of the fourth century, officially brought Christianity to the Kingdom of Axum in Ethiopia. The Egyptian church and the Ethiopian church have preserved their ties to our very day, even in their profession of the monophysite christological faith. In Roman Africa, the Christian presence is documented from the end of the second century and produced writers, theologians, and bishops such as Tertullian (second and third centuries),

Translated from Italian by Robert R. Barr.

1

Cyprian (third century), and Augustine (fourth and fifth centuries), whose works belong to the very core of the great corpus of ancient Christian literature. Augustine testifies: "The gospel was received in all regions of [Mediterranean] Africa" (Ep. 43, chap. 7).

With the inception of the Arab conquest in the seventh century, the spread of Islam in North Africa began to sweep away Latin African Christianity. The process was not sudden, but gradual, and lasted from the seventh to the twelfth centuries. Effective resistance was mounted by Egyptian (Coptic) Christianity, which, together with Ethiopian Christianity, lives yet today, although these churches have not undertaken missionary endeavors elsewhere in Africa.

Christianity's disappearance from North Africa is one of Christian history's darkest enigmas. Historians adduce two series of causes. First of all, Latin African Christianity suffered from internal divisions originating with the typically African heresy of Donatism and with the Arianism introduced by the Vandals who finally penetrated the Roman Empire in the fifth and sixth centuries. Second, and most important, was the fact that the Christianity installed in Roman Africa was a Christianity of the Latin language exclusively. As Archbishop Teissier of Algiers writes today:

> The existence in ancient times of a translation of the Bible into Berber, or of a Berber liturgy, has never been able to be verified . . . Here is the basic difference between North Africa and the ancient East. In the East, Christianity was implanted betimes in the local languages (Syrian, Coptic, Ethiopian, Armenian, Greek). In some cases this meant actually bestowing on these languages a system of writing. In North Africa, Christianity retained an exclusively Latin expression.

Still, the puzzling question remains:

> How can a Christianity established in some seven hundred different dioceses, some of them so closely neighboring on Christian Europe, with all their rich doctrinal legacy thanks to Augustine and Cyprian, a Christianity steeped in the blood of martyrs, have simply and completely disappeared?[1]

As for the Christian mission in Africa, the Arab conquest and the spread of Islam in North Africa ultimately prevented it from reaching the rest of the continent.

Beginning in the seventh century, Islam, which controlled the lands of the Sudan and the routes of the Mediterranean, long closed the Black Continent off from the gospel. We must await the day the Atlantic Ocean becomes the new center of European civilization and point of departure for European expansion in the world, to see Christian missions once more make their appearance in African climes.[2]

With the age of the great oceanic and transoceanic voyages and the age of discovery beginning in the fifteenth century, a new period was under way. Now Christianity came to the lower continent. However, the Christian presence there was limited, at first, to the western coasts, and then to the eastern and western coasts, of tropical Africa. No genuine penetration to the interior of the vast African continent occurred. Indeed those immense territories remained all but unknown to Europeans until the exploratory voyages of the eighteenth and nineteenth centuries.

It was in the spirit of conquest that Europe now sent forth its missioners. We need only attend to the text of the bull of Nicholas V, *Romanus Pontifex*, addressed to King Alfonso V of Portugal and his son Henry the Navigator under date of January 8, 1454 (or 1455, according to another dating). Therein, the Portuguese sovereigns are granted the right of conquest of Guinea (which, for all practical purposes, covered a huge region, stretching from Mauritania to Angola) for the purpose of converting "souls" to the Catholic faith. The document expresses the hope that Portuguese expeditions might even reach the Ethiopians ("Indians," in the bull), upon whom it calls to honor the name of Christ by striking an alliance with the newcomers to do battle with the Saracens and the other enemies of the faith. The bull *Romanus Pontifex* had been preceded by another bull, the *Dum Diversas* of June 18, 1452, authorizing the conquest of Morocco and conferring upon the Portuguese sovereigns, at their request, papal authorization for the conquest of Africa's Atlantic coast.[3]

The conquest of the Atlantic coast and then one region of southeastern and eastern Africa after another along the route to the East Indies meant the beginning of the traffic in human beings, which the principal European powers plied for four centuries, from the first half of the fourteenth to the second half of the eighteenth, transporting black Africans to slavery in America. The major raids were perpetrated on the western and southwestern coasts of Africa (Senegal, Gulf of Guinea, the Congo, Angola). The process that led to the abolition of slavery began in France, with the French Revolution, to be completed in Brazil only in 1888. As for the concrete meaning that this phenomenon had for black persons, Polish historian of slavery M. Malowist makes the following evaluation, based on the most reliable scholarly studies:

> According to Curtin . . . by the time slavery was abolished, the forced emigration to America had involved nine to eleven million persons. Some contemporary scholars, among them Hopkins, reckon the number of victims of the slave trade to have surpassed eleven million. While smaller by half than the estimates proposed in the past, these figures nonetheless indicate that, over the course of four centuries, from the fourteenth to the eighteenth, Africa must have suffered gigantic human losses, with negative consequences for social and economic development.[4]

Until nearly the end of the seventeenth century, Africa remained, for Europe, little more than a coastline, and for that matter "a coastline not very representative of the interior."[5] But eighteenth- and nineteenth-century European exploration of the African interior not only opened the way "to Christianity and commerce"—the goal of the great missioner and explorer, the author of *Missionary Travels and Researches in South Africa,* David Livingstone—but also to the occupation and colonization of these enormous expanses. The latter process was officially sanctioned by the Berlin Congress of 1884-85, at which the European powers (Great Britain, France, Portugal, Belgium, and Germany, later to be joined by Italy and Spain) reached formal agreement on an out-and-out partition of Africa. At the outbreak of World War I in 1914, only two of the some sixty now independent African countries had achieved that status—"Liberia" (formerly known as the Pepper Coast), created in 1821 at the initiative of American philanthropists as a land of asylum for North American black slaves liberated and repatriated to Africa, and the ancient Christian Kingdom of Ethiopia, a member of the League of Nations, which Italy, in a barbarous and anachronistic act of aggression, invaded and subjected in 1935-36.

It was in the colonial context of the nineteenth century that the Christian mission in Africa started up once more. "The same vessels transported men of commerce, colony, and the cloth."[6] The success the endeavor met in black Africa was astonishing, especially by comparison with the missions of Asia. According to the 1980 censuses—with the process of decolonization complete—of the 456 million inhabitants of Africa, Christians numbered 203 million (or 41 percent), 56 million (12.4 percent) of these being Catholics.

But events that occurred since decolonization call for a reexamination of the situation.

Of African Christianity, two historians write:

A fact is a fact: Christianity in Africa was the "religion of the whites." (It is untrue that it had ceased to be such.) African Christians had never been given the opportunity to be genuinely "at home" in Christianity—a chance to live in it as in a house of their own, which they might remodel on an ongoing basis through the contributions of their particular talents. The reasons for this state of affairs are inscribed in history. How could a church that had swept in on the coattails of colonial conquerors fail to seem, for good and all, a foreign world? And how could its representatives, swelling with the importance of their mission, as well as, perhaps, of the lofty culture they thought themselves to represent, place any confidence in the creative initiative of communities that had to be taught everything?[7]

Africa's encounter with Christianity has also produced a kind of collision, which the decolonization process—beginning in black Africa with the independence of Ghana in 1957 and concluding, for all practical purposes, some twenty years later in the mid-1970s—has brought out in the open.

We have no intention of putting the work and accomplishments of the missionaries on trial. "It is thanks to these persons that the Word first resounded through the African savannas and forests, ringing over the boom of the cannons and the bawling of the caravan drivers, with their bloodshot eyes."[8] We only mean to take account of the fact that the Christian mission in the colonial era unfolded in the context of a "logic of empire" and an "Occidental absolute," which colonialism's aftermath is already busy dismantling. And the dismantling is a challenge to church and theology, as well.[9]

The dawn of black awareness and the African personality had already occurred, say authors, historians, and students of culture, in the colonial period—at the close of the past century and in the first decades of our own—with the development, in Anglophone Africa, of the *African personality* (E. W. Blyden, S. Williams) and in Francophone Africa, of the concept of *négritude,* "blackness" (L. Damas, Aimé Césaire, Léopold S. Senghor), not to mention the appearance of a *pan-African consciousness* in the black diaspora of the United States (W. E. B. Du Bois, Marcus Garvey) and the French Antilles (R. Maran, J. Price-Mars).[10] In the same vein, once more in testimony to an

African cultural renaissance, Belgian missioner Placide Tempels comes forward with his *Bantu Philosophy* (1945), documenting the existence of a specifically African "worldview" or "philosophy." And then there are works of other European missionaries and scholars such as Sundkler, Taylor, or Barrett.[11]

It is against this backdrop of an African cultural rebirth that the problem of an "African theology" arose in the 1950s and 1960s. It received its first formulation in 1956, in a "dossier" of contributions entitled *Des prêtres noirs s'interrogent* (*Some Black Priests Wonder* . . .), in which certain young black priests, amid the political and cultural process of decolonization, posed themselves some questions about the future of the church's mission in Africa. Now the process was under way that would lead to the demise of the "mission theology" of a *salus animarum* and a *plantatio ecclesiae*—the theology of the colonial era—to give place to the beginnings of a "theology of adaptation"— the theology of an "Africanized Christianity." Finally, today we witness the birth of a "critical African theology" that means to be the organized faith-reflection of an authentically African Christianity.[12]

If the title of the very first sketch of an African theology published in 1956 reads *Some Black Priests Wonder* . . . , then the present collection of studies might be called *African Theologians Wonder . . . and Make Some Proposals.* The proposals made here are composed in the key of inculturation and liberation, those twin foci of theological reflection in Africa in the second half of the twentieth century. Our volume gathers contributions from eleven African theologians most noted across the continent for their writings and activity. The studies here presented have been prepared expressly for this volume (even when based on previous work); their purpose is to supply an overview of the "trajectories" of African theology today.

Our series of contributions opens with a piece by Alphonse Ngindu Mushete (Zaire), a brief but documented historical panorama of the origins of African theology and the guidelines it adopts in its reflection. There follow six articles whose principal concern is with the problem of the relationship between evangelization and African culture. These studies are in the area of biblical theology (John S. Mbiti, Kenya), christology (Justin S. Ukpong, Nigeria; Charles Nyamiti, Tanzania/Kenya), liturgy (François Kabasele Lumbala, Zaire; Elochukwu E. Uzukwu, Nigeria), and spirituality (Patrick Augustin Kalilombe, Malawi).

The second part of the book begins with the essay by Cameroonese theologian Jean-Marc Éla, author of *Le cri de l'homme africain*, 1980 (*African Cry*, 1986), which may well be regarded as the most expressive document of an African theology of liberation. It includes four essays on the liberation problematic in the African context (Jean-Marc Éla, Cameroon; Engelbert Mveng, Cameroon; Mercy Amba Oduyoye, Ghana/Nigeria, for the African feminist theology of liberation; Simon Maimela, South Africa, for black theology of liberation).

Both outlooks are intended to be integrated into a Christianity that will be no longer imported or simply adapted, but authentically African, a Christianity lived and experienced against a horizon of Catholicity and ecumenicity amid the new concrete historical—cultural and social—dimensions of Africa.

I wish to thank these African theologians, whom I have met in theological meetings in Europe or Africa and who have accepted my invitation to collaborate in this volume, most especially Professor A. Ngindu Mushete, with whom I discussed the project in its early stages. In the bibliographical appendix, I have included a list of major texts in African theology, with an indication of their specific relevance and their historiographical and theoretical orientation.

Notes

1. Henri Teissier, "La scomparsa dell'antica Chiesa d'Africa," in *La Chiesa nell'Africa del Nord,* by various authors (Milan: Paoline; Cinisello Balsamo, 1991), pp. 40, 42.

2. Jean-Marc Éla, *African Cry,* trans. Robert R. Barr (Maryknoll, N.Y.: Orbis Books, 1986), pp. 10-11.

3. See C. M. de Witte, "Les Bulles pontificales et l'expansion portugaise au XVe siècle," *Revue d'Histoire Ecclésiastique* 48 (1953):683-718; 49 (1954):436-61; 51(1956):413-53, 809-36; 53 (1958):5-48, 443-71.

4. M. Malowist, *La schiavitù nel medioevo e nell'età moderna* (Naples and Rome: Edizioni Scientifiche Italiana, 1987), p. 89.

5. Roland Oliver and J. D. Fage, *A Short History of Africa;* in Italian, *Breve storia dell'Africa,* 4th ed., rev. (Turin: Einaudi, 1974), p. 140.

6. C. Alix, in *Les Églises chrétiennes et la Décolonisation,* ed. M. Merle (Paris: Armand Colin, 1967), p. 17.

7. Louis-Vincent Thomas and René Luneau, *La Terre africaine et ses religions* (Paris: Larousse, 1975), pp. 327-28.

8. O. Bimwenyi-Kweshi, *Discours théologique négro-africain* (Paris: Présence Africaine, 1981), p. 81.

9. See Meinrad Hebga, *Émancipation d'Églises sous tutelle: Essai sur l'ère post-missionnaire* (Paris: Présence Africaine, 1976); Fabien Eboussi Boulaga, *Christianity without Fetishes: An African Critique and Recapture of Christianity,* trans. Robert R. Barr (Maryknoll, N.Y.: Orbis Books, 1984); Achille Mbembe, *Afriques indociles: Christianisme, pouvoir et État en société postcoloniale* (Paris: Karthala, 1988).

10. See A. Irele, "Négritude et Personalité Africaine," in *Colloque sur la Négritude,* from the colloquium held at Dakar, Senegal, April 12-18, 1971 (Paris: Présence Africaine, 1972); Bimwenyi-Kweshi, *Discours théologique négro-africain,* pp. 190-262.

11. See John Parratt, *Theologiegeschichte der Dritten Welt: Afrika* (Munich: Kaiser, 1991), pp. 20-53.

12. See Rosino Gibellini, *La teologia del XX secolo* (Brescia: Queriniana, 1992), pp. 490-510.

1

AN OVERVIEW OF AFRICAN THEOLOGY

A. Ngindu Mushete

African theology is an immense topic. Similarly, African society and its present evolution are marked by a growing complexity. Any broad view of such a complex structure runs the risk of appearing superficial. The following exposition, therefore, makes no pretense about being definitive or totally up-to-date; rather, it treats a wide variety of materials that must, of necessity, be related to a given moment. Otherwise the labor of documentation could be extended indefinitely. Nor is there any pretense of being exhaustive. It is not my intention to do an inventory of African theology or award a merit badge to theological products of the last twenty years. Rather I want to describe the currents that seem to be prevalent today and will provide some sense of direction in the coming years.

The first part of this essay focuses on the context of the question and makes reference to the manner in which theologians and church people perceive the African reality and its religious ramifications. The second part seeks to present the principal currents of theology of Africa.

The Context: Perceiving the African Reality
and Its Religious Repercussions

It has become almost commonplace to say that the evangelization of Africa

Translated from French by Robert R. Barr.

has always been closely tied to colonialism and that it still suffers from that dubious situation today.[1] No less commonplace is the observation that the notion of the implanting of the church and the concept of the universality of the church—two concepts at the core of the mission theology—were fraught with colonial overtones and connotations. What could be more evident? For so many Africans, the churches of Africa were defined by a state of subordination and subjection to Western societies, whose self-assigned task was to represent, at one and the same time, Christianity and "civilization." The texts are crystal clear. I am unable to resist the temptation to cite two passages at some length. Canon Riches declares, for example:

> Christianity came to Africa far more frequently as a colonizer than as a servant, and even when it came as a servant, it was as a servant with preconceived notions about what services it ought to render and what persons it ought to serve. The servant felt superior to the one to be served, and therefore deemed itself to have nothing to receive. It had no intention of listening.[2]

Engelbert Mveng specifies and broadens this observation.

> In the nineteenth century, the order of the day practically everywhere was the anti-slavery struggle. Yesterday the slaves had been baptized; today they were emancipated before being baptized, and freedom villages were founded. At Freetown, Libreville, Bagamoyo, philanthropy wrought wonders . . . Africa emerged from slavery, only to be plunged into colonization. The Berlin Conference of 1884-85 partitioned Africa into some thirty territories, or groups of territories, for exploitation and administration. The representatives of the states of Europe and America, invited by Bismarck to Berlin, regarded the blacks as minor children in need of the tutelage of whites. The colonial pact, finally, and the "indigenate," or native protectorate, established in Africa in the name of human rights, stripped our peoples of any rights or dignity . . . It was in the desert of this desolation of ours that the voice of the missionary resounded. Practically everywhere, the missionary was the ally of the colonizer, if an ally that the latter sometimes feared.[3]

This judgment might seem severe. Actually it is historically correct and altogether well-founded. Not that we should forget that the African churches were born of the missionary zeal of the churches of Europe. Christians in Africa feel at liberty to emphasize that evangelization was carried out in tandem with colonization. There was no possible way for European missionaries to escape the ambiguities of their historical situation. The mission church, in its personnel, its culture, its daily life and its daily actions, gave the impression of having struck a treaty of mutual assistance with colonialism. Thereby a heavy, painful ambiguity prevailed, and attempts were not always made to resolve this, whether in concrete fact or in the underlying theory. As Hans Küng has pointed out, the church of Jesus Christ has remained a European and American affair (see his *The Council: Reform and Reunion*, Sheed & Ward, 1962). It is often wedded, willingly or unwillingly, to the political contours of the colonizing country.

> When Germany lost its colonies in 1919 did not the German missionary congregations depart, along with their administrators, and did not the French, Belgian and British arrive in the same ships with their new administrators? And when Italy conquered Ethiopia how many Italian congregations suddenly discovered a missionary vocation in Ethiopia? ... And this is how it went. It was not at all strange to hear natives speak of the Congregation of Propaganda Fide as the ministry of colonies of the Vatican or the spiritual ministry of colonies of Europe.[4]

Thus perceived and analyzed, the problem of pluralism inevitably leads African theologians to pose other questions concerning what is fundamentally at stake in the proposition of the Christian faith in Africa and what its major articulations are. How solid are the results of evangelization in Africa? What is the value of the methods that have been applied? And especially, what objective do missionaries pursue? Doubtless the missionaries are for the most part filled with lively, generous intentions. But do they have a precise idea of what it is they strive to accomplish? Supposing this idea is precise, is it in conformity with the design of Christ and the church? Is it pure, without ulterior considerations that might be alien or harmful to its essence?[5] Formulated so insistently twenty years ago, these questions were all taken up *ex professo* and with the desired breadth in 1974 by the African bishops attending the Fourth World Synod of Bishops, the synod devoted to the problems of evangelization in the contemporary world.

More specifically, the African theologians present at the synod were asked to prepare a synthetic reflection on the pastoral problems that seemed to them most urgent for the churches of Africa.[6] The experts then indicated a series of urgent pastoral questions. First, they pointed out general problems:

1. Christianity's novelty and specificity as a historical, revealed religion;
2. The legitimation of evangelization (dialogue between Christianity and the non-Christian religions, evangelization and religious freedom, ecumenism, and so forth);
3. Autonomy and responsibility of the local churches;
4. Oneness of faith and multiplicity of theologies;
5. Representation of local non-Western churches at the level of the church's central administration;
6. Integration of foreign missionaries into the African churches.

Then they indicated some special questions:

1. Marriage and family;
2. Ministries and services in the church, especially the problem of the nonordained ministries;
3. Christian faith and human advancement;
4. Christian faith and political commitment (church and state);
5. Priestly celibacy and, especially, the possibility of admitting married persons to the priestly ministry.

By way of concluding their work at the synod, the African bishops in attendance similarly expressed themselves on the problems of evangelization in Africa.[7] These problems concern practically the whole gamut of questions arising today with regard to the notion of "local church." The bishops' questions were grouped under two rubrics: those emerging from the African political and religious context and then questions bearing on communion and co-responsibility in the church.[8]

To construct African churches which encompass all the means of salvation and are rooted in social structures and local cultures, fully responsible for the spiritual destiny of their people—this appears to be universally perceived as the fundamental problem facing African theologians and pastors. In face of this problem, the positions of theologians have been and are diverse, according to the specific ambience, person, and the center of interest.

Main Currents of Theology in Africa

Pending a more in-depth analysis from theologians whose works are still in progress or about to appear, we may define three broad currents of theology prevailing in Africa, up to the present time:

- mission theology
- "African" theology
- black theology or black South African theology

Mission Theology

To the question "What is the goal of mission?" generally three answers can be given: 1) the goal of mission is the conversion of unbelievers; 2) the goal is the planting or implanting of the church; and 3) the goal of mission is the birth and growth of a church as it becomes genuinely and fully itself, in order to live in complete responsibility and in communion in Christ with all other churches.

The first goal, *a theology of the salvation of souls,* ruled unchallenged in missiology for centuries, right up to the beginning of the twentieth century. During this long period of time this theology was seen to express the proper and specific aim of mission activity. The champions of mission as saving souls reject the theology of the implanting of the church because, they say, it has no basis in Saint Paul. "The 'implantation' theory," writes Karl Müller, "finds no confirmation in Saint Paul. And yet, Paul is utterly and absolutely a missionary. He has no intention in the world of making of a *plantatio ecclesiae* the proper, specific, theological goal of his apostolic activity."[9] For this theology, "the essential role of the missions is to heal, to convert, to Christianize," and "the missionary's essential task is to proclaim the gospel—to be the herald of the good news of Christ."[10] Staunchly loyal to the adage *extra ecclesiam nulla salus* (outside the [Roman] church there is no salvation), the theology of the salvation of souls logically leads its partisans to an across-the-board rejection of the cultural and religious traditions of the African peoples.

As Maurier writes:

The language that mobilized vocations and Christian charity was based first and foremost on the pity that ought to be inspired by the sad supernatural, moral, and human state of the "savages." There was no question of acknowledging the intrinsic values of other religions—which, for that matter, were little known. The very "values" of these religions, if indeed they had been perceived, were obstacles to the uniformistic, salvationistic Romanization that prevailed.[11]

Carried away by excessive zeal to defend the oneness of Christianity and distinguish it from what was commonly but improperly called "paganism," the theoreticians of the salvation of unbelievers forgot that the saving God is omnipresent and that there exists a universal revelation above and beyond the bounds of any "special" revelation (meaning the Judaeo-Christian one) and that salvation can be obtained through non-ecclesiastical channels as diverse as the various ideals and humanisms nurtured by human beings.[12] Another disadvantage of this theology deserves mention. Fashioned on the basis of a dualistic anthropology, this particular theology ran the dangerous risk of disregarding the concrete, historical dimension of the integral salvation brought by Christ. It thus lent credence to the Marxist thesis that religion is the opium of the people, as I have tried to show elsewhere.[13]

A second form of mission theology began in the 1920s. Some European theologians developed and exported to Africa a theology of mission known as the *theology of the implanting of the church.* While the theology of unbelievers had seen the souls of the blacks as the souls of those "who sit in darkness and in the shadow of death" (Luke 1:79), the theology of the implanting of the church reveals a different concern—a frankly ecclesiastical, even ecclesiocentric one. On the *tabula rasa*—the blank (indeed erased) slate—of people without culture and without civilization, the church is to be implanted, constructed as it has materialized historically in the West, with its personnel, its works, and its methods. Maurier describes this process:

[Missionaries] have indeed worked to implant the Roman Catholic Church in countries where it was not, and which, to boot, no longer belonged to themselves. Missionaries tend to be utterly unaware of the fact that they are agents of a Western Christian *romanité.* They say they work to save souls, extend the true faith, preach the gospel. And doubtless this is what they do. But they do so by working for the implanting of the Roman Church, its doctrine, its liturgy, its discipline, its organization, and its mentality. They do so unawares, since, after all, it goes without saying in the common consciousness: the Roman Catholic Church is the only true church of Jesus Christ, the sole depositary of salvation.[14]

This theology, one of whose theoreticians is Father Pierre Charles, S.J., sees the implanting of the church as the purpose of mission. The protagonists of this theory reproach the defenders of converting unbelievers with assigning to mission the specific goal of an activity that is the general goal of the church. Everywhere and always, they reminded their theoretical adversaries, the church must preach and must convert sinners, baptized or unbaptized.

For the theologians of the implanting of the church, mission ought to strive to "plant" the church in regions where it does not yet visibly exist. That is, it should endeavor to organize there, in stable, permanent form, the means of salvation: clergy, laity, religious, and Christian communities.

When it comes to evaluating the results of mission as thus conceived, two contrary opinions appear, one optimistic, the other pessimistic. The optimistic note is sounded by Mons. Delacroix, one of the most recent historians of mission:

> The expansion of the Church in the first centuries . . . had been limited to the confines of the Roman Empire. Missions in the Middle Ages . . . had not managed to forge beyond the Mediterranean world at all, except for expeditions without a morrow. The missioners of the fifteenth and sixteenth centuries had sowed the Church in the three Americas . . . Contemporary missions have succeeded in extending the radiance of the cross not only to countries that had been temporarily closed to it— China, Korea, Japan—but to regions until then unexplored, from the great North and extreme South of the Americas, to lands but recently discovered, on the African continent, in Indonesia, in Australia, and in far-flung Oceania. Except for a few countries, such as Afghanistan and Tibet, contemporary missions have installed the Church at the remotest ends of the earth.[15]

The results cited are irrefutable, and Mons. Delacroix's opinion is well based, as far as the facts are concerned. Without denying these facts, others evaluate them differently. Hans Küng writes, for example:

> While the Church, after the example of Paul, had become Greek with the Greeks and barbarian with the barbarians, it had become neither Arab with the Arabs, nor black with the blacks, nor Indian with the Indians, nor Chinese with the Chinese. The Church of Jesus Christ, regarded as

a whole, remained a European and American affair (*The Council: Reform and Reunion*, New York: Sheed & Ward, 1962).

Raimondo Panikkar, cited by Küng, goes further: "It is almost indisputable that, despite the gigantic, incessant effort of the Churches, maintained and financed by an enormous public in Europe and America, Christianity in Asia has suffered a resounding defeat."[16] This is not the place to examine the validity of these theses. Let me emphasize only that the theology of the implanting of the church has given birth to paralyzed Christian communities—copies ground out on a European model, deprived of initiative, creativity, and originality, praying with borrowed words and thinking by proxy, via Rome, Paris, London, and other capitals of Europe.

African Theology

Contrary to what we are taught by the missiologists of the conversion of unbelievers or the implanting of the church, this theology called *African* intends to take account of its African location—its culture, its religion, and its problems of civilization. We Christians of Africa demand the right to "think Christianity," to reflect on the truth of Christianity. In a work of powerful historical impact, *Des prêtres noirs s'interrogent* (*Black Priests Wonder*), appearing in 1956 from Editions du Cerf, the authors wrote, in a foreword:

> The African priest, for the advancement of the Reign of God, must say what he thinks of his church in his country. Not that the black priest has simply never been heard. But in the tumult of voices discoursing upon the missions, his word has been rather discreet, and easily missed, whereas it would seem that he actually ought to have the first vote in chapter (p. 16).

For the sake of clarity and easy recall, I shall distinguish two steps in the problematic of an African theology: first, a theology of adaptation or of stepping stones, and then a critical African theology.

Theology of Adaptation or Stepping-Stones

When it comes to evangelization, as we have observed in passing, only two methods are possible. Either we consider that what is at stake is an encounter between the church, such as it has historically evolved in the Western context, and the African peoples—in which case we shall try to adapt the practices of this church as well as possible to the sociocultural life of the African peoples; or else we deem that what is occurring is that the members of an African community have heard and accepted the message of Christ and now sincerely strive to proclaim this message, live it, and have it lived by others, in their own sociocultural life. Any purification or transcendence of this latter approach must necessarily occur slowly and gradually, under the influence of the life of faith and in all freedom. This purification and transcendence prepare and effectuate a new, perhaps unprecedented, incarnation of the gospel message.

The latter method is the one that conforms to the doctrine of Vatican II. This is the method that has brought about the incarnation of the gospel in the Western cultures of Europe. The former method has been and still is that of numerous bishops and priests in Africa: the method of adaptation.

Those who hold the theology of adaptation dream of a church of African color, a Christianity with an "African face." This is in fact the title of a book that expresses and signifies this tendency perfectly: *Un visage africain du christianisme (An African Face of Christianity)*, by Vincent Mulago (Paris: Présence Africaine, 1965), one of the great inspirers and promoters of African theology. Mulago writes:

> The herald of the gospel should be but an agent of transmission between the Roman Catholic Church and the people to be won to Christ. A people can be Christianized only when we have first understood them—unless we are willing to be satisfied with a merely superficial Christianity.

He goes on:

> Of course, we must not stop at a simple understanding. We shall need to raise our sights. Having penetrated the mentality, culture, and philosophy of the people to be conquered, we shall have to graft the Christian message onto the proselyte's soul. Only this method will yield a lasting result (p. 23).

And he adds: "The word 'adapt' may shock the ears of some. Suffice it to recall that it is merely a matter of presenting dogma in such a way that it will be accessible to the people" (p. 24).

The champions of this stepping-stone theology are numerous. Purely by way of example, we may cite Tempels, Mulago, Lufuluabo, Nothomb, and Kagame. The principal merit of these theologians is that they have reminded us, in season and out, of the urgency of the problem of incarnating the gospel message in cultures other than the European one. Nor is that all. The theology of adaptation has also had an influence, which it would be wrong to minimize, on the "Africanization" of ecclesiastical personnel, catechesis, and liturgy, to cite but a few familiar areas.

But this being said, the stepping-stone approach seems to have made only a modest contribution to a properly scientific theology. In a word—albeit a word deserving of lengthy commentary—the major shortcoming of the theology of adaptation is its *concordism,* which consists in confusing Christian revelation with the systems of thought that have historically served to express it. To what depths of religious truth can we be led by a comparison between Christianity considered in the abstract—Christianity regarded as a static system of truths—and certain African cultural elements isolated from their overall context? Hurbon has perceptively observed:

> The "adaptation to cultural values" of which we hear so much is often but a process of the indigenization of a Roman Church glued to its old positions, outfitted as it is with the designations of an antecedent history (a history itself historicized with a view to this subsequent enablement)— in the form of a structure and tribunal at once defined, definitive, and defining.[17]

Critical African Theology

In order to escape the danger of concordism, a considerable number of theologians, African or working in Africa, have been attempting for nearly twenty years to build a dynamic, critical African theology. Instead of looking for positive African values that cry out for baptism, these theologians seek to take up theological problems anew, from the ground up, and to manifest their presence in the field of serious scholarly theological research.

Two major concerns dominate this current. On the one hand is a desire for closer contact with the primary sources of revelation (the Bible and tradition). On the other is a determination to be completely open to the African world and its problems. Let us examine each of these two elements in turn.

The former—a concern for the new vitality that can flow from contact with the word of God as proclaimed and explained in the church—has produced a number of works of value in the areas of fundamental, historical, and biblical theology. To limit ourselves to Zaïre alone, and with the warning that our list is far from complete, we may cite the works of Archbishop Tshibangu concerned with theological methodology, Father Ntedika's painstaking research into Christian origins, and Monsengwo's work in biblical exegesis.

The desire for a "return to the sources" has culminated, naturally enough, in an excited—and exciting—debate over "African theology." Too little noticed, it seems to me, is the fact that through their historical and exegetical studies—whose fruitfulness is incontestable—African theologians have gained a lively awareness of the historical, living nature of theology. All theology is culturally and socially situated.[18] Nor could it have been otherwise. There is an interplay between God's word and human society, between theological development and social analysis, and we would do much better to be aware of this rather than to pretend not to know it. This is not the moment to describe the genesis and development of the debate on African theology, which has been done on a number of occasions. Let us only observe that in their sensitivity to the social and cultural "conditions of production" of any theological discourse, African theologians lament the cultural imperialism of certain of their Western colleagues who, without batting an eye, and even explicitly defending their view, assign an unmerited priority to European culture as the locus of human universality.

Universal theology is as mythical as universal philosophy. It has no foundation in revelation, faith, or history. As Wackenheim puts it:

Nothing could be more normal than a multiplicity of theological approaches. There is no such thing as one theology. There are only Christian theologies. The factors of diversification flow from the difference in cultures, in conceptualities, indeed in individual temperaments. Whoever may have been the author of such and such a writing or fragment, we are struck by the great diversity prevailing among the theological elaborations collected in the New Testament. This diversity of Christian thought becomes even more accentuated from the second century onward, in function of the differentiation of the cultural atmospheres reached by the proclamation of the Gospel.[19]

Archbishop Tshibangu specifies:

Ever since its beginnings, Christianity has been characterized by two theological currents. We have "Western theology" and "Eastern theology." These two theologies have found themselves in mutual opposition.

Here was an occasion, if not one of the causes, of the schism of the Eastern Church, as the Second Vatican Council has itself acknowledged.[20]

Let us become aware of this contingency and retain that awareness. Against the proponents of a theology of universal or worldwide value, Africans assert the right or requirement of an African theology to be authentically itself. African theology will not necessarily be a theology based on the philosophy of the Greeks and their neighbors. It will be one that validly operates on the basis of the cultural and religious experience of the African peoples, a theology responding to the questions posed by African society in its contemporary evolution.[21]

This will explain the second trait of current African theology: its openness to the world. African theologians strive to offer an African response to the new questions raised by the African situation, a response in conformity, nonetheless, with the essentials of Christian revelation.

We see this trait in the attention Africans devote to the theology of the local church, the laity, and non-Christian religions. We see it in Christian expressions of African origin, like the prophetical movements. The customary content of African pastoral and theological periodicals such as *African Ecclesiastical Review, Au Coeur de l'Afrique, Cahiers des Religions Africaines,* or *Revue Africaine de Théologie* is very significant in this regard. A concern for openness to the world is also manifested in the success of the Kinshasa Theological Week, which regularly gathers pastors and theologians for a study of some question of currency for the churches of Africa.

This same will to presence is apparent in our theologians' more technical works, through which they openly manifest not only a concern to overcome the constant temptation of concordism, but likewise a most resolute appeal to the human sciences. I want to mention only by example the work of J. S. Mbiti on African religious philosophy (*African Religions and Philosophy,* London, Heinemann, 1969) and his African theology (*Concepts of God in Africa,* London, SPCK, 1970; *New Testament Eschatology in an African Background,* Oxford University Press, 1971).

I would not be doing justice to these efforts if I said that they represent merely an "Africanization" of forms. Still, if we consider the committed research being carried on by certain African theologians, there are other studies that go more directly to the heart of the matter. From this outlook, I must point to the efforts of researchers such as Bimwenyi,[22] whose aim is to do a theology in which African culture is not only described, but genuinely assumed and integrated into a vaster conceptual whole, so that it will be possible for Africans to undertake a critical resumption of the fundamental data of Jewish and Christian revelation.

A typical example of this orientation, doubtless, is Laïnnex Hurbon's excellent *Dieu dans le vaudou haïtien* (Paris, 1972). Considering Christianity and voodoo as they are experienced in Haiti's concrete historical situation and its particular economic and social context, the author has recourse to phenomenological, structuralist, and hermeneutic methods in his search for paths to a reciprocal transformation of voodoo and Christianity as he seeks the liberation of the Haitian human being. God, declares the African theologian, is in the background of the intercultural confrontation:

> If, even as we are, settled on the soil of a Christian tradition, we must speak of the voodoo practitioner's relationship with God, then we shall have to take seriously the interpretation already made of Christianity by voodoo itself. Under pain of falling into abstractions, it is in the already constituted field of the encounter between voodoo and Christianity that God is available for reflection as the eschatological promise of the encounter of cultures. This already constituted field is nothing other than syncretism. It testifies to Christianity's failure in Haiti in its effort to uproot voodoo as in its effort to adapt to voodoo. Thereby it obliges us, on the one hand, to rethink the universality of the Christianity whose pretensions it contests; and on the other, precisely on the basis of the collapse of Christianity's pretensions to universality, to rethink the notion of God against the background of the final encounter of the cultures (p. 217).

The attempt now under way to incorporate the idea of "integral development" into the theology of evangelization is a remarkable example of this current effort to bring Christianity into confrontation with African reality. Archbishop Tshibangu writes:

> We must remember that human beings, created in the image and likeness of God, are fulfilled and realized in history through their world-transforming labor according to the spirit of Christ. "World," here, is intended in its positive, good sense. It signifies the created realities here below, where human beings have been placed by God as the center of these things and as God's lieutenant. It is concrete African human beings, then,

rooted in their history and their culture, who have been redeemed by Christ.[23]

In this perspective, a certain Christian theology of the supernatural must be considered. The opposition between nature and the supernatural is simplistic and keeps Christians from fruitfully reading the scriptures. In its true sense, the Christian supernatural is not something that is added to nature from the outside, or juxtaposed to it, or superior to it. It is, instead, a relationship in depth with God and with our fellow human beings.

A theology of the supernatural must take its point of departure and arrival in the dogma of the incarnation; otherwise it will have no foundation. African theologians like to draw attention to several themes: bringing together all things in Christ, the perfect human being (Eph. 1:10); Christ, the Alpha and the Omega of the universe and history (Rev. 22:12-13); the new heavens and the new earth (Rev. 21; 2 Pet. 3:13); and that of Christ, the image of the invisible God (Col. 1:1-5).[24] This all comes from Vatican Council II, which locates the church in the midst of the world and not in opposition to the world. These human problems of our time impassion both Christians and the church. The church does not pretend to carry a solution with the authority of the Magisterium that will be admitted by all as already complete. The church instead attempts to search with all human beings of good will, according to that wonderful phrase of John XXIII, making itself ready not only to learn from specialists on technical matters concerning these problems but also to work in common with all those who reflect on our times with the inspiration of the gospel of Jesus Christ (*GS* 1, 2, 7, 13, 16, 40).

Here we grasp the essential intent of African theology. The Christian ought to reflect upon the future of the Christian faith and the necessary conditions for the presence of that faith in today's Africa. Here too, with noticeably different overtones, is all that is at stake in South African black theology, which ultimately consists in this existential experience of Christian hope.

South African "Black Theology"

As a movement of thought and action at the same time, South African black theology appears on the scene as a critical review of racism as a global phenomenon historically bound up with the expansion of European capitalism. It is further inspired in the social situation of oppression and segregation known to blacks in America and South Africa.

The term *black theology* appeared in South Africa around the 1970s, arriving from North America, where it had been launched and popularized by James H. Cone.[25] In the American context, black theology sought, among other things, to respond to the challenge thrown down by Muslims who declared Christianity to be fundamentally incompatible with the aspirations of American blacks to dignity, justice, and equality.

The first public manifestation of black theology in the African context took place in March 1971, when a group listened to a recording by James Cone entitled "Black Theology and Black Liberation."[26] Since then, four major orientations have materialized in South African black theology.

Black Theology

Originally represented by a white theologian, Basil Moore, head of the Universal Christian Movement, this first current is in basic accord with the positions of black American theologians such as James Cone. Taken up and maintained by African theologians such as Manas Buthelezi, this current establishes a close link between a raising of black consciousness (racial, political, economic, and cultural consciousness) and black theology, and distinguishes the black theology of a total liberation of the black from an African theology which, according to Manas Buthelezi, is expressed in purely cultural terms and calls for a return to the past, while tending to justify the current situation of the people of the blacks.

African Theology

A second current has been vigorously expressed by Douglas Makhatimi, colleague and friend of Manas Buthelezi. This theology is founded on a biblical faith and adopts the mental and verbal categories of the philosophy of a "people of the blacks." Here the distinction between the white human being and the black human being is not only sociological; it is also, and primarily, of a cultural and philosophical order. Accordingly, this current deliberately distances itself from the European theologians who have inspired Cone, such as Moltmann and Tillich.

African Religions

A third current, based on the African religions, challenges Christianity's pretensions to uniqueness and novelty. It is represented by clergy who claim to discern a basic harmony between the African religions and Jewish and Christian religion. Okot p'Bitek went even further in this direction, asserting the need for a pure and simple return to the traditional African religions, which he regarded as superior to Christianity.[27]

The Independent Churches

The fourth and last current takes its point of departure in the independent African churches, which it regards as the privileged locus of black theology. Victor Mayatula, of the Bantu Bethlehem Christian Apostolic Church of South Africa, is among those who have vigorously expressed the bond between black theology and the independent African churches, both of which employ a discourse of liberation from the colonial situation.

Even with its negative aspects, which seem to me to constitute serious difficulties, black theology appears as an authentic theological development. Beyond any doubt, it is a contextual theology that proposes to raise the consciousness of the African people by analyzing their sociocultural experience in the light of Christian revelation.

Conclusion

In concluding this overview of African theology, it should be noted that for a long time Westerners have not noticed that there is not one world that exists, but worlds; there is not one history, but histories; not one culture, but cultures; not theology, but theologies. The fact is that every people, every human community, conceives and organizes its historical existence not according to a universal, immutable model, but according to its own particular situation in space and time. A perception of the world and its values always depends on the locus from which that perception comes into being. Since persons live in different spaces, they experience and theorize their human relationships, their culture, and their religion differently. Let us be aware of this contingency and retain this awareness.

African theologians hope to be able to make their specific contribution to the *intellectus* of the word of God through a continuing effort of fidelity to the gospel and serious scholarly research into Christian practice—in other words, into the fundamental role of the African Christian communities. It is incumbent on these communities, incarnated and rooted in the life of their peoples, before anyone else at all, to plumb the depths of the gospel and to nourish the reflections of theologians by their life and their questions.

As has been noted before, the condition of the theologian is sometimes terrible, and always arduous. In this period of profound change and questioning, our situation as theologians and Africans poses for us some basic, disturbing, and at times agonizing questions concerning the future of Christianity on the black continent. In the next years, two fundamental problems need to be at the center of our attention.

The first problem is that of the essence of Christianity and, more concretely, the problem of the relationships between Christian life and secular activity. In Africa, greatly preoccupied with development, this question is very important. The great danger for the Christian faith in Africa lies not in dogmatic belief but rather in imperatives for action. Will Christians in Africa be counted among those agents who are inactive and ineffective in promoting social and human development?

The second problem regards the formation of an adult laity, a Christian elite, experts in both human affairs and divine affairs, able to assure the primacy of the spiritual in this Africa that is searching for its individuality. To make progress, theologians have need of the accumulated works of sociologists, philosophers, and linguists; in short, of Christian humanists. Thanks to these theologians, and with our strong support, Christian faith and human reason will be open to a theological discourse faithful to Christ and at the same time respectful of Africa.

Notes

1. For an explanation of African problems caused by colonialism, see G. Balandier, *La sociologie actuelle de l'Afrique noire* (Paris, 1963).

2. Cf. "L'Afrique et l'Église," in *La reconnaissance des différences, chemin de la solidarité* (Paris, 1973), p. 207.

3. Cf. Engelbert Mveng, "La rentrée de l'Afrique dans l'Église," in *Parole et Mission* 12 (1969), pp. 366-67.

4. A. Henry, "La mission sans frontières," in *Parole et Mission* 8 (1965), pp. 215f.

5. Cf. M. Dagras, *Théologie de l'évangélisation* (Paris, 1976).

6. Cf. A. Ngindu Mushete, "L'Afrique au synode et les problèmes d'évangélisation," in *L'évangélisation dans l'Afrique d'aujourd'hui: Actes de la Xe Semaine Théologique de Kinshasa* (Kinshasa, 1975), pp. 53-60.

7. Cf. *Documentation Catholique* 71 (1974), pp. 995-96.

8. Cf. M. P. Hegba, *Émancipation d'Églises sous tutelle* (Paris: Présence Africaine, 1976), esp. chapter 1.

9. Cf. Th. Ohm, *Faites des disciples de toutes les nations I* (Paris, 1964), p. 23.

10. Ibid., p. 272.

11. H. Maurier, "La mission demain à la lumière de la mission hier," in *Église et Mission* 207 (1977), pp. 9-23.

12. J. Dournes, *Dieu aime les païens* (Paris: Aubier, 1963); J. Dournes, *L'offrande des peuples* (Paris: Cerf, 1967). Also of interest is J. Kerkhofs, "Vers d'autres formes d'une assistance des croyants sur le plan international," in *Église et Mission* 202 (June 1976), pp. 5-12.

13. Cf. A. Ngindu Mushete, "Christianisme et authenticité," in *Le Monde Moderne* 12 (1976), pp. 41-59.

14. Cf. Maurier, "La mission demain à la lumière de la mission hier."

15. Delacroix, *Histoire universelle des missions catholiques III* (Paris, 1958), pp. 12-13.

16. Raimundo Panikkar, *L'Asie et la domination occidentale* (Paris, 1956), p. 400.

17. Cf. L. Hurbon, *Le Dieu dans le Vaudou haïtien* (Paris, 1972), p. 33.

18. See my "Unité et pluralité de la théologie,"in *Revue du Clergé Africain* 22 (1967), pp. 593-615.

19. Ch. Wackenheim, *Christianisme sans idéologie* (Paris, 1974), pp. 71-72.

20. T. Tshibangu, *Le propos d'une théologie africaine* (Kinshasa: Presses Universitaires, 1974), p. 5.

21. Cf. ibid., p. 26.

22. O. Bimwenyi, *Discours théologique négro-africain* (Paris: Présence Africaine, 1981).

23. T. Tshibangu, "L'engagement des laïcs dans la croissance et le développement intégral de l'Afrique," in *Actes de la troisième assemblée planière du Symposium des Conférences Épiscopales d'Afrique et de Madagascar* (Kampala, 1972), p. 97.

24. Cf. O. Bimwenyi,"Le problème du salut de nos ancêtres," in *Revue du Clergé Africain* 25 (1970), pp. 3-19.

25. James H. Cone, *A Black Theology of Liberation* (Maryknoll, NY: Orbis Books, 1990).

26. Later published as "Black Theology and Black Power" in Basil Moore, ed., *The Challenge of Black Theology in South Africa* (Atlanta: John Knox, 1973).

27. Cf. David Bosch, "Currents and Crosscurrents in South African Black Theology," in *Journal of Religion in Africa* 6 (1974), pp. 1-22.

2

THE BIBLE IN AFRICAN CULTURE

John Mbiti

The Bible is a strange and unique book. It is strange in that, written by one people, the Jews, it has become a universal book. It finds a home everywhere in the world, and many people find a spiritual home in it. It is a unique book in ways which are not duplicated by other sacred books of the world, for example, the long duration of its composition and its translation into two thousand languages of the world. The time and effort put into reading it have no parallel.

Africa has a long association with the Bible. Not only did some key events of the Bible take place in Africa, but the first translation of the Bible into the Greek language, the Septuagint, took place in Alexandria. At the time of Jesus, the Bible was being read in Africa.[1] The Septuagint was normally used as the Bible of the early church. Since then, the Bible has continued to be read in Africa, and by 1990 was available in some 600 African languages, which account for 30 percent of the worldwide translations. Projections indicate that there could be 850 translations of the Bible in full or in part by the year 2000. Translating the Bible into these African languages has meant, among other things, putting it right into the heart of African cultures. To read the Bible in African languages means in effect to read it, hear it read, discuss it, wrestle with it, and use it in countless ways, all within African cultures.

Professor Chaim Rabin of the Hebrew University in Jerusalem made a significant statement at the Jerusalem Congress on Black Africa and the Bible in April 1972.

> There is no doubt that from the point of view of its structure and its ways of thinking, its directness, its imagery, the average African language is closer, a great deal closer, to Biblical Hebrew than the Biblical Hebrew is to any of the modern European languages.[2]

Does this not mean that in and through African languages we get much closer to the Bible than is the case through English, Italian, German, French, or other European languages? I wonder where Asian and Pacific languages fall in this comparison. The remarkable point is that through translations, African and biblical cultures come to speak almost the same language—in terms of images, pictures, simplicity, rhythm, vividness, and beauty. Translating the Bible has the enormous impact of placing and integrating it into African culture. This impact continues to grow as more and more translations are made. One African scholar who has worked with the Bible Society in Nigeria hopes that "the process of Bible translating will continue until the Bible is made available to every person in his or her own language at a price he or she can afford."[3] The same sentiment is often expressed by the Bible Societies, but how far it will or can be realized in Africa in practical terms is another issue.

There is no doubt, nevertheless, that Bible translation is proceeding by strides in spite of difficulties and other limitations, thanks to the dedication of many Christians. The impact of the Bible in an African language is enormous, not only in the religious realm, but also in the areas of literature and the shaping of the language concerned. Often the Bible is the first publication in a given language and therefore comes to dominate the shape of that language. It enriches the language with new concepts and terms that are either borrowed or adapted from another language, and those that are purposely created to express a new concept. For example, it is obvious that biblical terms such as *angels, demons, church, Holy Spirit, Eucharist* (Holy Communion), *bishop,* etc., have to be introduced into African languages through the translation of the Bible, since these were not part and parcel of traditional African religion.

Oral Tradition in the Bible and African Culture

At the above-mentioned congress in Jerusalem, Father I. de Souza from the Ivory Coast presented a paper on the "Bible and African Culture."[4] One of the points he mentioned briefly was the place of oral tradition in both the Bible and African societies. More attention should be given to this significant area of contact. As Father de Souza reminds us, in many places of the Old Testament we hear, "Thus says the Lord," or "the word of the Lord." One may add that nowhere do we hear, "Thus writes the Lord," apart from the stone tablet with the Ten Commandments and a few occasions where Yahweh asks that some words be written down.

I do not wish to belittle written communication, but we need to remind ourselves that most of what is in the Bible started and continued for many generations through the oral tradition. As a collection of originally oral material, the Bible rings a very noble bell in African life. An American missionary scholar points out that, "Identification of Christianity with western schooling has hindered church growth among those who do not attend school."[5] To what extent this statement is true cannot be easily checked. Nevertheless, everyone has a mouth and a tongue, and schooling has not taken these away. Illiteracy has neither hindered nor stopped the spread of Christianity in Africa. It could even be argued and documented that there is a more rapid spread of Christianity among illiterate people than among those who read, even if schooling and conversion to Jesus Christ do tend to go hand-in-hand at the time of pioneer evangelization work. In any case, the proportion of Christians to the population in the southern two-thirds of Africa which are predominantly Christian today is far higher than the literacy rate of their respective countries. Statistics from a few countries (in 1980, unless otherwise indicated) illustrate this.

Country	Christians	Literacy Rate—Total Population 1980
Angola	90.0%	20% (cf. 15% adult, 1975)
Burundi	85.0%	25% (cf. 14% adult, 1962)
Central Afr. Republic	84.5%	18% (cf. 18% adult, 1975)
Ethiopia	57.0%	25% (cf. 6% adult, 1965)
Kenya	73.0%	40% (cf. 60% adult, 1975)
Madagascar	55.0%	45% (cf. 40% adult, 1970)
Nigeria	49.0%	25% (cf. 25% adult, 1975)
Zaire	94.5%	50% (cf. 31% adult, 1961)
Zimbabwe	58.0%	ca. 30% (cf. 39% adult, 1962)[6]

This means that something of the Bible percolates (perhaps to some extent automatically) into African societies through the facilities of the oral tradition. In this way, on the African scene the Bible relives a large part of its original setting with regard to the channels of communication and uses of language. Indeed, Dr. Climb and others claim that:

> Many people (in Africa) are rejecting Christianity because they have rejected literacy . . . It is not strange that young people should revert also to forms of Christianity that are largely dependent upon the use of written communication, and identified very much with it.[7]

These are some of the negative consequences of missionary evangelization that has put so much emphasis on written (school) forms of communicating Christianity. Even if the Bible as we have it today is in written form, its content is in danger of being imprisoned within that book form. To a large extent, the Bible is a closed book, kept away from many Africans because they cannot read. A lot of spirituality has been imported and is based on written liturgies, hymns, prayers, and other forms of service. The area of oral spirituality has been neglected, delegated to the margins of church life, or indeed despised. All this is detrimental to the church.

Yet, this is not to ignore the fact that many Africans who cannot read, or only read very little, actually know the Bible from hearing it read aloud in church or at home. They are not as illiterate in Bible knowledge as are millions of Christians and other people in Europe (where I have been working for many years), where Christianity has existed for nearly two thousand years and virtually everyone can read and has access to the Bible. Oral communication still has great power and potential in Africa. The Bible should be given free hand to circulate orally, just as it did in its original stage of development. Churches should facilitate and exploit oral tradition through more public readings of the Bible, more story telling from the Bible, more memorization of passages and verses, more songs and hymns based on and actually using Bible passages, more biblical plays, and naturally more scholarly studies comparing oral tradition in the Bible and African oral literature.

Christian missions introduced schools in most parts of Africa, and this became one of their greatest contributions to shaping modern Africa. Nevertheless, oral tradition is a much older and more deeply established factor of African life, which should neither be neglected nor despised. The oral tradition of the Bible, with all its beauty, can be better rediscovered on the African scene than in many other parts of the world where written tradition has subdued and almost killed the oral art.

At the time of our Lord, for example, it is estimated that 95 percent or more of the population of Palestine did not learn to read the written Law in Hebrew. They were the Am-ha-ares (people of the land). Nevertheless, this did not mean that

> they were completely ignorant of the traditions of Israel . . . The women were not expected to learn to read from the written text, but they were expected to participate enough in synagogue life to be able to teach the Shema to their children. This was oral learning and teaching.[8]

Jesus passed on his teachings orally, and we have no document written by Jesus, even though he knew how to write. For many years after his death and resurrection, his teachings, life story, and activities were preserved and handed down orally. Only later did these begin to be written and eventually collected and edited into the four gospels.

The Need To Include Both Illiterate and Literate

The great movement of establishing schools in all African countries is a noble task and in some places a very successful one. It should not, however, be at the cost of suddenly losing the riches and potential of our oral tradition, which through countless generations and millennia has been the central vehicle of African culture. This fact should be appreciated, exploited, and sustained. Millions of people who cannot read and write should not be put at the periphery of society; they have as much dignity and worth as those who read and write. The Bible does not despise those who cannot read. There is enough room for both literacy and oral tradition in Africa, and the Bible fits very well into that context. Its final shape took form under conditions that were not very different from twentieth-century conditions in Africa, as far as oral tradition and literacy are concerned.

Note should also be taken of those who suffer from being cast aside by too much emphasis on literacy. The late Okot p'Bitek of Uganda laments this in his satirical poem "Song of Lawino," in which a wife speaks about her school-educated, literate husband, Ocol.

> Husband, now you despise me
> Now you treat me with spite. . .

You say you no longer want me
Because I am like the things left behind
In a deserted homestead.
You insult me
You laugh at me
You say I do not know the letter "A"
Because I have not been to school
And I have not been baptized . . .
(My husband) says I am rubbish,
He no longer wants me! . . .
He says I am primitive
Because I cannot play the guitar,
He says my eyes are dead
And I cannot read . . .

Later on, the poet pours scorn on book culture that is without a human face.

Listen, my clansmen,
I cry over my husband
Whose head is lost.
Ocol has lost his head
In the forest of books . . .
My husband has read much,
He has read extensively and deeply . . .
And the reading
Has killed my man,
In the ways of his people
He has become a stump . . .
His eyeballs have exploded
And he wears dark glasses.
My husband's house
Is a dark forest of books.
Some stand there
Tall and huge
Like the tido tree
Some are old
Their barks are peeling off

And they smell strongly . . .
The papers on my husband's desk
Coil threateningly
Like the giant forest climbers . . .
My husband's house
Is a mighty forest of books,
Dark it is and very damp . . . [9]

The Benefits of Oral Communication

One of the strong areas of African oral communication is the involvement between the speaker and listeners. This is called "multidirectional communication." About it, Dr. Climb writes,

When we survey the lively level of audience participation in a traditional African audience it reveals a very healthy and multidimensional flow of communication. Signals are sent by the performer to the audience. Immediately the audience begins visually and audibly to share their reactions with each other and with the performer . . . (In comparison) the western church may be organized to facilitate good listening in a very large group, but most of the communication is one-way. The seating faces one way. For much of the service one person speaks to many who cannot express themselves individually . . . The people of God in more ancient times made good use of communal exercises and group singing . . . It would seem that multidirectional, communal, public, rhythmic praise to God is one of the aspects of African oral art that would be most useful in the African church today to make the message of Jesus more indigenous to the masses. It is instructive to note that many African Independent Churches are making great and effective use of these oral techniques.[10]

Quite clearly, many parts of the Bible are better or more effectively communicated through this multidirectional level of communication. This has serious consequences in the preaching and teaching ministry of the church. We do not need to duplicate the monologues of European church services in which the congregation often sits passively for one to two hours, listening to priests and ministers, some of whom speak very poorly and have little or nothing fresh to give to the churchgoers.

On the other hand, the active participation and involvement of the whole people of God at church services can be illustrated by the healing services conducted by the African Independent Churches. For example, in the Bantu Bethlehem Christian Apostolic Church of South Africa (Azania), the holy spot where the service takes place is a circle, with symbols of the cross, sun, moon, and stars. At the end of the regular Sunday service, patients take off their shoes and enter into this circle. The healer, who is either a man or a woman, and the assistants also enter the circle. During the healing procedure, which consists of praying, laying on of hands, and holding the prophet's staff over each patient, other members of the congregation sing, dance, and play the drums around the holy circle.[11] This and other healing procedures in the independent (indigenous) churches parallel the healing procedures in traditional African medicine, which also often draw on the presence and participation of other people. The community is involved in the health and welfare of the individual who, by definition, is part and parcel of the wider community. We remind ourselves that healings and exorcisms performed by Jesus were public acts. Independent churches that practice healings, as most of them do, are knowingly or unknowingly reliving biblical events in the life of Jesus and in the early church.

Time in the Bible and African Culture

The issue of time is important in the encounter between the Bible and African culture. Here we are confronted with concepts that are parallel at times—or even converging and opposing at other times. As a whole, African concepts of time emphasize the past and the present. Time is viewed as moving toward the ever-increasing past. The future is there in as far as it falls within the rhythm of nature, meaning the seasons (rainy or dry), day and night, procreation, birth, growth, death, and so on. Myths speak only of the past and not of the future. There is no end of the world or history. Many African languages are either incapable of expressing the distant and indefinite future or only manage to do so in a vague and indirect way. Biblical concepts of time put emphasis on this present age and the age to come, the present and the future. They carry a definite eschatology, according to which God is working toward a final fulfillment of all things in Christ Jesus at the point of the eschaton.

Thus, African concepts overlap biblical concepts at the present dimension of time. But they radically differ after that, in that one looks strongly to the ever-increasing past, while the other looks toward an eschatological goal in the future, in the world to come—different, not only in time but in quality.

Naturally these are very broad statements and oversimplifications that I risk to make here, knowing very well that the situation is more complex than what could be outlined in such a brief essay.[12] I mention the problem here to draw attention to the difficulties that Christians have in understanding (and misunderstanding) eschatological and apocalyptic texts of the Bible. Many times the basic reason for these difficulties lies in concepts of time. So far, no other African theologian has attempted to wrestle with this issue.[13] Serious problems are posed by the Bible when it comes onto the African scene and considerably different concepts of time are brought in touch with each other. One such example is that of the *parousia,* which many African Christians cherish and expect to occur soon. They consequently see (or interpret) many signs which, according to them (and some other Christians elsewhere in the world) potent the approaching end of the world. Such "signs" are, for example, the wonders of modern technology, instant communication, wars and rumors of wars, famines, earthquakes, and so on.

Communion and Community

The concepts of communion and community present close parallels in the Bible and African culture. The concept of community runs throughout the Bible—in the Old Testament as the people of Israel, in the New Testament as the church. The social-political life of Jewish tribes has many echoes in African life. Of course there are also differences, but when reading the Bible, people get more excited about the similarities than about the differences. The similarities make them feel that they have a place in the Bible, that the Bible speaks about their situation. In any case, they understand better the passages which "ring a bell" in their own culture, and such biblical passages have a greater impact.

Community in the Old Testament revolves around several points of reference: genealogical roots starting chiefly with Abraham, Sarah, and Hagar, going through Isaac, Jacob (Israel), and the twelve tribal ancestors; the covenants (with Noah, Abraham, Moses, and in Sinai); the land; the Exodus (liberation) event; and the priestly cult. Unfortunately, the patriarchal dominance ignores the equally important role of women in the history and life of Jewish society in the Bible. In the New Testament, the community revolves around Jesus: His life and teaching, His death and resurrection, the celebration of the Eucharist in memory of Him and in anticipation of the fulfillment of God's Kingdom. Because of the importance of this community orientation for the Christians (and the world), Jesus issued one and only one commandment: to love one another (John 15:12). Love is the binding force in community. The New Testament speaks in various forms about this love, to the point where it states categorically that "God is love" (1 John 4:16). Women have a significant role in the New Testament but, unfortunately, the leadership and official running of church life has been dominated by males, which distorts the whole concept of community. This is contrary to the original image of human beings, male and female, as made in the image of God.

In African culture, the community plays a leading role, with various points of reference, such as blood and marital kinship, land, tribal and clan roots, rituals (especially initiation, membership of societies and ranks, and conferring of honors or titles in some communities), and indeed common (communal) suffering through foreign domination, famines, and other catastrophes. Elsewhere I have further explored this African community orientation and summarized it with the formulation: "I am, because we are; and since we are, therefore I am."[14]

With its 3,200 or so groups of peoples ("tribes") and thousands of clans and subclans, which are further structured into extended and individual families to reflect the community orientation of society, African life is centered on community. Community is both vertical (including the departed, the living, and those yet to be born) and horizontal (with kinship and neighborliness playing their roles, which at times may mean conflicts and tensions). The Bible is read and interpreted under the umbrella of this community orientation, and biblical teachings are considered in the light of this pervasive awareness of community.

For example, the six of the Ten Commandments in the Bible that are concerned with human relations have strong parallels in African societies. The Fifth Commandment, "Honor your father and your mother," fits so well into African traditional life that Christians understand it to include honoring their departed parents, as is the case in African traditional religions. Here too, the Third Article in the Apostles' Creed, *communio sanctorum*, finds ready acceptance in the African context, where there is already an active communion between the living and the departed (those whom I have called "the living-dead"). Does the Bible not lend support to these African sentiments when, among other examples, it speaks so often of the God of Abraham, Isaac, and Jacob, or when our Lord reminded us that God is not the God of the dead but of the living? The very celebration of the Eucharist binds us, the community of Christ, which includes those who have died "in faith." Ephraim K. Mosotho-ane advocates inviting the congregation to the feast of making offerings in memory of and fellowship with the departed, but converting this into a Christ-centered feast, fellowship, and communion, thus extending the circle of the Christian community.[15]

In some areas of the church in Africa, it is significant that there is now a justifiable move, albeit at times cautious, in the direction of integrating the wider African community within the eucharistic liturgy. For example, in the eucharistic liturgy used in the diocese of Mount Kenya East (of the Anglican church of the province of Kenya), a prayer of intercession before the consecration reads,

> Let us thank God for the lives of those who have departed in Christ. Gracious Father, we heartily thank you for our Christian ancestors who have passed through death to the new life of joy in our heavenly home.

Before sharing the elements, the celebrant calls upon the people, "I am because we are," to which they respond: "We are because He is."

Similarly, one eucharistic prayer of the Roman Catholic church in Tanzania reads,

> You, Father God . . . We entreat your mercy.
> Also you, our Grandparents,
> Who sleep in the place of light
> All ancestors, men and women, great and small,
> Help us, have compassion on us,
> So that we can also sleep peacefully.

Another example comes from the All-Africa Eucharistic Prayer in which God is called upon to

> Give us kinship and brotherhood and sisterhood . . .
> With the living, and the living-dead,
> With children yet unborn,
> In Jesus, who was anointed with the Medicine of life.[16]

The Eucharist provides a fruitful area for meeting in fellowship, communion, and community, where biblical and African sentiments are most intensively possible and exercised.

I also need to highlight the integration of Nature into the concept of community, both in the Bible and in African culture. Human beings are very much part and parcel of Nature—the environment, the companionship, the dependence on Nature, and so on. The Bible portrays human beings as originating from the earth and returning to the earth. Many African myths of creation speak in similar images. Nature reveals God to humankind, Nature speaks of God, Nature bears witness to God's work and being. God uses Nature to communicate the wisdom, might, and Greatness of God. In the Bible, human beings are set in the world (Garden of Eden) as stewards of Nature to cultivate it, to take care of it, to be responsible for it—under the sovereignty of God. African religious sentiments and activities integrate Nature very strongly, even to the point where some natural objects and phenomenon are personified into spiritual beings in order that human beings may come to religious and mystical terms with Nature.

While the biblical prophets tell us, "Thus speaks the Lord," in African religions it is Nature that tells about God and reveals God. Accordingly, human beings are priests of and in Nature, in the world. Therefore Nature is the friend of human beings and the two should coexist in harmony, and if human beings injure Nature, it is also human beings who reap the scars of this injury. Events of Nature are seen as having a "message" for human beings and not merely as impersonal. Thus, community is community with God, with one another, and with Nature—both in the Bible and in African culture. Professor Kwesi Dickson is right in drawing our attention to the role of the land when he writes, "The African view shares something with the Israelite conception: the land, in African as well as Israelite thought, is the basis of group consciousness. Not only is the land not to be defiled, but it also plays a part in the African's awareness of group interrelatedness."[17]

Conclusion

Perhaps it is fitting to end this essay with these thoughts on community. After all, the Bible is a lived book and a living book, by the community, through the community, and for the community, whose foundation and goal is God. Nowhere else today is the world of the Bible as real or as alive as it is in Africa. Here it is being experienced, not as a world of two to four thousand years ago, but in many ways as the African world of yesterday, today, and tomorrow. Africa is living in the Bible, and the Bible is alive in Africa.[18]

Notes

1. Acts 8:26-40.

2. Chaim Rabin, "The Uniqueness of Bible Translation," in Engelbert Mveng and R. J. Z. Werblowsky, eds., *The Jerusalem Congress on Black Africa and the Bible, April 24-30, 1972, Proceedings* (New York: Anti-Defamation League of B'nai B'rith, 1972), p. 115.

3. Emmanuel A. Dahunsi, "The Problem of Translating the Bible into African Languages," in *The Jerusalem Congress,* p. 120.

4. I. de Souza, "Bible et Culture Africaine," in *The Jerusalem Congress,* pp. 81-99.

5. Herbert V. Climb, *Oral Communication of the Scripture: Insights from African Oral Art* (Pasadena, CA: William Carey Library, 1982), p. 36.

6. Statistics taken from David B. Barrett, ed., *World Christian Encyclopedia* (Nairobi, 1982); *World Annual Report 1980* (Stuttgart: United Bible Societies, No. 122/123, 1981); and John S. Mbiti, *Bible and Theology in African Christianity* (Nairobi: Oxford, 1986), pp. 235-241.

7. Climb, *Oral Communication of the Scripture,* pp. 37 ff.

8. Ibid., pp. 55 f.

9. Okot p'Bitek, *Song of Lawino* (Nairobi, 1966), pp. 13-15, 199-202.

10. Climb, *Oral Communication of the Scripture,* pp. 154-156.

11. M. West, *Bishops and Prophets in a Black City* (Cape Town, 1975), pp. 92 f.

12. Elsewhere I have discussed these problems in two books, *African Religions and Philosophy,* 2nd ed. (London: Oxford, 1990) and *New Testament Eschatology in an African Background* (London, 1971).

13. A German theologian, Werner A. Wienecke, has written a doctoral dissertation in which he makes a comparison between African and biblical concepts of time: *Die Bedeutung der Zeit in Afrika in den traditionellen Religionen und in der missionarischen Verkündigung* (Bern, Berlin, New York, 1992).

14. John S. Mbiti, *African Religions and Philosophy.*

15. E. K. Mosothoane, "Communion Sanctorum in Africa," in Theo Sundermeier, ed., *Zwischen Kultur und Politik* (Hamburg, 1978), pp. 62-77. I have discussed this issue further in my book, *New Testament Eschatology in an African Background,* pp. 144-151.

16. See Joseph G. Healey, *A Fifth Gospel: The Experience of Black Christian Values* (Maryknoll, NY: Orbis Books, 1981), pp. 146-148.

17. Kwesi A. Dickson, *Theology in Africa* (Maryknoll, NY: Orbis Books; London: DLT, 1984), pp. 160-166.

18. For further discussion of the role of the Bible in Africa, see John S. Mbiti, *Bible and Theology in African Christianity.*

3

CHRISTOLOGY AND INCULTURATION:
A NEW TESTAMENT PERSPECTIVE

Justin S. Ukpong

Issues of christology and inculturation in this context revolve around the question of the meaning of Jesus the Christ for the inculturation movement in the church today. The importance and relevance of this question are to be seen in the light of Gerald O'Collins's remark that "all Church reform remains theologically shallow and pastorally ineffective unless it clearly bases itself on the founder of Christianity himself and our faith in him as Son of God and Savior,"[1] and Karl Rahner's observation that "the mystery of the Church is only the extension of the mystery of Christ."[2] We are, therefore, led to ask in what way inculturation may be said to be founded on Christ or to be an extension of the mystery of Christ. My point of departure is that in his ministry, Jesus used what we have come to designate today as the inculturation approach to evangelization—he proclaimed the Good News to the Jewish people from within the perspective of the Jewish culture. I shall seek to show this by examining different aspects of Jesus' ministry as recorded in the Gospels. In this way, the modern movement of inculturation shall be seen to be a reflection of the missionary method of Jesus himself.

Inculturation is a new term in Christian theology, and its meaning is still developing. As used in this essay, it is understood as an approach[3] in mission/evangelization, and involves evangelizing a culture from within, that is to say, proclaiming the Good News to people from within the perspective of their culture. Three things characterize this approach in Christian mission. First is the utilization of the resources of the culture being evangelized in expressing the Christian faith. Second is that the Good News of Jesus is pronounced to challenge and animate the culture. Third is that all this is done from the perspective of the culture and through the agency of an insider or insiders in the culture.[4] It must be emphasized, however, that these constitute one process; that is to say, the same process whereby the Good News challenges and animates a culture involves also the expression of the Good News in terms of the culture.

Correctly understood, the church's mission is to evangelize human cultures and transform the human race through the gospel message.[5] This means effecting change in a Christian direction in the common meanings and values that inform the way of life of a people. It involves a challenge to the common thinking and shared meaning in society.[6] When this is approached utilizing the insights and resources of the cultures concerned, inculturation occurs.

Christology, the other key term in my essay, has been defined by Leander E. Keck as "a comprehensive term for the statement of the identity and significance of Jesus."[7] It involves an interpretation of the person of Jesus, his fate, what he did and what he said, and the meaning of these for humanity, the cosmos, and God-humanity relations.[8]

Current Approaches to the Issue of Christology and Inculturation

In contemporary African theological scholarship, five different approaches to clarifying the meaning of Jesus in relation to inculturation may be discerned. The *incarnational approach* is based on the doctrine of Christ, the eternal Word of God, taking human nature in Jesus. The logic of this approach is that just as the eternal Word of God became incarnate in a human culture to bring redemption to humanity and creation, God's word and the Christian faith must become "incarnated" in human cultures and attain expression through these cultures so that the redemption brought by Christ may be actualized in these cultures. The mystery of the incarnation, therefore, offers a christological model for inculturation. This model, already found in Vatican II (*Ad Gentes*, 22), was first clearly enunciated by the bishops of Africa and Madagascar during the 1974 Synod of Bishops in Rome.[9] On many occasions, Pope John Paul II has also used this image to express inculturation,[10] and many African theologians have used it, too.[11] In spite of its possible pitfalls as an inculturation image, which Aylward Shorter points out,[12] there is no doubt that, when properly understood in the historical context, the incarnation offers a strong christological grounding for inculturation.

Another approach to the issue of christology and inculturation is the *Logos Spermatikos (Seeds of the Word)* approach. This approach is typified by Efoé-Julien Pénoukou in his book *Églises d'Afrique: Propositions pour l'Avenir.*[13] Pénoukou uses the idea of the eternal Logos (Word), in whom all things were created, to show that Christ pervades all human cultures, even if he is not known or identified as such. He is, therefore, right from the beginning of creation, in solidarity with all creation. This was further expressed by the historical incarnation. Cultures need to be opened to the gospel and converted to Christ, and the gospel also needs to be opened to African culture so that it may attain fullness of meaning. Pénoukou's approach is, in fact, an application of the *Logos Spermatikos* theology of St. Justin, Martyr, and St. Clement of Alexandria to the modern problem of inculturation.

The third approach, which may be called the *functional analogy approach,* seeks to describe Jesus' redemptive functions in terms of analogous African thought categories. This is the approach found, for example, in the christologies of John S. Pobee, who sees Christ as the Greatest Ancestor or Nana of the Akan;[14] Bénézet Bujo, who calls Christ the proto-ancestor[15]; and Charles Nyamiti, who refers to Christ as our "Brother-Ancestor."[16] This approach has a parallel in the type of New Testament christology that studies the christological titles.

The fourth approach is the *paschal mystery approach* typified by Aylward Shorter in his book *Toward a Theology of Inculturation.* Following a modern christological approach (like that of Kasper, Moltmann, and Pannenberg) which uses the death and resurrection of Jesus as the center of christology, this approach takes the resurrection as the starting point for understanding the christological basis of inculturation. According to Shorter, Jesus in his earthly existence was limited in his contact with other cultures. But after the resurrection, he belongs to all cultures and can identify with them through the proclamation of the Good News. There is, therefore, a causal link between the resurrection and inculturation. Besides, the fact that Jesus died and rose points to the fact that inculturation involves challenging cultures to a new life. This approach, according to Shorter, does not deny continuity of Christianity with pre-Christian cultures.[17] The approach has a parallel in the biblical image of the church as the mystical body of Christ (Eph. 1:22-23; 4; Col. 1). Speaking to the Kenyan Episcopal Conference in 1980, Pope John Paul II declared, "Thus, not only is Christianity relevant to Africa, but Christ in the members of his Body, is himself African."[18] Commenting on this statement, John Mutiso Mbinda rightly observed that here the Pope was using "a new approach to the theology of inculturation based on the resurrection rather than on the incarnation."[19]

The fifth approach is *biblical* and is based on New Testament statements about the universal dimension of Christ and Jesus' identity with the Father. John S. Mbiti pointed out that the fact that Jesus existed before Abraham (John 8:58) and is the light of the world (John 8:12) shows that Jesus transcends any historicization of him and makes for the possibility of Christ's existence in Africa before the coming of Christian missionaries.[20] Since Jesus is one with the Father (John 10:30) and Africans do worship God, Jesus has actually been worshiped in African religion without a name. Similarly, Vital Mbadu-Kwalu points to the fact that Jesus is the revealer of God and to the basic similarities between the God known in the Yombe religion in Zaire and the God revealed by Jesus. He concludes that Christ must have been active among the Yombe of Zaire before they received Christianity.[21]

In this essay, I shall take a different approach from those delineated above. First of all, while the first four approaches may be described as systematic, mine is biblical. Second, my focus shall be the totality of the ministry of Jesus as the grounding of inculturation. This is distinct from statements of or about Jesus that is the focus of the fifth approach above.

Methodology

In contemporary theological discussions, christology may be approached as a theological reflection focused on the meaning of Jesus as a preexisting divine person who became human (christology from above) or on the life and ministry of the earthly Jesus (christology from below). I have adopted the latter method and seek to examine how Jesus in his ministry, as recorded in the gospels, evangelized the Jewish culture from within. Since this necessarily involves drawing historical conclusions from the gospels, it is important to clarify my approach to the gospel materials.

The gospels are a document of the faith proclamation of the early Christians, a faith understanding of the earthly Jesus, with whom some of them had come in contact. They are not a biography (in the modern sense) but a living testimony to the life of Jesus, a record of the way the earthly Jesus impressed himself upon the early Christians—perhaps the only way they understood him and could describe him and his ministry. What the gospels reveal is a life of Jesus presented in transcendental terms with eschatological as well as historical dimensions. It is very clear from the commitment expressed in the gospels that the evangelists saw the gospel stories as part and parcel of their faith and that of the early Christian communities. The stories grew out of the people's faith experience of Jesus as the living Lord, and it is this faith that gave them the impetus for their mission to preach Christ to others. This demands that for an appropriate interpretation of the gospels it is necessary to enter into and share the faith of the early Christians.[22] Thus, my starting point shall be the New Testament faith in Jesus the Christ.

Because the gospels are a faith presentation of the life of Jesus and not a biography, the problem of recovering the authentic image of Jesus behind the gospel materials and drawing historical conclusions from them arises in any investigation of the life of Jesus. This problem is at the heart of modern New Testament christological research, but it lies outside the scope of this essay. I do want to point out, however, that the fruit of this research shows that any interpretation that draws historical conclusions from the gospels is no longer possible without attention to the historical problems the gospels raise, and use of the historical critical method. This method seeks to identify, through the application of certain accepted criteria, what in the gospels can be authentically attributed to the earthly Jesus.[23] My investigation shall be informed by this method.

In spite of disagreement on many details, all four gospels are agreed on the basic outline of Jesus' ministry. It was itinerant in character and was made up mainly of preaching, teaching, and healing. Most of it took place in the open air and involved enthusiastic crowds of people. With a few exceptions, it was directed to the Jews, and most of it took place in Galilee.

James H. Charlesworth has remarked that in doing New Testament research "one must distinguish between what is in the New Testament from what is behind it."[24] In the New Testament, we have the Christian redaction of the message of Jesus. But behind this message stands Judaism and a historical Jesus who was a Jew and spoke the gospel message from within the context of Second Temple Judaism.[25] In the rest of this essay, I shall investigate how Jesus proclaimed the Good News to the Jewish people from within the perspective of the Jewish culture and how he challenged that culture to respond to the Good News by using its resources to express the message of salvation. This shall involve inquiry into the nature of Jesus' movement, Jesus' preaching, Jesus' attitude toward the Torah, Jesus' parables, and Jesus' miracles.

It is important to note here that the Jews maintained no separation between secular culture and religious culture, as we do today. For them, the religious was cultural and the cultural was religious. Besides, all facets of life were viewed from a religious perspective. Thus, the Torah, the Temple, and so forth were as much cultural as religious symbols.

Nature of Jesus' Movement

That Jesus was at the head of a movement in Judaism that sought to evangelize the Jewish culture and religion is well attested in the gospels. The gospels depict Jesus as making the repentance movement of John the Baptist the point of departure for his own mission, and as imbued with a sense of mission to evangelize the Jewish people.

Jesus started his public ministry by receiving baptism at the hands of John the Baptist. This was clearly an indication of the acceptance of and identification with that movement and what it stood for. The son of a Jewish priest, John the Baptist was recognized as standing in the tradition of the Old Testament prophets who sought to call Israel back to the spirit of the covenant religion. No doubt the age of the prophets had passed, but John's life and ministry took the pattern of an itinerant prophet. He called people to repentance and announced that God's day of reckoning was near. Those who accepted his message and identified with his repentance movement received baptism at his hands.

It would be a mistake to think that John's movement was about repentance by individuals for their sins. No doubt individual repentance was a strong aspect of the movement, but in Israel there was always a very strong understanding of corporate guilt. Sin was not just a matter of the individual sinner's conscience but had a corporate community dimension as well. The sin of an individual in certain circumstances could bring guilt and punishment on the people; so also could the atonement of one person win forgiveness for the people. Such understanding of both individual sin and corporate guilt is certainly behind the teaching about repentance in Matthew 3:1-12 and Luke 3:7-14. John's repentance movement was basically about corporate guilt, and individual repentance within the movement was participation in corporate repentance for Israel's corporate guilt. Confession of individual sins and reception of baptism expressed participation in this movement of corporate repentance for Israel's guilt. Such guilt was seen to be behind the oppression that Israel suffered at the hand of its enemies.

John's movement was a sectarian movement in Judaism. Like many other such movements at the time in Israel (the Essenes, for example), it sought to restore an authentic Israelite religion and morality against the backdrop of hellenizing influences and deteriorating religious and moral standards. John's mission was to inaugurate a vision of a new, repentant Israel and invite people to participate in its realization.

Jesus' baptism at John's hands had first of all the significance of Jesus' identifying himself with John's movement of atonement for Israel. Jesus therefore identified himself with those who sought a new humanity for Israel and with John's vision, which Jesus himself was to bring to realization. Second, Jesus' baptism had the significance of being the point of departure for his ministry, and it is significant that John's theme of repentance was also the theme of Jesus' ministry.

The gospels portray Jesus as showing a strong sense of mission to evangelize the Jewish people and their culture. All the gospels depict him not only as a preacher of the coming of God's kingdom but also as one who was aware that that was his special mission. The Gospel of Matthew in particular emphasizes Jesus' conscious authority in challenging the Jewish legalistic attitude toward religion. "You have learned how it was said . . . but I say to you" (Matt. 5 passim). Mark and Luke present Jesus as appropriating to himself the prophetic role of bringing the gospel to the poor and the needy (Mk. 6:1-6; Lk. 4:16-19). In the Gospel of John, there is constant reference to Jesus' consciousness of being sent by the Father (Jn. 5:23; 5; 37; 6:44, and so on). These are indications that Jesus' movement was a conscious effort to evangelize the Jewish people.

Jesus' Preaching

In his preaching, Jesus focused on the theme of the Kingdom of God, an already familiar and important theme in Jewish religious thought. Through the use of this familiar theme, he sought to evangelize his people. It is evident in the four gospels that Jesus' ministry was characterized by a proclamation of the Good News. In the widest sense, the proclamation comprised not only what Jesus said but also what he did and what happened to him.[26] For Mark, this was the Good News. Thus, Mark opens his work with the title "The beginning of the Good News of Jesus Christ" (Mk. 1:1), indicating that the whole work contains the Good News about Jesus. Luke also understood the whole of Jesus' ministry in terms of proclamation. In his programmatic presentation of Jesus' ministry (Lk. 4:16-19), he sees Jesus' actions in respect of the poor, the oppressed, captives, and the sick as a proclamation of the Good News. In the Gospel of Matthew, we find the narrow sense of proclamation. In this gospel, Jesus' ministry is identified as comprising teaching, proclaiming the Good News, and healing (Matt. 4:23). Thus, for Matthew, preaching (proclamation of the Good News) is one category among others in the activities of Jesus' ministry. In the Gospel of John, while the aspect of proclamation in Jesus' ministry is less obvious than in the synoptics, it is nevertheless very much present. Right from the very beginning, John's prologue presents Jesus as the eternal *Logos*, through whom everything came to be, and as the light that shines in the dark to enlighten all people. However, Jesus was not accepted by all, and those who accepted him were made God's children (Jn. 1:1-13 passism). Behind this christology is Jesus as the presenter/proclaimer of God's salvation, and all through the gospel we see how Jesus gradually reveals the mystery of this salvation.

It is well agreed among New Testament scholars today that central to Jesus' proclamation is the theme of the Kingdom of God/the kingdom of heaven (special Matthean terminology).[27] In many instances the issue was the conditions for entry into the kingdom (cf. Matt. 5:2; 7:21; Mk. 9:47; Lk. 18:24-27; Jn. 3:3, 5); in other instances the imminence of the kingdom was at issue (cf. Matt. 8:11, 12; Mk. 9:1; Lk. 12:32), while in still other instances its nature was explained by the use of parables. Also, Jesus' exorcisms meant the breaking of the power of the devil to establish the kingdom of God (cf. Matt. 12:28).

In terms of the mode of existence of this kingdom, we find in the synoptic gospels that the kingdom of God is a multifaceted reality. It is referred to as a present reality and a reality yet to be consummated (Matt. 13:36-43; 25:31-46). According to Bruce Chilton,

> The Gospels clearly demonstrate that Jesus was possessed of a message concerning the kingdom. He proclaimed it, acted upon it (cf. Matt. 12:28/Lk. 11:20), called disciples to help preach it, explained it in parables and other catechetical sayings and disputed its meaning with those with whom he disagreed.[28]

Did Jesus invent the language or the concept of God's kingdom? Even though we may find it difficult today to understand the meaning of the term in some texts of the gospels, in general, however, the way the term is used suggests that it was understood by the original hearers. The twelve, for example, were sent to preach "the kingdom" (Matt. 10:7; Lk. 10:9). In Mark 16:43 (Lk. 23:51) the expression "kingdom of God" is used as if its meaning is self-evident. In the Lord's Prayer, the term appears as a normal part of devotion. All this suggests that neither the language nor the concept of the kingdom of God was an invention of Jesus but rather that it was something already known to his hearers. Besides, a theme or an expression that was central to Jesus' ministry would have rendered his preaching completely meaningless if it was not to some extent already a familiar word or concept to his hearers.[29]

Jesus came from a background of Palestinian Judaism and carried out his ministry within that context. The earliest synoptic traditions also grew from these roots and were disseminated and reinterpreted there.[30] If, therefore, the language of the kingdom of God was pivotal to Jesus' preaching and was understood by his hearers, we must seek its origins in his background—Palestinian Judaism.

The idea of God's kingdom has its roots in the Old Testament. Thus, even though the expression *kingdom of God* may not be found as often in the Old Testament as in the New Testament, it is, however, rooted there. In the Book of Exodus and particularly in the Psalms, God is referred to as "King" and as the "Lord" that reigns over Israel (cf. Ex. 15:18; Num. 23:21; Ps. 5:2; 73:12). Reference is also made to God's throne (Num. 10:35; 1 Kg. 4:4) and God's dominion and kingdom (Ps. 21:29). However, as Rudolf Schnackenburg has observed, in the Old Testament the dominant idea is the experience of God's kingship in God's historical action in relation to Israel rather than the abstract notion of "sphere of communion."[31]

Apart from the idea of God being experienced as king in his historical relations with Israel, we also find the idea of God's eschatological kingship. This idea is expressed in such texts as Jeremiah 25:30-33 and Ezekiel 39:21, which portray God as coming in judgment of the earth. In the words of Sigmund Mowinckel,

> The fundamental idea in the future hope (of Israel) is always the kingly rule of Yahweh, his victorious advent as king and his reckoning with his enemies. Yahweh's victory is followed by the manifestation of his kingship. He appears as king and takes possession of his realm.[32]

In later Judaism, "the theme (of God's kingly reign) pervades the rich and highly differentiated Jewish eschatology and itself assumes various forms."[33] In the Jewish apocalyptic writings, there is reference to the kingdom of God concept in the Book of Daniel (2:44; 3:33; 4:31; 6:26). In the Books of Enoch, Baruch, and Jubilees, reference is also made to God who would intervene and establish his royal rule. In the Kaddish prayer, which was regularly in use in the Jewish synagogues immediately before the time of Jesus and is still being used today, the theme of God's kingdom occupies a central place, just as in the

Lord's Prayer.[34] All through the history of Judaism, the kingdom of God concept as an expression of God's kingly rule over Israel was prominent. The concept, according to John Bright, "lay within the vocabulary of every Jew. It was something they understood and longed for desperately."[35]

Jesus did not, therefore, invent the concept of the kingdom of God. This was already an important and significant theme in the history of Jewish religious thought. Adopting an already existing and important theme like that as the medium for transmitting the Good News means that in his mission, Jesus was set on evangelizing Jewish culture and religious thought from within by utilizing the resources of the culture.

Jesus and the Jewish Torah

The Jews had an essentially religious view of the world and life. They had one body of laws, the Torah, which was religious but governed both the religious and secular aspects of life. The Torah was regarded as the manifest will of God for Israel, the central expression of God's election, a special gift from God, and a way of life for the Jews.[36] The Torah had deep theological significance for Israel and was an object of deep meditation (cf. Ps. 1:3) and a unifying religious force. Those who lived by it were to receive power and blessings from God.[37]

Because it was an important constitutive element in the daily life of Israel, the Torah was constantly being interpreted. At the time of Jesus, there were varying schools of interpretation of the Law. Jesus himself claimed to be the authentic interpreter of the Law. He was also acknowledged as a competent interpreter of the Law, hence, the various cases we see referred to him in the gospels. It would seem that the texts of Mark 12:28-34, Matthew 22:34-40, and Luke 10:25-28 offer a starting point for understanding Jesus' approach to the Law. In these texts we are led to see that the Law—indeed, the whole of the scriptures (the Law and prophets)—hinge on the ethic of love. And love of God must be understood in terms of a response to a God who loves all people and makes the sun and rain available to both the good and the bad. Such love is the ethic of the family of God and the basis of love of neighbor. Those who would be God's children must prove their "legitimacy" by loving as God loves—both the good and the bad, the friend and the foe.[38] A constitutive element of love, in antithesis to the demands of the letter of the Law, is mercy (Matt. 9:13). Bearing this in mind, let us consider Jesus' teaching on the Law and his encounter with the Law in practice.

More than any other evangelist, Matthew shows great interest in Jesus' teaching on the Law. In the Gospel of Matthew, Jesus' teaching on the Law is presented as part of the Sermon on the Mount (chapters 5-7). For Matthew, the Sermon on the Mount parallels God's presentation of the Ten Commandments to Moses in the Old Testament. Thus, Jesus is presented as teaching with divine authority. Earlier, in Matthew 4:17, Jesus had called for repentance in view of the coming of the kingdom he had come to inaugurate. Here he lays out the ethical demands of the kingdom. In fact, the Sermon on the Mount is a distillation of Jesus' ethical teachings.[39]

Matthew first presents the beatitudes, which challenge conventional human values. Lest this would seem like relativizing the Law, the section of the teaching on the Law opens with the reassurance, "Do not imagine that I have come to abolish the Law or the prophets. I have come not to abolish but to complete them" (5:17). The rest of the Sermon on the Mount is devoted to explaining how the Law is to be fulfilled, for the Law will retain its validity until it is fulfilled (Matt. 5:18). From the Sermon on the Mount and many incidents in the gospel, we come to the understanding that fulfillment of the Law by Jesus meant restoring the original divine intention of the Law (for example, Matt. 9:4, 8).

In presenting Jesus' ethical teaching on the Law, Matthew identifies five areas of the Law. The first is the law forbidding killing (5:21-26, cf. Ex. 20:13). This law must be understood to forbid not only killing in the literal sense but also all actions liable to injure people's reputations or feelings. It also demands early settlement of quarrels. Next is the law forbidding adultery (5:27-32, cf. Ex. 20:14). The basic teaching here is that sin begins in the conscience. The third area is the teaching on oaths. Here again the teaching centers on the basis of swearing, which shows lack of trust among people. People of the new regime must be trustworthy people whose yes is yes and whose no is no. The law of retaliation is the focus of the next teaching (5:38-42; cf. Ex. 21:23-25). The Ancient Near East law in general permitted revenge. In adopting that law for their use, the Jews limited retaliation only to what was equal to the original offense.[40] Thus, rather than positively encouraging retaliation, the intention was to limit its extent. It was, therefore, a law that sought to protect the offender. The new ethical demand is that one should not respond to violence with violence. In this way the intention of the law—that of protecting the offender—is better satisfied. The demand that if one is struck on one cheek one should offer the other actually implies passive resistance.[41] The same holds for giving up one's cloak or going an extra mile. The idea is to break the chain of evil by not meeting violence with violence. This new teaching on retaliation is often seen as abolishing the Law, but in line with the above explanation it is in actual fact transcending or perfecting the Law.

The next teaching is on the law of love (5:43-48). It is commanded in Leviticus 19:18, "you must love your neighbor as yourself." But the Jews tended to interpret *neighbor* as "kinsman," and this implied permission to hate a nonkinsman. In the new regime, even enemies are to be loved, for all are children of the one Father who loves all equally.[42] This exposé on the Law is closed with a call to be perfect (5:48).

It will be clear from the above that Jesus brought a new understanding of the Law and a new way to approach it. Central to this new approach to the Law was love—the fact that God loves all persons, both good and bad, as children, and we must likewise love all other persons to prove that we are God's children.

If Jesus recognized the Law as having validity until its complete fulfillment, what about those instances in the gospels which portray him as apparently showing very little regard for the Law? In Mark 10:1-12 and Matthew 19:1-9, for example, it would appear that Jesus abrogated the Law of Moses permitting divorce. Though the text of Deuteronomy 24:1-4, on which the Pharisees apparently based their argument, does not directly spell out permission for divorce, the practice of divorce is, however, assumed. According to Matthew's formulation of the question, the intention of the questioner was to draw Jesus into the Shammai-Hillel controversy on what constituted the reasons for divorce (Deut. 24:1). Jesus' answer was that permission for divorce was not part of the Law originally intended by God but only a dispensation from that Law. He took time, therefore, to explain the original divine intention as contained in Genesis 1 and how that was suspended on account of human weakness.[43] Fulfillment of the law of marriage, therefore, meant returning to God's original intention of a permanent union of husband and wife without divorce. The focus shifted from a dispensation from the Law to the fulfillment of the Law itself.

In John 8:3-11, a woman who deserved to die for committing adultery (Deut. 22:22-24) was brought before Jesus. If Jesus followed the Law and condemned the woman to stoning, he would appear to be heartless. On the other hand, if he showed mercy and released the woman he would seem to show no regard for the Law. In view of Jesus' new perspective on the Law in terms of love and mercy, there is no doubt that his intention was to show mercy to the woman. He did not, however, do this directly but turned the episode into an indictment of the character of the woman's accusers before releasing her. In that way, without attracting confrontation, Jesus implemented his perception of a new interpretation of the Law based on love and compassion.

A superficial reading of the Sabbath polemics between Jesus and the Pharisees would seem to give the impression that Jesus had no respect for the law of Sabbath observance. But if it is understood that there were different schools of interpretation of the Law at the time of Jesus and differing opinions on what constituted violation of the Sabbath, the matter becomes quite different.[44] Added to this is the fact that Jesus himself was an authoritative interpreter of the Law who identified himself as the supreme arbiter of God's will such that his interpretation of the Law surpassed and superseded that of the Scribes and Pharisees.[45] This is the framework in which we read of these controversies.

Matthew 12:1-8 (Mk. 2:23-28; Lk. 6:1-15) recounts the incident of disciples plucking corn on the Sabbath. (It is to be noted that it is Jesus' disciples that were involved and not Jesus himself.) The action was regarded as a breach of the Law of Sabbath observance. Why did Jesus allow his disciples to do this if he had regard for the Law? A careful reading of the text in question shows that Jesus' attitude was based not on disrespect for the Law but on an inner understanding of God's will in relation to the Law; Jesus' interpretation was also a reaction against a false evaluation of the Sabbath.

In the Matthean text, Jesus draws three arguments from scripture to support his position (Mark and Luke have one). The first is the case of David in 1 Samuel 21:1-6. When David and his companions were hungry, they ate the holy bread of God that they were not supposed to eat. This presupposes a wider interpretation of the Law in the case of human need. If David could do that, this would be even more true for the Son of David, the Messiah. The second case used was that of priests who can perform their duties in the temple on the Sabbath even though such duties constitute a breach of the Sabbath. Jesus points to himself as being greater than the temple; therefore, the disciples should be considered exempt while serving him, just as the priests are exempted while serving in the temple. The third argument is based on the superiority of mercy over sacrifice. This means that the law of love and mercy supersedes the law of the temple and of the Sabbath.[46] Similar to this incident are the accounts of healing on the Sabbath (Matt. 12:9-14; Mk. 3:1-6; Lk. 6:6-11). Again Jesus shows how in such cases mercy supersedes a legalistic attitude toward the Law.

While it is true that in the gospels Jesus was accused a few times of breaking the Law, in all those instances, he was able to show that rather than breaking the Law, he was offering a new approach to and a new understanding of the

Law. However, it is true that this new approach to the Law meant a new attitude toward the conventional Jewish Halakan, the interpretation of the Law. These were customs or laws about absolutions before meals (Mk. 7:1-23), eating or associating with people regarded as public sinners (Matt. 9:9-13; Mk. 2:15-17; Lk. 5:27-28), fasting (Matt. 9:14-17; Mk. 2:18-22; Lk. 5:33-39), and so on. Jesus engaged in polemics against these ceremonial laws because they were opposed to the new vision of the Law he offered.

Joseph Klausner has expressed dissatisfaction with such polemic. According to Klausner, Jesus seemed to have overlooked the fact that it was those ceremonial laws that made Israel as a people distinct and different from other peoples. By these laws Israel maintained her identity and distance from others.[47] But for Jesus the question was if a people's identity should be a barrier of separation. It is very clear from the gospels that in the new regime Jesus came to inaugurate, while Israel's identity is recognized (Jesus came to save the lost house of Israel, Matt. 15-24), this should not be a barrier of separation, because all peoples everywhere are children of the same Father.

From the above it will be clear that Jesus' attitude toward the Torah was basically positive and transcended prevailing Jewish attitudes. Jesus introduced a new understanding of the Law and pointed to himself as its fulfillment. He revealed God's love and mercy toward offenders and emphasized what was already in the Old Testament—that God wants repentance, mercy, and love rather than the ritualistic observance of the Law (see 1 Sam. 15:22; Ps. 40:6-8; Ps. 51; Amos 5:21-24; Mk. 12:33). This is how Jesus evangelized the Jewish religious world with the Good News and the new vision of God's Kingdom— he reinterpreted the people's religious perceptions in a new way. This is the inculturation approach to mission.

Jesus' Parables

Even a cursory acquaintance with the synoptic gospels will reveal the parable as characteristic of Jesus' approach in preaching. Not only is most of Jesus' recorded preaching couched in parables, but also a great part of the synoptic material as we have it today comprises Jesus' parables. Thus, the parable is seen to be a very significant feature of the synoptic gospels and of Jesus' ministry. As to the extent the parables may be attributed to the historical Jesus, no less an authority than Joachim Jeremias has this to say.

The student of the parables of Jesus, as they have been transmitted to us in the first three Gospels, may be confident that he stands upon a particularly firm historical foundation. The parables are a fragment of the original rock of tradition . . . we stand right before Jesus when reading his parables.[48]

Among the arguments offered by Jeremias are the fact that the parables reflect the clarity of Jesus' Good News and the eschatological nature of his message, the presence of Aramaisms in the parables, and the pictorial element that helped to make the parables easily remembered by people. This does not, of course, mean that individual parables have been transmitted to us exactly the way Jesus spoke them. That would be to expect the impossible, first of all, because these parables were transmitted orally and were bound to lose much of their originality in the process. Second, the early church used these parables for instruction, just as Jesus did, and so they were bound to undergo some reinterpretations to suit the new life situation of the early church.[49] Thus, what is affirmed here is not the preservation of the *ipsissima vox Jesus* in the parables as they appear in the gospels as much as the authenticity and reliability of the gospel parable tradition as a whole. Hence, while it cannot be doubted that Jesus spoke the parables reported in the gospels, it cannot be affirmed that he spoke them in the precise way they are reported. Historical critics such as Joachim Jeremias and C. H. Dodd have identified and isolated elements of the parables in the synoptic gospels that can be traced back to Jesus and elements that may be attributed to the early church and the gospel redactors.

Since Jeremias, there has been a scholarly consensus that Jesus' parables belong in the tradition of the Hebrew *masal* and the Aramaic *Mathia* rather than in the Greek tradition of *parabolé*. Thus, the Hebrew concept and use of *masal* must be seen as the appropriate background for understanding Jesus' parables.

The root meaning of *masal* is "to represent" or "be like."[50] In the Old Testament, while its usage involves comparison in most cases, whether directly or by implication, its range of meaning goes beyond comparison. It embraces proverbial sayings, by-word, figurative discourse, similitude, wisdom sayings, and so on.[51] *Masal* refers to a literary expression that is not plain speech. *Masal* always has two meanings: one is the straightforward meaning expressed in what is said; the other is the metaphorical meaning veiled in what is said. Thus, in addition to fables, stories whose meanings are veiled or have something else as referent come under the general notion of *masal*. Hence, as Timothy Polk well observes, "the term *masal* is notable for its interactability to definition, having become something of an embarrassment to well established critical methods, not least to form criticism."[52] However, there seems to be a scholarly consensus today that *masal* is not to be understood as a form-critical *Gattung*, at least not in the sense of grammatical literary form. Rather, it is to be seen as a term applicable to many different literary types, such that it does not have a fixed literary form.[53] Thus, *masal* is constituted not by type or form but by content and function, and what is basic to all *mesalim* is the element of resemblance that permits recognition of a variety of examples as belonging to one family. Such resemblance may or may not be in terms of comparison.[54]

In late Judaism, *masal* appears in the apocalyptic literature such as Ezra 4, Enoch 1, Baruch 2. In this literature, *masal* functions as a means of giving eschatological instructions or revelation, the significance of which needs the interpretation of the divine speaker.[55] In rabbinic literature, *masal* functions as a method of expounding the Law by the rabbis and refers to a wide range of literary genre. John Drury has pointed to a wide use of *masal* within the literary tradition of Second Temple Judaism,[56] and Priscilla Patten has shown how Mark's understanding of Jesus' parables follows the understanding of parables found in such apocalyptic literature as Ezra 4, Enoch 1, and Baruch 2.[57]

In using parables as the principal mode of teaching, Jesus was availing himself of an already existing mode of teaching that had a long tradition in the Jewish culture and was current in his time. This was only reasonable; otherwise his teachings would not have been understood.

In recent years, there have been interesting and significant approaches to the study of Jesus' parables. Since Adolf Julicher, the allegorical method of interpreting the parables has been abandoned as the form-critical school attempted a classification of the parables according to categories. In the classification, the parable proper was distinguished from metaphor, simile, similitude, allegory, or illustration. Thus, only one literary type of what is designated as *masal* was given the same *parabolé*. Today the popular understanding of *parabolé* in the gospels follows this approach, which is a departure from the broad understanding found in ancient writings. In this restricted sense, *parabolé* refers to "an implied comparison between an experience or event from ordinary, everyday life, and a reality of the moral or religious order."[58] Very often it involves a fictitious story.

New Testament scholarship today has been able to show that Jesus' use of parables, whether in the broad or narrow sense, was markedly different from what may be discovered among contemporary rabbis. Jesus used parables with creativity and new insight. The rabbis used parables to clarify points in their teaching and explain the meaning of the written Law. Parables were an instrument of teaching for them. But Jesus used parables differently. For him, parables did not merely serve the function of explaining a teaching, they made up Jesus' preaching itself.[59] This shows that Jesus not only adopted a resource already present in the culture but also transformed its usage in the process of transmitting the Good News. In his hands, the parable attained a new mode of usage.

It is also significant that Jesus drew his parable images from contemporary Jewish way of life. Most of his parable images remain at the level of daily life experience. Because he ministered mainly in the countryside, most of his images were drawn from rural patterns such as farming, fishing, trading, and so forth. In that way, Jesus made the message of salvation available within the life context of the people without demanding a special skill or training.

Jesus' Miracles

As noted above, Jesus exercised his ministry mainly by preaching and working miracles. Just like the parables, the miracles of Jesus provide one way of understanding the extent to which Jesus shared and made use of the worldview of his people and thus evangelized from within their culture.

Only very few radical scripture scholars today question that Jesus performed such miracles as healing the sick and driving out evil spirits. This does not, however, mean vouching for the authenticity of every miracle story in the gospels. Because these stories were handed down by popular report, they must be seen as containing interpretations, exaggerations, and generalizations. Rather, what is meant is that Jesus actually healed, yet we cannot rule out the possibility of occasional specific memories of actual incidents.[60]

The twentieth-century scientific mind would tend to deny the possibility of miracles. But if we understand that Jesus' miracles had faith as their context and took place generally on request, it becomes easier to understand how Jesus healed people. The fact is that those who had faith and saw God in Jesus were very likely to experience a new personal well-being in the form of healing. It must also be remembered that the sociocultural context in which Jesus worked was that of first-century prescientific-age Palestine. The worldview of the period assumed that God and demons could act directly on human beings. Thus, certain occurrences were ascribed to supernatural intervention, and people's experiences of God through Jesus were interpreted in that context. Jesus probably concurred with such interpretation.[61]

Jesus was not the only person in his time who was known to have worked miracles. There were Jewish and non-Jewish miracle workers in Palestine around the time of Jesus, and among the Greeks, miracles were reported to have taken place at the temple of the gods. Pheme Perkins has noted how the stories of these miracles resemble the gospel miracle stories in certain aspects, but she also notes how the motives of Jesus' miracles are significantly different from those of other miracle workers.[62]

The miracle stories show how Jesus shared the most fundamental aspect of the Jewish culture, its worldview. As we observe in the Old Testament, the Jewish worldview posited the existence of spirits that were good and bad and could influence human life and action.[63] In the Old Testament, good spirits influenced the judges, giving them wisdom, courage, and strength, and in the cases of Moses (Num. 11-25) and Elijah (2 Kg. 2:9, 15), they were "personal" and could be transferred to other people.[64] In the New Testament, it is the Holy Spirit that influences people to good action. In the Old Testament, evil spirits come generally under the name of Satan (1 Chron. 21:1), and in the New Testament they are called demon, devil, Beelzebub, and also Satan. In the New Testament, these spirits are depicted as constituting a kingdom in opposition to the Kingdom of God, and Jesus' ministry is seen as set on establishing God's kingdom and destroying the kingdom of Satan. Those miracles of Jesus that involve casting out evil spirits express this motif. People suffering from convulsions, mental illness, and psychosomatic disorders were considered to be possessed by the devil, and Jesus' healing consisted in casting it out. In many instances, the gospels report that those evil spirits themselves acknowledged Jesus' divinity. Thus, in the Jewish worldview certain kinds of illnesses were considered as spirit possession. Jesus shared this worldview and utilized it through his healing miracles in communicating the Good News of the Kingdom.

Conclusion

Jesus was a Jew. He was born into Judaism, subject to the Law of Moses, and lived within the limits of that Law. The movement he founded stood in the tradition of the Old Testament prophetic movement and that of John the Baptist. It was a sectarian movement whose purpose was to call Israel back to God and restore the true meaning and observance of the Law. Later the movement developed into an independent religion of its own—Christianity. The Law of Moses, sacred to the Jews, was also for Jesus the sacred Law of God. But Jesus had come as a fulfillment of this Law. New Testament scholars would agree that Jesus did not introduce any new set of laws or commandments. The

Old Testament Law of love of God and neighbor was central for him, and he gave a new and wider interpretation of it. The Ten Commandments, a norm of Christian morality today, is an inheritance from the Old Testament. But Jesus did something new: He revealed the intimate bond between God and humanity that transcends all laws. This may be said to characterize Jesus' approach to evangelization.

Contrary to the popular Christian image of Jesus as one who constantly went against the Jewish culture and society to condemn the Law and the Jewish religion, the above study shows a different image. Central to this image is that Jesus did not destroy or condemn the Jewish culture and religion as such but sought to evangelize them. Using elements of Jewish culture, he sought to instill into the Law and the Jewish religion a new vision based on the Good News that he preached. This involved a challenge to the Jewish culture and religion to respond to the Good News and a challenge to people to rethink their basic beliefs, hopes, and institutions. Jesus issued this challenge from within the culture itself and not from outside it. This is the inculturation approach in evangelization.

It is significant for the inculturation movement today that in evangelizing the Jewish culture from within, Jesus also preached a universal kingdom, which eventually inspired the disciples to undertake a universal mission to evangelize all peoples.[65] Understandably, the disciples were, among other things, to do this as Jesus himself did, that is, these people were to be evangelized from within the perspectives of their cultures. One may not argue here that this was all right for the Jewish culture, which already had divine revelation, but not for other cultures. The logical conclusion of such an argument would be that Jewish culture should be imposed on all Christians. But historical experience shows that such a line of thinking cannot be correct, since Jewish culture today does not determine the shape of Christianity. Even during the time of the New Testament, we see Paul in the Letter to the Galatians[66] and other letters fight against such imposition. This is also Luke's point in Acts 15. We must, therefore, accept that Jesus left a model of approach to evangelization that was to be applied in all cultures to the extent any model can be applied to particular situations. Paul seems to offer us the best example of this approach when he talks of being "all things to all people" (1 Cor. 9:22) in the process of bringing the gospel message to people.

Notes

1. Gerald O'Collins, *Interpreting Jesus* (Mahwah, NJ: Paulist Press, 1993), p. 4.

2. Karl Rahner, *Foundations for Christian Faith: An Introduction to the Idea of Christianity* (New York: Seabury, 1979), p. 213.

3. The problem with most current definitions of inculturation is that they do not distinguish the process of rooting the Christian message in a culture, which is mission or evangelization, from the different approaches or methods employed in that process, one of which is inculturation. It is important and necessary to make that distinction, as the history of mission shows that different approaches have been employed over the years in the process of evangelization.

4. "Insider" here means anyone who has acquired knowledge, experience, and the insights of the worldview of the culture.

5. Cf. Pope Paul VI, *Evangelii Nuntiandi*, no. 19.

6. Cf. George A. Napoli, "Inculturation as Communication" in *Effective Inculturation and Ethnic Identity: Working Papers on Living Faith and Cultures*, ed. Arij A. Roest Crollius (Rome: Gregorian University Press, 1982), p. 84.

7. Leander E. Keck, "Toward the Renewal of New Testament Christology," *New Testament Studies* 32 (1986), p. 362.

8. Cf. ibid.

9. Cf. *AMECEA Documentation Service*, no. 11 (1974), p. 2.

10. Cf. Encyclical Letter *Slavorum Apostoli*, 1986; Address to Biblical Commission, April 26, 1979; Address to Kenyan Bishops, May 5, 1980; *Catechesi Tradendae*, no. 53.

11. Cf. P. Sarpong, "Inculturation," *Shalom* 6 (1988), p. 78; Justin S. Ukpong, *African Theologies Now: A Profile. Spearhead*, No. 80 (Eldoret: Gaba Publications, 1984), p. 27; Ngindu Mushete, "History of Theology in Africa" in *African Theology En Route*, ed. Kofi Appiah Kubi and Sergio Torres (Maryknoll, NY: Orbis Books, 1979), p. 27.

12. Cf. Aylward Shorter, *Toward a Theology of Inculturation* (Maryknoll, NY: Orbis Books, 1988), pp. 79-82.

13. Paris: Desclée, 1994.

14. See his *Toward African Theology* (Nashville: Abingdon Press, 1979), pp. 94-98.

15. See his "Pour une éthique africaine-christocentrique," *Bulletin de Théologie Africaine* 3 (1981), pp. 41-52.

16. See his *Christ as Our Ancestor* (Zimbabwe: Mambo Press, 1984), pp. 1-93.

17. Cf. Aylward Shorter, *Toward a Theology of Inculturation*, pp. 84-87.

18. *AMECEA Documentation Services*, No. 5 (1980), p. 203.

19. John Mutiso-Mbinda, "Inculturation and African Local Church" in *Word of God-Human Languages: Reports of the Yaoundé Meeting, Ecumenical Association of African Theologians, Sept. 24-28, 1980* (Yaoundé: Collection of African Theology, n.d.), p. 37.

20. John S. Mbiti, "Is Jesus Christ in African Religion?," a seminar on Confessing Christ in Africa Today at the Ecumenical Institute, Bossey, Switzerland, 1988.

21. Cf. Vital Mbadu-Kwalu, "Dieu Connu en Jésus Christ: Une approache Paulinienne après l'épître au Romains" in *Chemins de Christologie Africaine* (Paris: Desclée, 1986), pp. 229-246.

22. Cf. Peter Stuhlmacher, *Historical Criticism and Theological Interpretation of Scripture* (London: SPCK, 1979), p. 89.

23. For a discussion of these criteria, see M. Eugene Boring, "The Historical-Critical Method's Criteria of Authenticity: The Beatitudes in Q and Thomas as a Test Case," *Semeia* 44 (1989), pp. 9-44.

24. James H. Charlesworth, "Research on the Historical Jesus Today: Jesus and Pseudepigrapha, the Dead Sea Scrolls, the Nag Hammadi Codices, Josephus and Archaeology," *Princeton Seminary Bulletin* VI (1985), p. 103.

25. Cf. ibid., p. 100.

26. Cf. Jack Dean Kingsbury, *Matthew as Story* (Philadelphia: Fortress Press, 1988), p. 61.

27. Cf. ibid., pp. 61-62.

28. Bruce Chilton, "Introduction" in *The Kingdom of God,* ed. Bruce Chilton (Philadelphia: Fortress Press, 1980), p. 3.

29. Cf. John Bright, *The Kingdom of God* (New York: Abingdon Press, 1963), p. 17.

30. Cf. Michael Lattke, "On the Jewish Background of the Synoptic Concept 'The Kingdom of God'" in *The Kingdom of God,* ed. Bruce Chilton, p. 75.

31. Rudolf Schnackenburg, *God's Rule and Kingdom* (New York: Herder and Herder, 1963), p. 13.

32. S. Mowinckel, *He That Cometh* (Oxford: Oxford University Press, 1956), p. 143.

33. Rudolf Schnackenburg, *God's Rule and Kingdom,* p. 41.

34. Cf. Norman Perrin, "Jesus and the Language of the Kingdom" in *The Kingdom of God,* ed. Bruce Chilton, p. 96.

35. John Bright, *The Kingdom of God,* pp. 17-18.

36. Cf. Sean Freyne, *Galilee, Jesus and the Gospels: Literary Approaches and Historical Investigations* (Philadelphia: Fortress Press, 1988), pp. 247-248.

37. Cf. Gerhard von Rad, *Old Testament Theology, Vol. 1: The Theology of Israel's Historical Traditions* (New York: Harper & Row, 1975), pp. 200-201.

38. Cf. John P. Meier, *Matthew,* New Testament Message, no. 3 (Collegeville, MN: Michael Glazier, 1980), p. 55.

39. Cf. Robert Knopp, *Finding Jesus in the Gospels: A Companion to Mark, Matthew, Luke and John* (Notre Dame: Ave Maria Press, 1989), p. 116.

40. Cf. ibid., p. 119.

41. Cf. Pinchas Lapide, *The Sermon on the Mount: Utopia or Program of Action?* (Maryknoll, NY: Orbis Books, 1986), p. 121.

42. Cf. John P. Meier, *Matthew,* pp. 54-55.

43. Cf. Wilfrid Harrington, *Mark,* New Testament Message, no. 4 (Collegeville, MN: Michael Glazier, 1979), p. 154.

44. Cf. Sean Freyne, *Galilee, Jesus and the Gospels,* p. 256.

45. Cf. Jack Dean Kingsbury, *Matthew as Story,* p. 64.

46. Cf. John P. Meier, *Matthew,* pp. 129-130.

47. Cf. Joseph Klausner, *Jesus of Nazareth* (New York: Macmillan, 1925), pp. 370-377.

48. Joachim Jeremias, *The Parables of Jesus* (New York: Macmillan, 1972), pp. 11-12.

49. Cf. John P. O'Grady, *The Four Gospels and the Jesus Tradition* (New York: Paulist Press, 1989), p. 49.

50. Cf. Francis Brown, S. R. Driver, C. A. Briggs, *A Hebrew and English Lexicon of the Old Testament* (Oxford: Clarendon Press, 1951), p. 605.

51. See my "The Nature and Function of Gospel Parables," in *Gospel Parables in African Context,* ed. Justin S. Ukpong (Port Harcourt, Nigeria: CIWA Press, 1988), pp. 3-4.

52. Timothy Polk, "Paradigms, Parables, and Mesalim: on Reading the Masal in Scripture," *Catholic Biblical Quarterly* 45 (1983), p. 564.

53. Cf. M. Landes, "Jonah: A Masal?" in *Israelite Wisdom,* ed. J.G. Grammie, et al. (Missoula: Scholars Press, 1978), p. 138; D. Suter, "Masal in the Similitudes of Enoch," *Journal of Biblical Literature* 100 (1991), p. 196.

54. D. Suter, "Masal in the Similitudes of Enoch," pp. 197-198.

55. Cf. Priscilla Patten, "The Form and Function of Parable in Select Apocalyptic Literature and Their Significance for Parables in the Gospel of Mark," *New Testament Studies* 29 (1983), p. 257.

56. Cf. John Drury, *The Parables in the Gospels: History and Allegory* (New York: Crossroad, 1985), pp. 7-38.

57. Cf. Priscilla Patten, "The Form and Function of Parable in Select Apocalyptic Literature and Their Significance for Parables in the Gospel of Mark," *New Testament Studies* 29 (1983), pp. 246-257.

58. Madeleine I. Boucher, *The Parables,* New Testament Message, no. 7 (Collegeville, MN: Michael Glazier, 1981), p. 17.

59. Cf. Gunther Bornkam, *Jesus of Nazareth* (New York: Harper and Row, 1975), p. 69.

60. Cf. R. H. Fuller, *Interpreting the Miracles* (London: SCM Press, 1966), pp. 32, 39.

61. Cf. Peter de Rosa, *Jesus Who Became Christ* (London: Collins, 1974), pp. 144-146.

62. Cf. Pheme Perkins, *Reading the New Testament: An Introduction,* 2nd ed. (New York: Paulist Press, 1988), pp. 65-66.

63. Cf. Justin S. Ukpong, "Pluralism and the Problem of the Discernment of Spirits," *Ecumenical Review* 41 (1989), p. 420.

64. Cf. Ze'ev Weisman, "The Personal Spirit as Imparting Authority," *Zeitschrift Teir die Alttestamentliche Wissenschaft* 93 (1981), pp. 225-234.

65. Cf. Donald Senior and Carroll Stuhlmueller, *Biblical Foundations of Mission* (Maryknoll, NY: Orbis Books, 1983), pp. 145-158.

66. Cf. Justin S. Ukpong and Kingsley Asahu-Ejere, "The Letter to the Galatians and the Problem of Cultural Pluralism in Christianity," *Revue Africaine de Théologie* 12 (1988), pp. 66-67.

4

CONTEMPORARY AFRICAN CHRISTOLOGIES: ASSESSMENT AND PRACTICAL SUGGESTIONS

Charles Nyamiti

Elsewhere I have written on "African Christologies Today."[1] In an effort to avoid repetition, I will not include here a detailed presentation of the christologies of various African theologians; instead, I would like to critically assess contemporary African christologies, with a view to providing some suggestions as to what remains to be done.

In order to better appreciate these christologies, I will situate them within the general structure and trends of today's African theologies. This will highlight some neglected areas, as well as the need for a systematic approach to the topic. I shall also discuss the importance of, and urgent need for, African christological textbooks designed for teaching purposes for our seminaries and other theological institutes.

African Christologies in Today's African Theology

There is a close link between contemporary christologies in the African context and today's African theology. The latter is, indeed, partly determined by such christologies. Hence, for the sake of a better appreciation of our subject, it is useful to describe briefly what is meant by African theology, and to expose the various trends in that theology. This will pave the way for an examination of how African christologies are related to the concept of African theology and its different methods of approach. It is important to note that the term *African* refers here chiefly to black Africa, south of the Sahara.

Rightly understood, African theology comprises various definitions. In its broadest (etymological) sense, African theology can be defined as *discourse on God (theo-logos)*—and on all that is related to Him—in accordance with the mentality and needs of the people in the black continent. Thus understood, African theology is of different types: 1) African traditional (or non-Christian) theology, as is found in African traditional religions; and 2) African Christian theology (meaning African theology in its narrow sense).

This latter type can also be understood in a broad or narrow (strict) sense. In its broad sense, African Christian theology can be defined as the understanding and expression of the Christian faith in accordance with African needs and mentality. In its narrow or strict sense, African Christian theology is the systematic and scientific presentation or elaboration of the Christian faith according to the needs and mentality of the African peoples.

A particular type of African christology corresponds to each of these definitions. Thus, the definition of African theology in its broadest or etymological sense is parallel to African christology in its broadest meaning. This can be defined as *discourse on Christ in accordance with the mentality and needs of the people in the black continent.* When so understood, African christology (like African theology) is of various types.

First, there is African traditional (non-Christian) christology. At first, this appellation seems contradictory, but it refers to an important reality, for it designates what one might call "the discourse on the hidden Christ in African traditional religions and cultures."[2] It is an undeniable fact that even before the advent of Christian missionaries in black Africa, Christ was already at work among the Africans. The well-known theology of the *Logos spermatikos* supports this view. It is in a similar sense that we speak today of Christian theology of non-Christian (including African) religions. All this confirms the affirmation that there is a latent "non-Christian" African christology in the traditional religions and cultures of the African peoples. This christology must have existed since Africans were on the black continent.

Second, when one considers African theology in its narrow, or Christian, sense, this can also be understood in a broad or a strict manner, as already noted. Broadly defined, it would include the simple understanding and expression of the gospel message in keeping with African needs and mentality. This definition is large enough to cover both systematic (or scientific) and nonsystematic African Christian theology. As we shall soon see, the latter exists in the African churches and ecclesial communities in a somewhat latent form—mainly orally, and in an unsystematic fashion. Obviously, such theology must also contain an unsystematic sort of African christology found in the African traditional churches and the so-called African independent churches. In a later section, I shall speak more about this type of christology.

As already mentioned, African theology in its narrow or strict sense is the systematic and scientific elaboration of the Christian message in accordance with the requirements and mentality of the Africans. Again, to this type of theology correspond the African systematic and scientific christologies that are being elaborated by various African and other theological writers. It is this type of christology that is my primary concern here.

Briefly, therefore, various forms of African christologies correspond to different kinds of African theology: the "non-Christian" (traditional) and Christian African christologies, of which the latter comprise the nonscientific and scientific types.

However, pluriformity in African theologies and their corresponding christologies is determined by factors other than those mentioned above, including the following that deserve special mention.

1. *Denominational differences* found, for example, between Catholic and Protestant theologians;
2. *Political and cultural differences* existing between writers belonging, for example, to independent and South Africa, or to French- and English-speaking Africa, or tribal or national differences;
3. *Personal differences* among the individual theologians, due to varying academic formation, temperament, personal choice, or interest.
4. *Variety of theological approaches.* Such variety is largely determined by the factors previously mentioned.

With regard to the various approaches, two main types are currently employed in African theology and christology: the inculturation method and the one of liberation theology.

Inculturation

Inculturation involves an effort to incarnate Christian teaching in African cultures on the level of theology or christology. Various schools are found in this way of procedure.

The philosophical or speculative school is characterized by a critical and philosophical approach to African religions or sociocultural realities, as well as to biblical and traditional Christian teaching. Stress is put on the noetic aspect of theology, primarily understood as *intellectus fidei*. Both the Bible and church tradition are directly confronted with African traditional wisdom, problems, and aspirations. The approach to Christian mysteries is both ontological and functional, analytical and practical. This school is especially found among Catholic theologians.

The sociocultural and biblical school emphasizes direct dialogue between the biblical message and African traditional teachings. Generally speaking, the approach is largely pragmatic (functional), with little sympathy toward speculative problems. More importance is given to the Bible than to the teaching of church tradition. This trend is found especially among English-speaking Protestant theologians, although one finds it also among some Catholic writers, particulary those in favor of mythopoeic or narrative forms of theology characterized by the systematic use of African traditional myths, symbols, and proverbs.[3]

Another kind of methodical divergence in inculturation christologies is made by authors who take the biblical teaching on Christ as their point of departure and relate that teaching to African sociocultural contexts. But most writers start from the African reality in order to see how this reality can be utilized to present Christian teaching on Christ in an African way.

At times the African worldview is taken from the African context, but more often one of several African themes or categories is chosen for the purposes of christological elaboration.[4] Such themes include ancestor, chief, elder-brother, healer, hero, life, initiation, name, and so forth. These categories are either taken from one or a few ethnic groups, or are envisaged in the light of their constitutive elements found in the majority of the African communities. Among these themes or categories, ancestor, healer, initiation, and life are perhaps those that have been most frequently utilized. Christological subjects taken from the Christian sources include Christ's incarnation; his birth, baptism, death, and resurrection; his eucharistic sacrifice; his qualities as Victor, Savior, Son of God, and others.

Compared to the christologies of liberation—to which I shall now turn—African inculturation christologies are more widespread, more developed, and exhibit more originality and variety of method.

Liberation

There are two types of liberation theology in Africa: South African Black theology, centered chiefly on racial or color factor (apartheid) and African liberation theology, found especially in the independent part of Africa, which has a broader perspective than that of South Africa. Liberation theology in independent Africa endeavors to integrate the theme of liberation in the rest of the African cultural background. Liberation is not confined to modern socioeconomic and political levels but includes emancipation from other forms of oppression such as disease, poverty, hunger, ignorance, and the subjugation of women.

Both types of liberation theology and their corresponding christologies bear many features similar to South American liberation theology and, in some cases, with North American Black theology, although they differ from both types in various ways.[5] In view of the present situation in South Africa, one is led to presume that South African Black christology will become more and more affiliated with liberation christology in the independent part of Africa. Given the general discredit of Marxism, it is to be hoped that African liberation christologists will draw their philosophical inspiration chiefly from African traditional and contemporary wisdom.

Neglected Areas

These definitions of African theology and their corresponding christologies bring to light not only the pluriformity of such theology and christology, but also the aspects or areas of African christology that have been neglected by African and other theological writers. This neglect is often the result of our narrow conception of African theology and christology, which is often limited to systematic and scientific types understood exclusively in their Christian sense. Neglected areas of African christology include those below.

African Traditional (non-Christian) Christology

It is commonly agreed that even before the coming of Christianity into black Africa, Christ was already at work among its citizens, revealing himself to them and drawing them to the Father through his Spirit in ways known only to himself. This being the case, one should expect to find traces of Christian teaching—and even of christology—in African religions or cultures that manifest Africans' religious experiences. One should also remember that Africa had contact with Christianity from the first centuries of church history. Such contact must have been diffused in various degrees among African peoples, including those in the black region, long before Christianity arrived here. One can reasonably assume, therefore, that rigorous systematic research in the traditional religions and cultures of black Africa might reveal latent forms of African Christian theologies, and even christologies, which were in existence long before the advent of Christianity in this part of the continent.

One should carefully examine African traditional myths, proverbs, and symbols that involve the incarnation of divine personages and other supernaturals. Special investigation should also be made of African beliefs and teachings on divine names and attributes, as well as the plurality of divinities, their birth and death. Research should be extended to African symbolism of the descent into hell, the ascent into heaven, and other eschatological myths. No less important are African cosmogonic myths and those of the human primordial Fall and bringers of salvation.[6] In sum, African traditional religions and cultures should be systematically and scientifically examined in order to detect traces of Christian teachings on Christ and how such teachings have been inculturated in African contexts.

African Nonsystematic Christologies

When defining African theology and christology, we noted that African theology and its corresponding christology can be understood as the simple understanding and expression of the Christian teaching in accordance with African needs and mentality. It was also mentioned that this definition is large enough to include both scientific and nonscientific African theology and christology, and that the latter exist in the African churches and ecclesial communities in a somewhat latent form, chiefly orally and in an unsystematic way.

The existence of this kind of christology can be accounted for if one remembers that African christology is taken here in the sense of simple understanding and presentation of the Christian teachings on Christ to adapt them to the problems, needs, and ways of thinking of the African peoples. It is in this sense that I say that African christology may be said to have existed since the beginning of Christianity in our continent, although, to a great extent, in a somewhat hidden form: mainly in spoken and unsystematic forms of language. Indeed, in spite of colonial attitudes of the past, missionaries and others were not infrequently led in one way or another to present the Christian doctrine to answer to the problems and even to fit it, at times, with the ways of thinking and approach proper to the Africans. And these latter, being human beings and not inanimate objects, received the Christian message and assimilated it within themselves not only in the Western form according to which it was mainly delivered, but also in keeping with their African way of experience. The so-called African independent churches may be cited as an example of communities where such christology can be more easily observed. Hence, a serious scientific investigation in this field might reveal a christology that is perhaps, in some aspects, more authentically African than any contemporary African systematic christologies produced so far.

As far as I know, systematic scientific investigation in this topic has not yet been made. Yet the subject is important. It could throw more light to the path along which African systematic christology should proceed, and it might indicate some limitations of today's African academic christologies. For this reason, I offer some general hints and guidelines that might be useful in undertaking this kind of research.

The first point I wish to mention is that this type of christology is bound to be pluriform, similar to the pluriformity of contemporary African systematic christologies. In its own way, therefore, it must include African christologies of inculturation and liberation. At this juncture, I would like to draw attention to a new form of African theology that is gradually emerging. According to V. Salvodi and R. Sesana, this theology—which they call the *theology of community development*—"provides the theoretical basis for pastoral action in the basic communities and the conscientization of development." Its architects are "bishops directly engaged in pastoral work and their theology is a response to the problems they meet in their everyday life as pastors."[7] Hence, any researcher should not lose sight of this important and promising phenomenon.

It is out of place to give here a detailed list of hints and guidelines as to how scientific investigation in the subject should be made. A few suggestions should suffice.

One of the classical ways to begin research of this type is to prepare a list of questions to be addressed to individuals (or groups) of different age, social status, sex, and religion about their understanding of Christ and his relevance to their various needs or problems and life at large. It goes without saying that the questionnaire should not be drawn arbitrarily without some guiding principles. A sound knowledge of the African traditional worldview, problems, needs, and aspirations is essential. For this purpose, the list of "typically African themes" given by Pope Paul VI in his message to Africa (*Africae terrarum,* October 1967) could be useful.[8] These themes included:

1. A spiritual view of life, including "the idea of God, as the first or ultimate cause of all things."

2. Respect for the dignity of human beings, particularly manifested in the traditional way of educating within the family, in initiation rites, and the traditional social and political life.

3. The sense of the family, evidenced by the attachment to the family and the bond with ancestors.

4. Closely linked with the family is *patria potestas* of the father of the family, implying authority and demanding respect; it is sometimes accompanied with a typically priestly function.

5. The sense of community life expressed by participation in the life of the community into which the individual is introduced by various initiation rites.

A second profitable area of research would be to study the sermons and catechetical or religious instructions on Christ of early (and even present) missionaries, catechists, and others. A researcher should examine these didactic discourses for various presentations of the mystery of the God-man, the particular aspects of christology that were stressed, the African symbols used to express the mystery, and so forth.

Third, a close investigation of the christologies of the many "African independent churches" is indispensable in this type of research. One can rightly expect more genuine Africanness in these christologies, all the more so because such christologies are the result of the spontaneous expression of the experience of Christ's mystery by Africans in their various sociocultural contexts.

In addition, the investigation should include the African christologies of inculturation and liberation. In researching liberation christology, one should first study the different forms of oppression found in the African traditional cultures and the modern sociocultural context of the African continent. The investigator should try to find out (either through direct questions or other-wise) how Africans associate Christ with these types of oppression.

Finally, one of the most effective methods is investigation through direct contact with the people by taking part in their daily life, as far as possible, in view of discovering their inculturation and liberation christologies. Apparently this method is employed by many Latin American liberation theologians, who claim that the resulting theology is not theirs, but that of the people with whom they live in close contact who are actively committed to the struggle for liberation of the poor.[9]

Need for a More Adequate Approach

Christology is undoubtedly the most advanced subject in African theology today. Much writing on this issue has progressed beyond pointing out some general wishes or methodological directives as to what should be done to actually doing it. Yet, with the exception of some academic dissertations, many essays in this field remain on the rudimentary level. This is true of both inculturation and liberation christologies. With regard to the former, the method currently used rarely goes beyond pointing out some similarities and differences between certain African cultural items and their christological parallels. The conclusion is then drawn that the African analogical pendants are found eminently in Christ (such as, Christ is the Chief, the Ancestor, the Healer, *par excellence*). This is usually followed by some practical suggestions with regard to our present African sociocultural context. As to the theological methodology that is employed in liberation christologies, in the majority of cases, it is borrowed from the Latin American way of doing liberation theology. There are some approaches that might contribute to achieving more significant and more original results, both in inculturation christologies and those of liberation.

Inculturation Christologies

There are many possible ways of approaching African christologies of inculturation, but the comparative analogical method currently used by many African writers is one of the most fruitful and useful. This method could be pursued more profoundly. Although I will make only a few brief suggestions here, the reader is referred to other writings on the subject for more details.[10]

This method, which I call the intrinsic employment of African cultural themes in theology, involves the identification of African cultural items or categories with the Christian mysteries. This permits African culture to enter internally into the theological elaboration, presentation, and formulation of the Christian mystery. Such employment of cultural themes comprises two main processes: the identification of the African element with the Christian mystery and the explication of the implications underlying such identification.

Identification is realized when the African theme fuses together with the Christian mystery to form one theological entity, such as in the statement, "Christ *is* our Ancestor" (in the African sense). This sort of identification is currently being made by African writers. The identification that is usually made is analogical. However, it can also be dialectical, as in the statement, "Christ is *not* a sorcerer" (in the African meaning). In this case, the African item (sorcerer) is joined to the Christian theme (Christ) to form a theological composite of two opposed entities, previously interpreted as irreconcilable elements. As far as I know, this kind of identification has not yet been used in African christologies of inculturation.

Explication involves the effort to understand the implications underlying this identification. Two main steps are involved: a comparative approach and a creative interpretation. The comparative approach requires a close and detailed analysis of the components of the African and Christian items that have been joined together, to determine to the extent possible the similarities and differences between them. In many cases, this analysis has been inadequate or superficial. This is an important lacuna. As I noted in one of my papers, "This type of examination will bring more fruit in the measure it is made from the perspective of each of the various components of the African category, rather than from the angle of such category in its general or global sense alone."[11]

Creative interpretation requires several steps, the first of which is the theological interpretation of the parallelisms and differences between the African cultural category and its Christian counterpart. Such interpretation is often missing in African christological essays. Even in cases where it occurs, such interpretation often does not go beyond pointing out that similarities indicate what is good and what is preparatory for evangelization in the African theme. Similarly, differences show the erroneous elements or limitations in the African category and its need for accomplishment in Christ.

At present, this kind of interpretation alone sounds almost banal, owing to its self-evidence. More is certainly required than is offered by this kind of explanation. It is thus possible to interpret the parallelisms and divergences "by accounting for their existence in terms of philosophy, cultural anthropology (e.g., diffusionism, evolutionism, Jungian archetypes, ecological environment, etc.) or theology (e.g., the presence of *logos spermatikos*)."[12] Moreover, in order to obtain more fruitful results, the search for similarities and differences should not be done in a hasty or superficial manner. It is advisable to endeavor to ascertain differences in the similarities discovered, and similarities in the differences.

The second step is the theological interpretation of the Christian mystery in terms of its African counterpart. At this stage, the theologian plunges into the heart of creative interpretation, and it is here that many African writers fail.

What is demanded in this stage is theological acumen, imagination, and originality. Theological interpretation requires the drawing, to the degree possible, of "all of the implications of the consequences and insights which are revealed by the examination and interpretation of the Christian mystery in the light of the African categories."[13]

The third step involves the principle of interconnection of the Christian mysteries.[14] To my knowledge, few African writers use this most fecund principle of theologizing. African christologies should be elaborated in the light of their close link with the mysteries of the Trinity and ecclesiology. A profound and pastorally fruitful christology is impossible without such linking.[15]

Equally significant are the pastoral implications of this process. Luckily, most African writers endeavor to indicate the practical implications of their christologies. We could wish, however, that this enterprise be pursued in a more adequate and profound manner and be extended to the spiritual life of the people; sometimes it is limited to their material welfare.

Metaphysics is also a useful resource. One of the most efficient means to acquire depth (and better results) in theological work is to participate in sincere dialogue with various theological schools in the tradition of the church. Through such dialogue, theologians will perceive better the contribution and limitations of their theology. It is always desirable and recommended to integrate the positive data of other writers in a consistent and organic manner. African theologians cannot hold dialogue with traditional and modern christologies without being involved in metaphysical problems. Besides, a theological task is to interpret the christological dogmas of the ecumenical councils in an African way. Again, it is impossible to accomplish this task properly without involvement in metaphysical questions.

Nor should the use of metaphysics be excluded from African theology under the pretext that it is foreign to the African way of thinking. Every human being has an inborn inclination to metaphysical inquiry. The African traditional beliefs in the existence of supernatural meta-empirical realities strongly indicate this fact. As Vatican II prescribes, African speculative christology, "under the tutelage of St. Thomas," is required for didactic purposes in all seminaries and other theological institutes of higher learning, including those of Africa.[16] The metaphysical approach is, moreover, a useful means to acquire theological depth.[17]

Christologies of Liberation

In spite of few differences from North American Black theology and Latin

American liberation theology,[18] African christologies of liberation are, methodologically speaking, basically similar to those of Latin America. There is, however, a pressing need for originality in this field. This is true partly because of what I feel to be questionable methodological principles of liberation theology in Latin America, but especially because the African sociocultural situation possesses an almost inexhaustible number of potentialities that can be actualized in original and authentically African liberation christologies. Indeed, it is surprising that few, if any, of the African liberation christologists have availed themselves of these potentialities to any appreciable extent. For this reason, it is highly desirable and most important that African liberation christologists should hold closer dialogue with African inculturation christologists, who appear to make use of more cultural originality.

Above all, African liberation christologists should shun reductionism—a vice shared by many liberation theologians. What is required is integral liberation, with particular stress on liberation from sin as the root cause of all oppression. Among these lines, I have suggested a method whereby the theology of liberation takes Christ's primary goal and mission on earth (that is, the supernatural salvation of humanity and the glorification of God) as a point of departure.[19] I believe that when this approach is developed consistently and deeply, with the help of African traditional and modern wisdom, it is apt to produce a more balanced and integral liberation christology that is also authentically African.

Relevance of African Christological Textbooks

There is a relevant and urgent need for African theological textbooks in our major seminaries and other higher theological institutes.[20] Even today, the theological books used in our seminaries are mostly of Western origin. Moreover, of all the books and articles written on African christology so far, none suffices for teaching purposes in our senior seminaries. These writings develop christology only with regard to some of its aspects. For the needs of teaching senior candidates for the priesthood, the whole of christology from the Bible and church tradition must be rethought from the African viewpoint before it can be used for instruction. This is another important reason for the relevance and utility of such textbooks: their construction pushes the African theologian to reflect, from an African perspective, on the totality of the Christian message on a particular mystery, and not only on some of its aspects. To my knowledge, no such treatment of any Christian theme or mystery has been carried out in writing by an African theologian.

For the sake of clarity, I am going to present a scheme for African christology. I have tried to follow the prescriptions of Vatican II with regard to how dogmatic theology should be taught in the seminaries (*Optatam Totius,* 16).

Scheme for African Christology

I. Positive Part
    A. Revelation of Christ in non-Christian religions (especially in African religions and cultures)
    B. Christ in African independent churches and "folk" Christianity (latent christology in African traditional churches)
    C. Christ in Judaeo-Christian religion
        1. The Bible
        2. Church tradition (the patristic epoch to the contemporary period, including African christologies today)

II. Systematic Part
    A. The Incarnation as redemption
        1. Incarnation in the light of christologies from above and from below
            a. Summary of biblical teaching and official position of the church
            b. Traditional theological positions (Catholic and non-Catholic)
            c. Modern theological views
            d. African theological views
                i. Already given answers (if any)
                ii. Author's views
                iii. Practical relevance (spiritual and bodily)
        2. The hypostatic union
            a. Summary of biblical teaching and official position of the church
            b. Traditional theological positions (as above)
            c. Modern theological views
            d. African theological views (as above)
        3. Inferences from the hypostatic union (natural divine sonship of the man Jesus, Christ's right to adoration, communication of idioms, christological *perichoresis*)
            a. b. c. d. (as above)
        4. Incarnation as establishing the reconciling Mediator, Ancestor, Healer, Elder Brother, Liberator, King (Chief), and so on
            a. b. c. d. (as above)
        5. The role of the Trinity
            a. b. c. d. (as above)

6. Perfections and limitations of Christ's humanity (his true humanity, holiness, knowledge, liberty, power, passibility, *kenosis)*
   a. b. c. d. (as above)
B. Redemption as continuation and fulfillment of the Incarnation
   1. Redemption in general
      a. b. c. d. (as above)
   2. Realization of redemption through the events of Jesus' life (his virginal conception, birth, circumcision, presentation in the temple, flight to Egypt, life in Nazareth, public ministry, culminating in his passion, death on the cross, descent into hell, resurrection, and ascension)
      a. b. c. d. (as above)
   3. The event of Jesus' life as ancestral, onomastic, initiatory, liberative, and vitalistic mysteries
      a. b. c. d. (as above)
   4. Realization of redemption through Christ's offices (teaching office, pastoral office, healing office, priestly office)
      a. Theology of sacrificial death and the cross and descent to hell
      b. Theology of Christ's exaltation and its relation to the eschato logical transformation of humanity and the cosmos
      a. b. c. d. (as above)
   5. Incarnation viewed from the African ancestral, onomastic, initiatory, vitalistic, liberation points of view

The above scheme needs little comment. In the systematic part, the Incarnation is inseparably linked with redemption, not only because the two mysteries are presented as indissolubly joined together in the Bible, but also because, as shown by most of (if not all) today's African christologies, these two mysteries cannot be treated separately when viewed from the African perspective. The last subdivision of this part (5) is related to what has been written on these issues by modern African christologists. For a bibliography relevant to these issues, the reader is referred to *Jesus in African Christianity* (J. N. K. Mugambi and L. Magesa, editors) and to the bibliography in this essay.

Needless to say, this scheme makes no claim for perfection. Nor is it the only possible scheme for African christology. Besides, it would be possible to construct a similar scheme based on *one* African category (for example, ancestor, healer, or liberator) as a point of departure. Nevertheless, in my opinion, the above scheme appears to be a better alternative.

On account of the intimate link between christology and the Trinity, ecclesiology and eschatology, any course on African christology should be preceded by one on the Trinity and should be followed (preferably immediately) by courses on ecclesiology (including Mariology) and eschatology.

In conclusion, I would like to emphasize what I wrote in another essay. "With the exception, perhaps, of Black christology in South Africa, none of the existing African christologies has had any appreciable influence in the life of the African churches."[21] In order to achieve such influence or impact, African christology must be taught to our seminarians, who are the future propagators of christology in our churches.

Notes

1. This article was published in *Jesus in African Christianity: Experimentation and Diversity in African Christology*, J. N. K. Mugambi and L. Magesa, eds. (Nairobi: Initiatives Publishers, 1989), pp. 17-39. For more complete information on today's African christologies, the reader should turn to that essay as well as others in the book.

2. Naturally, this recalls to mind the title of Raimundo Panikkar's books, *The Unknown Christ of Hinduism* (Maryknoll, NY: Orbis Books, 1981) and *Worship and Secular Man* (Maryknoll, NY: Orbis Books, 1973).

3. In this school, one could perhaps include what may be termed the gradually emerging *German symbolic school* of African theology, in which stress is put on the need for systematic scientific employment of African traditional symbols. Examples of writers belonging to this school are H. Rucker (see his *Afrikanische Theologie: Darstellung und Dialog*, Innsbruck-Vienna, 1985), and G. Hasenhuttl (see *Schwarz bin ich und schon*, Darmstadt, 1991). However, neither of these two writers has provided a noteworthy African christology.

4. See my article in *Jesus in African Christianity*, pp. 17ff. As regards the bibliography in that article, the following may be added: L. M. Ntumnba, *La Nomination Africaine de Jésus Christ: Quelle christologie?* (Doctoral dissertation, Louvain-la-Neuve, 1988); P. N. Wachege, *Jesu Christ Our "Muthamaki" (Ideal Elder): An African Christological Study Based on the Agikuyu Understanding of Elder* (Nairobi: Phoenix Publishers Ltd., 1992); K. Bediako, "Biblical Christologies in the Context of African Traditional Religions," in *Sharing Jesus in the Two Third Worlds*, V. Samuel and Cristopher Sugden, eds. (Grand Rapids, 1983), pp. 81-121; Charles Nyamiti, "The Incarnation Viewed from the African Understanding of Persons," in *African Christian Studies* (March 1990), pp. 3-27; (June 1990), pp. 23-76; (March 1991), pp. 29-52; (June 1991), pp. 41-68; D. W. Tomilyan, *Christ the "Matat" (Chief): A Christology from the Perspective of Kuku Culture (Sudan)* (mimeographed) (Nairobi: CHIEA, 1991).

5. Charles Nyamiti in *Jesus in African Christianity*, pp. 27-29.

6. On these issues, useful information can be obtained from L. V. Thomas, *"Généralité sur l'ethnologie négro-africaine,"* in *"Ethnologie Regionale,"* Encyclopédie de la Pléiade, vol. 1 (Paris, 1972); in the same volume see also *"L'Afrique anglophone orientale, centrale et méridionale,"* pp. 335-380; L. V. Thomas, *Les religions d'Afrique Noire* (Paris, 1969); A. A. Ruch Omi and K. C. Anyanwu, *African Philosophy. An Introduction to the Main Philosophical Trends in Contemporary Africa* (Rome, 1981); J. Mtugambi and N. Kirima, *The African Religious Heritage. A Textbook on Syllabus 224 of the East African Certificate of Education* (Nairobi, 1976); F. M. Sergounioux and J. Goetz, *Les religions des prehistoriques et des primitifs* (Paris, 1958); E. Dammann, *Die*

Religionen Afrikas (Stuttgart, 1963) and *Grundriss der Religionsgeschichte. Theologische Wissenschaft* (Stuttgart-Berlin-Cologne-Mainz, 1972), pp. 10-26; H. Gravrand, *Meeting the African Religions* (Rome, 1968); G. Parrinder, *Religion in Africa* (London, 1969) and *African Mythology* (London, 1975); K. Wiredu, *Philosophy and an African Culture* (London, 1980); B. C. Ray, *African Religions: Symbol, Ritual and Community* (New Jersey, 1976); W. Hirschberg, *Volkerkunde Afrikas* (Mannheim, 1965); J. V. Taylor, *The Primal Vision* (London, 1969); J. Mbiti, *African Religions and Philosophy* (London, 1969); R. J. Gehman, *African Traditional Religion in Biblical Perspective* (Nairobi, 1989); M. Eliade, *Patterns in Comparative Religion* (New York, 1958) and *The Sacred and the Profane: The Nature of Religion* (New York, 1961).

7. The authors mention Bishop Malula, Sanon, Kalilombe, Mwoleka, and Sarpong, among others. They also note that the AMECEA Pastoral Institute (Eldoret-Kenya) and the Lumko Pastoral Institute in South Africa are important sources for this kind of theology (V. Salvodi and R. K. Sesana, *Africa: The Gospel Belongs To Us* (Ndola, Zambia, 1986), pp. 119-120.

8. See R. Hickey, ed., *Modern Missionary Documents and Africa* (Dublin, 1982), pp. 176ff. For a list of some items in the African traditional worldview, see my article "The Incarnation Viewed from the African Understanding of Person," in *African Christian Studies* (March 1990), pp. 5ff.

9. One wonders, however, how this close contact is effected by the Latin American liberation theologians. The forms of oppression from which the poor in Latin America are suffering certainly include more varieties than socioeconomic and political oppression from Western powers and local civil authorities, as is generally claimed by these theologians. Why do these writers fail to disclose those other varieties? Besides, if these theologians communicate closely with all the poor in their country, it is surprising that apparently they have so far failed to discover the latent inculturation theologies among the indigenous Indians, who are certainly among the poor alongside whom these theologians live and work.

10. See my following essays: *African Theology. Its Nature, Problems and Methods,* Gaba Pastoral Papers, no. 19 (Uganda, 1971); *The Scope of African Theology,* Gaba Pastoral Papers, no. 30 (1973); "A Critical Assessment on Some Issues in Today's African Theology," *African Christian Studies* (March 1989), pp. 5-18; "My Approach to African Theology," *African Christian Studies* (December 1991), pp. 35-53.

11. "My Approach to African Theology," p. 44.

12. Ibid., p. 45.

13. Ibid.

14. Cf. *Vatican I,* DS (Denzinger-Schönmetzer), *Enchiridion Symbolorum,* 3016; *Vatican II, Optatam Totius* (Decree on Priestly Formation), 16. For more details on the use of this principle in African theology, see my article: "My Approach to African Theology," pp. 45-46.

15. More details on this issue can be found in my essay in J. N. K. Mugambi and L. Magesa, eds., *Jesus in African Christianity,* pp. 30-32.

16. *Vatican II, Optatam Totius,* 16.

17. For more details on the relevance of metaphysics in African theology, see "My Approach to African Theology," pp. 47-50.

18. See my essay in J. N. K. Mugambi and L. Magesa, eds., *Jesus in African Christianity,* pp. 28-29.

19. J. N. K. Mugambi and L. Magesa, eds., *The Church in African Christianity,* pp. 156-162.

20. More details on this issue can be found in my *Scope of African Theology,* pp. 33-38.

21. J. N. K. Mugambi and L. Magesa, eds., *Jesus in African Christianity,* p. 34.

5

AFRICANS CELEBRATE JESUS CHRIST

François Kabasele Lumbala

Why are ritual and worship the most appropriate expression of our experience of God? Represented in symbols, the experience of God fascinates us, attracts us, and yet always withdraws. Simultaneously veiling and revealing, symbols summon us to move beyond what is visible. Hence the importance of liturgy in any church, especially in a church intent on a mission of inculturation.

In the following pages, I shall consider certain African cultural experiences—namely, celebrations of salvation in Jesus Christ. The rituals described here are not all approved by the Roman Dicastery for Divine Worship, nor are they employed throughout all of Christian Africa. They do, however, enjoy at least the tolerance of the local ordinary, if not provisional approval restricted to certain dioceses or parishes in the spirit of no. 40 of the Second Vatican Council's Constitution on the Sacred Liturgy. In a dynamic of experiment and quest, Africans seek to express and profess Jesus Christ, celebrating salvation in Christ, in terms of who they are and how, in their daily lives, they perceive Jesus. Official approval has always been consequent upon the concrete life of communities, not antecedent to it; nor is a rite authenticated at a theologian's desk. Liturgical ritual delivers up its secrets only when celebrated in a community.

However, the dynamism at work here need not give way to anarchy.

Translated from French by Robert R. Barr.

Christian celebration always transpires in communion with the hierarchy of the church. After all, the liturgical act is a community act, and hence subject to approval by an organization. Thus, various initiatives are submitted to the local or regional hierarchy so that hierarchy, prudently, but without quenching the Spirit, can preside over their implementation.

My analysis will be divided into four parts. First, I will show how an African liturgy responds to the need for liberation, acting as a leaven in the dough of the liberation, for which Africa is striving at the present moment. Then I shall address certain experiments currently in progress in inculturated liturgy, beginning with Easter. I will then discuss Christian initiation, and finally, survey some African sacramentals.

African Liturgy: Leaven of Liberation

It seems to me that a certain amount of criticism and resistance directed against African experiments in new rites and new ways of celebrating originate in a faulty comprehension of the notion of incarnation. The incarnation of God in the history of human beings occurred at a particular moment—in Jewish space and culture. In this dimension it is unique and constitutes a monument and jewel in the history of humanity. That monument, that jewel, is cut and fashioned in a Jewish style of two millennia ago. We leave it to the "archaeologists" to admire and love it from afar. We Christians are interested in this monument because we see it as an archetype of a continuing phenomenon in the history of human beings with God. The Jewish history of Jesus interests us only because it is a starting point, a dynamizing force, that since that time has rendered the history of all human beings the place where the Word of God takes flesh and becomes Emmanuel. The Jewish Christ interests us only because, instead of making Jews of us all, he has transcended the concrete context of his incarnation to become the Alpha and the Omega of all human history.

Had Jesus himself not transcended Jewish culture? "You have heard . . . What I say to you is . . . It was also said . . . My command to you is . . ." (Matt. 5). "The sabbath was made for man, not man for the sabbath" (Mark 2:27). "An hour is coming when you will worship the Father neither on this mountain nor in Jerusalem," but "in Spirit and truth" (John 4:21-23). In the incarnation, God has seen to it that the pathways of humanity converge, but God has done so only by going beyond them, always transcending all the models.[1] Never, then, must peoples be shut up in a "regime of Christendom"—Greek, Roman, or even African. "Christian Africanness" will itself be a new transcendence of

Africanness and of any Christendom. "Any confrontation of the faith with the human condition in one of its cultural realizations stirs the inexhaustible energy of the Incarnation, and can engender an unprecedented evangelical awareness."[2]

Other resistance to attempts at inculturation is fueled by the contempt manifested by some Africans for the quest for traditional values, which they characterize as "passéism" and "cultural archaeologism." One sometimes hears things like: "Yesterday's Africa is no more. Young people in the cities no longer know the traditions of initiation or the symbols that you evoke in your experiments . . . Are the real problems of the churches of Africa not economic and political ones? You lull the people to sleep by amusing them with your old-fashioned folklore." And so on.[3]

The notion that "yesterday's Africa is no more" is the fruit of a deficient, over-hasty analysis. We need only consider what we see and observe in the cemeteries of our African cities, at the door of our delivery rooms, and on the night tables of our patients in city hospitals, in order to observe that the old conception of the world and life continues, in new forms[4]: the "confessions" made to midwives by women in labor, the pebble a pregnant woman carries in her clothing and drops at the door of the maternity clinic before entering, the words pronounced at a tomb before a burial, the abuse heaped on the parents' heads by the companions of a young person cut off in the prime of life, the fetishes fashioned for success in studies and business affairs, or love, that the groom may be faithful, the growth in the number of marabouts and anti-sorcerers in our cities. We could go on and on. No culture remains static. In order to develop, any culture borrows exterior elements—but on condition that it can integrate them in a harmonious way by creating new syntheses on the basis of old elements.

A theology of these elements may appear to certain persons as a kind of "ethnotheology." But human beings are "situated" beings. They can begin only with what they have received. There is no "ideal Christianity" on this earth. Any Christianity, even that of the fathers of the church, is but an approach to be transcended. If a rite is "beset with traps," then it ought to be taken seriously, and the experiment being conducted by "this black priest in the headdress of a traditional chief, surrounded by warriors armed with lances," should not be trivialized or written off as superficial and idle.[5]

Our cultural elements have been rejected and disparaged by colonialism. To explain these elements in a new light constitutes a step toward liberation. Such an elucidation restores to our people not only an awareness of their worth and dignity, but provides instruments for the development of new syntheses. This is no narcissistic dabbling in inculturation but a new consciousness-raising of what we are, which we can apply to the building of a new future.

Accordingly, we must recover and place at the disposition of our young people cultural elements whose transmission has been hindered, or even prevented, by colonization. Our youth will see to it that they develop along new paths for future syntheses. The effort to cultivate our values and refresh the memory of young generations is not "passéism." It is a universal necessity of culture. A people's symbols and ideals are not inborn. They must be transmitted and taught to the young. The young, in turn, will preside over the development of symbols into new, concrete forms relevant to current situations and cultural elements.

The traditional Bantu chief wore a band of leopard skin at his belt or on his arm. But that is no longer in keeping with our modern dress, so in Zaïre, the president of the Republic wears a leopard-skin toque. Here is an example of an evolution in harmony with the past. Again, instead of a lance, an instrument of power, he carries a baton, a symbol of his function as guardian of the people. Instead of sacrificing chickens or goats around the ancestors' tree, new generations surrender their first wages to the eldest of the family, who represents the ancestor, or perhaps make a gift to that person from time to time as a sacrificial offering. Instead of donning a white garment for funerals, young persons wind a white cloth around their heads. This is not "passéism," but the harmonious evolution of a cultural symbol. This step is at the foundation of our liberation. After all, if the individual is alienated and no longer has any self-esteem, he or she cannot make progress. There is no starting point. Unless one is oneself, no true encounter with another—someone different from oneself—can occur.

Not only do I maintain that an inculturated liturgy is a path to liberation, but I also believe with Vatican II that liturgy is the priority task of the church (*Sacrosanctum Concilium*, 10). Granted, the churches of an Africa that has been victimized by political dictatorships and economic domination at the hands of foreign powers must assume the task of guiding the peoples to sociopolitical liberation. But it would be a mistake to think that this is the church's main job and all of the others are conditioned by it. Wherever the management of the temporal becomes a church's main enterprise, we may doubt the Christian authenticity of that church. The economic and the political are part of life, yes. Therefore the Christian church should be interested in them and arouse the faithful to take active part. But the economic and the political are not the whole of life. The battle for sociopolitical changes constitutes a part of witness, and so all authentic liturgy must embark upon this combat. After all, liturgy involves life. Suffice it to cite the number of pastors called on the carpet by African governments for celebrating "subversive liturgies." But to stake every-thing on "sociopolitical battles" seems to me to be a mistake. Christ has come to liberate human beings and to save them. That liberation goes far beyond health, nutrition, and political liberation, which are but manifestations of the coming of the Reign of God. We are created for God, we have been made to live with God, and we have been gathered together for the praise of our divine Parent. To achieve an "inculturation" of the liturgy that succeeds in this in the churches of Africa is to seize upon the activity that provides a foundation and gives meaning to all the other activities and witnessing of our churches.

African Easter Celebrations

Just as the altar is the heart of the church, so Easter is the sanctuary of Christian liturgy. Hence the importance and, at the same time, the delicacy of the subject of Easter in the effort of inculturation.

Initiation as a Symbol of Easter

The Christian Paschal feast is the celebration of Jesus' passage from this world to his Father, his act of total offering and total praise of God, his act of intercession for the world, crowned by his death and his resurrection. In passing from this world to their divine Parent with Jesus, Christians die to sin to live a life in conformity with the will of God, in a kind of "rebirth" by which they have a "new understanding" and become "enlightened" beings. They all become "Renés," "Renatas," "Christians."[6] They no longer belong to them-selves.

This vocabulary reminds us of the ancient initiations of the mystery religions, which supplied Christianity with some of its images and words for expressing and celebrating Easter. Christianity had borrowed from Judaism the images of the sacrificial lamb and the unleavened bread of misery, symbols that Judaism itself had taken from Canaanite harvest festivals.[7]

In black Africa, the image we Christians seize is that of initiation. It is a rite that brings us across a vital threshold to be born again and opens up to us a "new understanding" of the world and of life. This rite and image has the advantage of connecting us both to Christian tradition and to the current reality in our communities of black Africa.

Not infrequently, we hear the erroneous observation, after a hasty analysis, that initiation traditions have disappeared in modern Africa and that when the young hear us speak of initiation, they no longer understand what we are talking about! Granted, initiation can no longer be performed in its ancient, traditional structures. But initiation lives, strewn throughout the life of the individual and group: at birth, at weaning, at adolescence, upon taking up a trade, at marriage, at death. All their lives long, black African persons endlessly arrive, are fulfilled, become what they are. For example, in our cities today a series of traditional rites performed by members of the family always accompanies the oath of office taken by a public official. The feet of the new functionary may be rubbed with a white hen. Or again, the proclamation of the title may be followed by the family's outcry against evil (conjuration of evil). These are initiatory rites.

It has seemed to us that it would not be out of place, but actually ideal, to envisage Easter as image of initiation. As was true for the early church, this requires a celebration of the sacraments of Christian initiation at the Easter Vigil. Next, the image of initiation calls for a rite of community reconciliation. Finally, in the course of the Paschal celebration, this same image inspires a ritual reenactment of death and resurrection—an element we have reserved for technical reasons for those about to be baptized at the Easter Vigil. We have established the following celebrations.

Holy Thursday

Holy Thursday focuses on community reconciliation and the family bond among those gathered at the Lord's Supper. Here the new family of Christ comes together on the basis of reconciliation in Christ and the meal. Christ is about to pass from this world to the Father. We must make the passage with him—allowing ourselves to be initiated, reconciling ourselves with God and human beings, and sharing in Christ's repast. This suggests the image of the departure of an eldest child. The latter gathers his siblings around him, lavishes on them his last counsels, and proceeds to the reconciliation of the group, with actions that vary with the particular conflicts that may exist within the group.[8] The service concludes with the meal.

After the readings, we celebrate a solemn rite of reconciliation. The main element of the ceremony consists in everyone's coming to dip his or her hands in a bowl of blessed water that the priest will carry outside the church after the ceremony and empty as a sign of the community's rejection of the conflicts that poison it.[9] After communion, the priest and ministers don aprons, fetch bowls of peanuts, roasted maize, bananas, or pistachios, ready to eat, which have been carried to the altar by the faithful together with the bread and wine. They move among the faithful, serving them. This gesture replaces the washing of feet, which functioned in another culture to signify service in the performance of the ministry of the church. Another reason we have eliminated the washing of the feet is that it originated in the Jewish custom of bathing before a meal, a rite of purification. Finally, we do not expose the Blessed Sacrament on Holy Thursday, the day of Christ's arrest. It is not the day of his arrest that we wish to commemorate with a vigil, but the day of his death, the day of mourning, and so we postpone the vigil of prayer and adoration to Good Friday.

Good Friday

Some African Christians have borrowed very eloquent gestures and images from the traditions of the mourning of a great chief. We are celebrating the death of Christ. The service opens with brief scenes from Christ's passion and death, each at its respective station along the Way of the Cross around the outside of the church. Between the stations, we pause for silent meditation. Then we return to the church, the president of the assembly solemnly places the cross on high in view of all the faithful and covers it with a white cloth. Women, with their heads wrapped in white cloths, sit around the cross. Warriors then step forward to make gestures of combat, a sign of the veneration and honor paid to a defender of the people, while a Bantu christological hymn is proclaimed by one of the members of the assembly. As the hymn reaches its climax, a rifle shot rings out, and the warriors' miming is at an end. They lay their instruments of war at the foot of the cross, making traditional gestures of veneration. The assembly follows in procession, making these same gestures. Thus concludes the veneration of the cross.

The prayers of the faithful follow. Then the president solemnly retires the cross to the sacristy, returning to the altar carrying the consecrated Host. He places the Host on the altar for adoration, thus binding the void of death with the continuing presence of the One who has been raised. Now vigil is kept, community after community, till morning comes.

Holy Saturday

The core and kernel of Holy Saturday is the celebration of baptism, confirmation, and eucharist. The celebration opens with the explosion of joy of the resurrected Christ in the lighting of the new fire and the declamation of traditional heroic hymns, now applied to Christ Victor. After the readings and homily come the baptisms. In celebrating our baptisms at the Easter Vigil, we are returning to the original custom of Christian initiation and its step-by-step progress through the Paschal night. The first important element in our celebration is the profession of faith. Next comes a reenactment of death and resurrection, consisting in having the candidates lie down on mats (as a symbol of death), face down, covering them with banana leaves (representing burial and hope of life), and then raising them to their feet and announcing to them that they have been raised with Christ. Now comes the pouring of the water with the proclamation of the Trinity; the anointing with holy chrism, accompanied by the blessing of the work tools of the godparent and godchild; and finally, the anointing of the newly baptized, with white kaolin, by the godparent and the president of the assembly together. The neophyte is welcomed by the assembly with applause and shouts of joy. The eucharist continues, and the newly baptized receive communion. This eucharist, like the one celebrated on Holy Thursday, is accompanied by an invocation of the ancestors and a eucharistic prayer composed in accordance with an oral tradition in the form of a dialogue between the celebrant and the assembly. The eucharist employs local eucharistic products.

The invocation of the ancestors is not something we casually insert into the ritual. It is postulated by a conception of the world as a place of sharing and mediations between the Supreme Being and other beings visible and invisible. We are like communicating vessels. Any pressure exerted on our own portion of the liquid that is life is transmitted integrally throughout that liquid to all beings living on earth as well as to the ancestors, our "living dead." Anything that influences my life will have an effect on the life of the ancestors in the beyond. The eucharist is an important event in my life, and so I call on my ancestors when I celebrate it so that they can participate in the harmony and totality of my being.[10] As for the "matter" of the eucharistic bread and cup, an adequate treatment will have to await another moment. Here, let me say briefly that there are two currents of thought on this subject. I like to refer to their proponents as, respectively, the theologians of the Transcendent and the theologians of Emmanuel. The former[11] insist on the importation of Mediterranean food, the better to mark the special nature of the Lord's supper and to remain in closer contact with the historical act as such. The latter[12] reproach these with historical fetishism and urge the use of local materials—the better, they say, to mark that our God does not come among us carrying his "picnic" under his arm! Indeed, the Mishnah lists five kinds of cereal from which the unleavened Passover bread may be baked, and among the five is millet, an African grain.[13]

Finally, we should note the birth of new prayers and christological hymns in African celebrations of the eucharist. Books such as *African Faces of Jesus (Chemins de la christologie africaine)* or doctoral dissertations such as "Nomination africaine de Jésus" and "Le Christ initiateur,"[14] are important echoes of this inculturation.

African Christian Initiation

Let us take a more detailed look at the rites of Holy Saturday. The conciliar renewal of the past twenty years has greatly emphasized the bond among the three sacraments of Christian initiation. For example, the *Praenotanda* of the Roman Ritual recommend that the three be celebrated in conjunction.

In borrowing the term *initiation* from the pagan worship of the mystery religions, despite fundamental differences between these and Christianity, our forebears in the faith capitalized on resemblances they had observed between pagan cults and Christian rites. Similarities had been perceived both in the ritual processes themselves (fasts, retreats, special formulas, purification, sacrificial offerings, new understanding, and the like) and in their finality (in the present case, union with the Beyond—with the gods—and immortality). But this was only an analogy. The purpose of Christian initiation was mainly to express the unity among the three sacraments, which made faithful of catechumens in the course of the Paschal night; the three sacraments manifested the realities of faith.[15]

In black Africa, traditional initiations have offered analogies as well as divergences. The first enterprises of inculturation steadfastly rejected our mystical initiations with their phenomena of preternatural possession. Pastors relied exclusively on the category of initiations by which young boys or girls acceded to the status of men or women in society. But for us, initiation is a good deal more than a passage from the life of a child to that of an adult. The aim of initiation is to integrate the person into the world as a whole, situating him or her formally and publicly in life as a gradual journey to the world of the ancestors. It seeks to bring a person to rebirth by leading him or her through a death and a resurrection, and this by way of asceticism and instruction.[16]

A typical schema of a traditional initiation in Africa can serve as a reference point to understand current efforts in inculturation. First, *reclusion,* which can last from three weeks to six months. Next, *asceticism* involves sleeping on the ground, eating small amounts of unusual foods, and undertaking exercises calculated to increase physical endurance. Third, *instruction* is required in the customs and history of the people, morality, and various techniques. Fourth, a *number of rites* take place, including the reenactment of death and resurrection, circumcision, excision or its opposite (lengthening of the labia minora), imposition of a new name to signify the acquisition of a new status and new role in the community, and the laying aside of old garments with a ritual toilette. Finally, the *return to the village occurs,* with an anointing with white kaolin, the donning of a new garment, and a festive community repast to which the ancestors are symbolically invited.

Some pastors have attempted a rapprochement. Father Du Fonteny, for example, in Lower Zaire, superimposed the Christian rites on the pagan rites.[17] Others preferred to rehabilitate the ancient rites in the form of sacramentals of confirmation.[18] The latter have added a blessing by the priest as a parallel to continuing traditional practices.[19] With various communities at Cijiba, we have developed a ritual of Christian initiation that is more of a synthesis. We have used it for four years now with adults who can manage to be free of their usual tasks for an entire month. These persons come to the parish center to live for three weeks. Since they are adults, there is no question of circumcision or labial extension (excision is not practiced in Kasayi), since these initiation rites have already been performed. We no longer attempt to perform the ancestral initiation at the same time as the Christian initiation. Instead, our aim is to reconcile the two in a new way.

Following the pattern of our ancestors, the initiation of a human being never ends; it is a continuing journey. Here is the schema that we follow.

1. *Reclusion:* For the last three days of Lent, the catechumens withdraw from their ordinary life and come to live at the parish church. There they follow a program of intensive prayer (in the morning, at the beginning of the afternoon, later in the afternoon at the eucharist, and in the evening).

2. *Asceticism:* They devote themselves to hard work in the service of various parish committees, such as working in the community fields or the maintenance of public springs and toilets.

3. *Religious instruction:* The group has already received religious instruction in their respective communities at the hands of "elders" and "catechists." Now the instruction is in depth. We study together the history of our peoples and the usages and customs of our ancestors, comparing the latter with Christian faith and morals. The catechetical committee leads the catechumens through a survey of salvation history and the articles of the

Profession of Faith. Then the liturgy committee conducts the initiation to worship. Each day the catechumens take part in the eucharist.

4. *Rites:* On Saturday evening we celebrate the rites. First, immediately after the homily, the catechumens recite the Profession of Faith and renounce Satan. For the symbolic reenactment of death-resurrection, the participants lie on mats that have been placed on the floor. We cover them with banana leaves and intone the chant of mourning. Then we raise them up, saying, "Christ has come out of the tomb, alive forever. You, too, you are alive with him!" After this reenactment, water is poured over the candidates' heads, with the proclamation of the Trinity. The priest incenses the candidates, and the rite proceeds with the adoption of a new name.

A new name is chosen by each new Christian. It may be from the ancestral tradition (provided it be representative of the call of God or a translation of the name of a Christian mystery) or in memory of a saint. The priest asks the godparent what the newly baptized's new name is to be, and the godparent responds with the recitation (or chant) of the godchild's genealogy, ending with the new name. Thereupon the priest solemnly and festively greets the newly baptized person, pronouncing the new name in a loud voice, and the two shake hands.

Confirmation follows. Before the anointing, the godparent fetches a work tool used by the godchild in his or her work or trade. The godparent dances around the godchild, carrying the tool, and presents it to the celebrant, who blesses the tool, anoints the forehead of the neophyte with the holy chrism, and performs the laying on of hands. Finally, the celebrant smears white kaolin on the neophyte's arms, cheeks, and feet, proclaiming that this person is a new being, with a new status. He shakes hands with the newly confirmed person, who turns toward the assembly to receive the applause of all. Then the eucharist proceeds, opening with the invocation of the ancestors. The eucharistic prayer, composed of the classic elements, is structured as a dialogue between the celebrant and the assembly.

Some Sacramentals in Africa

Rites of Religious Consecration

Although it would be good to describe a number of different efforts along these lines, I must limit myself to a rapid survey.

In Cameroon, one religious community, the Congregation of the Beatitudes, employs the symbolism of the makabo plant, whose leaves grow in such a pattern that when it rains, it waters the plant next to it. As a sign of their commitment, candidates for religious profession carry this plant to church with them to hand to the celebrant to indicate they have consecrated their lives to the ministry of the gospel in community life.

In Malawi, the Convent of Poor Clares of Lilongwe has adopted the use of maize flour, a symbol of life (as it is used to make *nsima,* the staple Malawian food) to express the gift of themselves from their parents. The parents present the flour to the celebrant as a symbol of the life of their child. The convent, for its part, makes a gift of fire to represent their contribution to and cooperation in their sister's act of consecration. Finally, one of the religious in charge (or a superior) sprinkles the candidate's forehead with a bit of oil, recalling the traditional initiation rite, in which the woman who gave a child its name sprinkles the child with this oil.

In Zaïre, the rites center on three elements: the intervention of the parents and ancestors, the pact in blood, and certain rites of initiation. In Kinshasa, the main focus is on the pact in blood. The celebrant addresses the candidates for profession:

> Now you will offer a drop of your blood on the linen cloth. This piece of cloth, with its spots of pure blood, will be placed beside the altar stone and kept there to symbolize the daily offering of your life for the glory of God our Father and for the service of human beings, our siblings. At communion time, Christ will give you to drink of his most holy and most pure blood. Thus a pact of friendship will have been struck between you and Christ.

At these words, each of the candidates has her fingertip pricked, so that a drop of blood comes forth. Then she approaches the piece of linen, which the bishop holds draped across his knees, to spot it with her blood. Next, the master of ceremonies displays the cloth to the assembly of the faithful, unfolding it before them. The bishop then rises, turns to the people of Christ, and recites the prayer of blessing. Finally, the master of ceremonies carries the cloth to the altar and places it alongside the altar stone.

The rite celebrated by the Sisters of Charity gives significant attention to parents and elders, and through them, the ancestors. The rite opens with a dialogue between the parents and the bishop concerning their dispositions with regard to their daughter's undertaking. This dialogue extends to the whole congregation in a traditional stylized conversation. Finally, before pronouncing the formula of the vows, the candidate receives her parents' blessing. In Kasaya, parents impart this blessing by applying white kaolin or ashes from the fireplace of the family home while pronouncing the following words:

> We thy family hold naught against thee, but without malice or spite allow thee to depart. May thy path be as white as this kaolin. May thy feet tread upon no scorpion or serpent, but only soft, sweet earth.

At Matadi, in Lower Zaïre, this blessing is given with a kola nut, palm wine, a lifting of the hands, and words spoken by the father or aunt. This person first invokes the Supreme Being, then the line of the ancestors. Then he or she chews a kola nut, takes a sip of palm wine, and spits the mixture on the candidate's hands and arms, finally lifting his or her hands on high three times, praying that the candidate may have a life *"sambuka, kinda, siama"*—strong, fruitful, and persevering. And the young woman responds, *"Yobo"*—so be it.

The Mothers of Bethany include the parents in the ceremony of the vows and celebrate the pact in blood at communion time. But they add a special rite by presenting three symbols at the moment of profession.

> In the name of the Father, and of the Son, and of the Holy Spirit. Before you, our bishop, I, [name], in all liberty of mind and heart, bind myself by vow to God and the Blessed Virgin Mary: [lifting a pearl necklace] a vow to withdraw my heart from the things of earth; [lifting a bunch of banana leaves bound with a white cloth thong] a vow to don my undergarments as for my Lord alone, who wears the leopard skin as I the banana branch; [lifting a piece of rope] a vow to dispose my heart to obey as a goat that never rejects her master's halter, however rude, according to the Rules and Constitutions of the Mothers of Bethany: this vow I make this [day, month, year].

In the ritual of Mbandaka, certain elements of initiation have simply been added. While the candidate pronounces her vow, she holds a cord of raffia in her hands. With each vow, she ties a knot in the cord, so that after she has pronounced the three vows she has tied three knots in the cord, which henceforward will be preserved in a sacred place. As an emblem of her consecration, an ivory bracelet is placed on the new sister's wrist by the bishop.

At the conclusion of the eucharist, the family awaits the newly consecrated young woman at the church door, where the initiation dance begins. Horns are placed around her neck, and she is given a special knife for her right hand and a spear for her left. The hide of a totem animal, or monkey, regarded as very strong or the mightiest in the region, is wound around her hips as a loincloth. She skips about in this "armor," first around the churchyard, then back into the church, to the applause of the multitude.

The men of the Congregation of the Son of God, at Luiza, also use a special knife as the symbol of initiation and maturity. The weapon is conferred on each newly professed by the bishop.

In each of these rites, the key moments specified by the Roman Ritual that we have from Vatican II are all included: call and interrogation, commitment or profession of vows, admonition and prayer by the celebrant and the assembly, and finally, conferral of emblems. But these various elements are distributed quite differently, depending on the concrete symbols utilized and their specific traditional meaning and impact on the participating group.[20]

Blessing of Fields and Sowing

The work of the fields occupies great numbers of persons in black Africa. It is a labor of survival, surrounded with traditional rites to ensure its success. These rites consist essentially in an attempt to remove any handicap to life—anything infertile, any kind of division that would entail death in any form—from the place and the time of planting. For a Christian to bless a thing, a person, or an activity is to call down the divine grace on that thing or person in the name of Jesus Christ and his salvation. All the signs of the moment must be set in parallel with salvation history, and that history must be expressed as the human being's supreme good, the finality of all the other graces sought at this moment. Here is a ritual that adheres to these principles.

The faithful arrive for the celebration of the eucharist carrying a little earth from their fields along with a few grains of the seed to be sown. Two pots have been placed on a small table before the entrance of the church, and the assembly gathers around them. The priest joins them, wearing his liturgical vestments, accompanied by an altar server carrying a vessel of holy water. The introductory hymn reminds the assembly, "But for the Lord, we could do nothing, nor would anything be fertile." The priest invites the faithful to come forward with their offerings of earth and seed and to place the earth in one of the pots and the seed in the other. Then the priest blesses the earth that has been placed in the pot, praying that all accidents and danger be removed from the soil—any thorns, wounds from hoes, and so on. Then he blesses the seed, praying that they may bring forth fruit a hundredfold. Finally, he sprinkles both the earth and the seed with holy water, begging of God such rain and fine weather as will be conducive to a plentiful harvest. The entire assembly then processes into the church singing Psalm 51, and the two pots are placed at the foot of the altar. The greeting of peace follows, then the readings, and finally, the rest of the eucharist.

This rite blends an animistic conception of the world with the Christian notion. When you bring a bit of soil from your field to the church, you have brought the whole field. If you place a grain of your seed grain in the pot, you have brought your entire store of seed to the altar. And this is true of everything you offer in ritual. But "God gives the growth" (1 Cor. 3:7), and this is what is emphasized by the readings for this occasion (Gen. 1:27-31; Ps. 125; John 12:23-26).

Blessing of Bewitched Children

The premise of the blessing of bewitched children is that sorcery is a widespread social phenomenon. Sorcery consists essentially in the will to harm the life of another by evil spells of a preternatural, diabolic order. Children are often placed in thrall by malevolent adults, and they must be delivered from them. This ritual, which takes place at the eucharist after the reading of the word, consists of five steps.

1. Summons of the interested parties and interrogation as to what they have done and what they now desire.
2. Prayer and blessing with holy water. The parties prostrate themselves before the altar as Psalm 51 is sung. The priest then sprinkles them with holy water, citing the grace imparted to them at baptism.
3. A tonsure, a traditional sign in rites of deliverance, is now performed by the priest, who begs of God the grace of the "non-return" of the evil and the strengthening of these persons' desire for the good.
4. The cry of solidarity against evil (a traditional rite in the process of deliverance) is raised. The assembly is invited to cry out against the evil, to curse it. Then the prostrate persons are raised to their feet.
5. Prayer and laying-on of hands: the priest lays hands on the persons involved, with a prayer recalling Christ's mission of liberation and deliverance (Luke 4:18-19).

Conclusion

God is the same for all. Jesus Christ has come to save human beings as a group and each of them in particular. Thus, God's encounter with human beings will be both the same and different, among all persons and throughout all times. This is the logic of love.

The world over, lovers hold hands and kiss. But each couple expresses these gestures differently, according to their own respective ways of touching and kissing. We are different from one another. The way in which we enter into relationship and communion with God, with the same God, will be both different and alike. After all, each of us is unique, but we all stand before the same God.

If this is true for each individual, how true it will be for cultures! The prayer of African Christians will sing of salvation in Jesus Christ and his Lordship. It will praise the Father, it will invoke the Spirit. But it will do these things differently. After all, African persons are themselves. They are different from everyone else, because they are situated differently. They are conditioned by different sociocultural situations. They will pray in other rhythms, through networks of orality, through a different theological discourse, through another mystique and spirituality.

This difference is not to be deplored. On the contrary, it is a benefit. After all, the Christian mystery is one of infinite richness. Sung and professed in different melodies, different rhythms and symbols, it will only be more splendid and magnificent.

Notes

1. François Kabasele Lumbala, "L'au-delà des modèles," in *Chemins de la christologie africaine,* ed. François Kabasele, Joseph Doré, and René Luneau (Paris: Desclée, 1988).

2. Giuseppe Alberigo, address to the Bologna Colloquium of 1988.

3. Jean-Marc Éla, trans. Robert R. Barr, *African Cry* (Maryknoll, NY: Orbis Books, 1986); Achille Mbembe, *Hérésies et dissonances: critique politique du christianisme africain d'aujourd'hui* (Paris, 1988).

4. *Tradition et modernisme en Afrique noire,* Bouake Colloquium (Paris, 1965); Van Bulck, "Existence et portée du monothéisme africain," in *Formation religieuse en Afrique noire* (Brussels: Lumen Vitae, 1955), p. 43; O. Bimwenyi Kweshi, *Discours théologique négro-africain* (Paris, 1983); Jean-Marc Éla, *La ville en Afrique* (Paris, 1984).

5. Eloi Messi Netogo, *Théologie africaine et etnophilosophie* (Paris, 1985), p. 70.

6. M. Jourjon, "Les pères de l'Église et le dialogue de l'identité chrétienne," in *Sacrements de Jésus-Christ* (Paris: Desclée, 1983), p. 47.

7. Roland de Vaux, *Institutions de l'Ancien Testament,* vol. 2 (Paris, 1982), pp. 383-94.

8. I have presented some of these ritual acts in "Sin, Confession and Reconciliation in Africa," *Concilium* 190 (1987), pp. 74-81.

9. Kabasele, "Pâques africaines," *Communauté et Liturgie* 2-3 (1987).

10. See my "L'inculturation sacramentelle au Zaïre," *Lumen Vitae* 42 (1987), p. 1.

11. Among them: A. Vanneste, in *Revue Africaine de Théologie* (6) 12 (1982); D. Notomb, in *Nouvelle Revue Theologique* (105) 1 (1983); L. Mpongo, in *Nouvelle Revue Theologique* (108) 4 (1986).

12. Among them: A. T. Sanon, "Dimensions anthropologiques de l'Eucharistie," in *Documentation Catholique* 79 (1981), pp. 721-28; Jean-Marc Éla, *My Faith as an African* (Maryknoll, NY: Orbis Books, 1988), pp. 47-50; Elochukwu Uzukwu, "Food and Drink in Africa and the Christian Eucharist," *B.T.A.* 2 (1980), pp. 171-187; Kabasele Lumbala, "L'inculturation sacramentelle au Zaïre," pp. 83-84.

13. Kurt Hruby, "Le geste de la fraction du pain ou les gestes eucharistiques dans la tradition juive," in *Gestes et Paroles dans les diverses familles liturgiques,* Conférences St. Serge, 24th week (Rome, 1978), p. 128.

14. The reader will find some elements of these hymns in *Chemins de la christologie africaine;* L. Museka, "Nomination africaine de Jésus" (doctoral thesis, University of Louvain, 1988); L. Luyeye, "Jésus l'initiateur: esquisse d'une christologie inculturée" (doctoral thesis, Toulouse, 1988).

15. F. M. Gy, "La notion chrétienne d'initiation: jalons pour une enquête," *L.M.D.* 132 (1977), p. 53.

16. Anselme T. Sanon and René Luneau, *Enraciner l'Évangile* (Paris: Karthala, 1982), pp. 184, 198.

17. Du Fonteny, "Évolution et méthodes d'apostolat en Afrique," *Bulletin des missions* 3-4 (1952), pp. 20-21.

18. C. Mubengayi Lwakale, *Initiation chrétienne et initiation africaine* (Léopoldville, Zaïre, 1966).

19. Cilowa, *Dipambidila baana* (Mbujimayi, 1977).

20. The reader may consult my *Alliances avec le Christ en Afrique* (Athens, 1987).

6

INCULTURATION AND THE LITURGY (EUCHARIST)

Elochukwu E. Uzukwu

The presence of many African and Asian bishops at the Second Vatican Council may have facilitated the strong position taken by the council with regard to culture: only through culture do human beings come to authentic and full humanity (*GS* 53). We may take this assertion as self-evident; however, there is no consensus among African local churches about how this "incultura-tion" is to be realized in practice. The orientations of the Nigerian and Zairean churches, the two largest conferences in Africa, project this absence of una-nimity.

In Nigeria, the Roman Catholic clergy shies away from a courageous rooting of Christian life into ethnic experience. Despite hundreds of theses, both published and unpublished, that explore ways in which Christianity should be practiced in Nigeria, the Nigerian hierarchy feels more at ease with promoting "orthodox doctrine and approved liturgical discipline."[1] The Yoruba, more than other peoples of Nigeria, have maintained their cultural heritage despite modernity and the Christian or Muslim presence. They may thus prefer spiritual churches such as the Aladura, which have room for culturally related patterns of ritual behavior (drumming, singing, clapping, ecstatic experiences), to the missionary churches.[2]

But despite the room for adaptation of the Roman liturgy to local situations (*SC* 37-38), very little has been done apart from translating Latin liturgical texts and permitting dancing during the offertory procession. Among the predominantly Roman Catholic Igbo, the liturgical texts have not been completely translated; gestural behaviors such as clapping or dancing are unknown in the eucharistic liturgy except during special fund-raising masses such as harvest festivals and bazaars. However, popular charismatic movements and healing ministries are gradually introducing into the Roman Catholic church symbolic objects and gestures that characterize the spiritual churches. The abundant use of holy water in healing masses, ecstatic experiences (interpreted as charismatic phenomena but with parallels in Yoruba *orisa* or Igbo *agwu* cults), along with clapping and dancing, are no longer the preserve of those churches called *uka mmili* (water churches) or *uka akulu-aka* (clapping churches) by Roman Catholic Igbos. Rituals have been devised spontaneously by many pastors to reconcile parties in a conflict, to reestablish confidence in families, clans, or villages. But these are yet to be coordinated as authorized liturgies of dioceses.[3]

When we turn to the Zairean local church, we notice a sharp contrast between the Zairean clergy's positive appreciation of their cultural heritage and the more ambiguous Nigerian position. Even during the preparatory stages of the Vatican II document on the liturgy, the bishops of Zaire had expressed dissatisfaction with the Roman liturgy. They felt that a return to the "sources" would help put in its place this liturgy that is foreign to Africa and then introduce fundamental adaptations responsive to the African situation. The result is the Romano-Zairean rite, which, in many ways, is a departure from the austere and precise Roman ritual.

It may be important at the beginning of this essay to highlight the possible causes of the divergence in attitude toward culture among the leaders of African local churches. The first cause may not be unconnected with different attitudes toward colonialism as supported by anthropology and the missionary enterprise. Mudimbe has exposed persuasively how colonialists, missionaries, and anthropologists labored to transform Africa into European dominions—socially, politically, economically, and spiritually. Whether the anthropologist operated with an evolutionary or functionalist model, whether the colonialist imposed his wish through indirect rule or by assimilation, or whatever the nationality of the missionary, they all believed that "Africans must evolve from their frozen state to the dynamism of Western civilization."[4]

Preoccupied with the "salvation of souls," the missionary systematically assailed the environment of the African in order to change the African person.[5] Converts to Christianity were made to embrace this negative attitude toward the African person and environment. The training of the local clergy was very strongly marked by the exclusion of Africa from any positive contribution to its reception of the gospel. In Nigeria this missionary-colonialist orientation was accepted and propagated by the church leadership, while in Zaire it was resisted and reversed.[6]

The second reason is related to the first. Anthropologists such as Griaule and Evans-Pritchard and missionaries such as Tempels started to distance themselves from the practice of imposing European models on the African situation and began to appreciate the positive value of African cultures. Tempels's effort resulted in the *Jamaa* experiment (a Christian community), which was later excommunicated by the hierarchy for unorthodoxy.[7] While this climate of openness to African culture was favored by missionaries in Zaire, no such openness was recorded in Nigeria, despite encouraging encyclicals such as Benedict XV's *Maximum Illud* (1919). Roman Catholic missionaries in eastern Nigeria, who were primarily Irish, were very insistent on and uncompromising about handing on, without change, whatever they practiced in their country (in true imitation of Columbanus' mission to Gaul in the sixth century). While the Zairean hierarchy carried forward its positive approach to culture in its Faculty of Theology founded in 1957 in the work of theologians and in church life, the Nigerian hierarchy simply clung to its inheritance.

Finally, the liturgical movement, which reached its peak after World War II, saw the monastery of Mont-César in Belgium as its center stage.[8] The impact of Mont-César on the Belgian church was not lost on the Belgian colony of Congo-Zaire. Ireland, on the other hand, did not play any significant role in this liturgical movement; subsequently, it had no impact on the Irish church or in areas where Irish missionaries worked. Thus, while the Zairean local church was receptive to adaptation, the Nigerian local church viewed it with apprehension as either a return to "paganism" or infidelity to Rome.

These preliminary suggestions about the causes for the divergence in the attitude of African local churches toward cultural heritage are useful not only for making an inventory of liturgical productions in Africa; they are also useful in understanding the various meanings attached to inculturation in the Roman Catholic church. Official Roman theology favors a situation whereby the gospel transforms and uplifts culture.[9] The model is still evolutionist (colonialist-missionary). The gospel is always carried by and communicated through a given culture—in this case, west European culture. Thus, the emphasis laid in Roman documents—and reflected in positions of the Nigerian bishops—on *purifying* and *uplifting* is not devoid of ambiguity; it is not clear where the "culture-free gospel" ends and Western culture begins. Furthermore, there seems to be a lack of appreciation of how the gospel becomes different as it is being sharpened by questions posed to it by the context and shaped by responding to the context in which it is received and how it remains the same, retaining its universal character.[10] But it is these two dimensions of sameness and difference that must be brought to the fore in the interaction between gospel and culture. In this essay I will make use of these two categories to assess the eucharistic liturgies celebrated creatively in Africa.

I shall approach celebration under two main rubrics: first, African eucharists as celebrative memorials and, second, verbal gestures in African eucharistic celebrations. First I will examine African celebrations that are characterized by a joy rooted in historical memory. In this way, the African traditional assembly/celebration becomes a vehicle to express gesturally the experience of redemption in the Christ. Then I will dwell on the power of the spoken word in rendering thanks to God for the Christ, as in African Christian eucharistic prayers. In the first part I shall use the Ndzon-Melen mass developed in Cameroon as a model; in the second part, the Gaba Pastoral Institute's eucharistic prayers will inspire my analysis. I make little reference to the highly developed Zairean liturgy, as it is described elsewhere in this book. I would have liked to examine texts of liturgies celebrated in South Africa, but did not have access to them. Furthermore, the dominance of the militant prophetic model in the South African Anglican and Protestant churches, which cause them to look askance at the culture-oriented positions of other sub-Saharan African churches, would present another point of view.[11] But I am limiting my study to the Roman Catholic liturgies; thus, the more ancient Coptic and Ethiopic liturgies and Anglican and Protestant liturgies, whether in South Africa or elsewhere, are not examined.[12] Finally, since the eucharistic celebration is my theme, I shall not refer to the rich experiments on Christian initiation, especially in the francophone churches of West Africa.[13]

The African Eucharist as Celebrative Memorial

Liturgical celebration is characterized by action. Celebrations that can be called creative in Africa are marked by the active participation of the whole celebrating community. When the intention for the convocation of the assembly is grasped, there is active participation. But, in addition, when the reasons for the convocation are acted out in assembly, the celebration becomes a tensive symbol—an environment for the creation and realization of life.

In trying to spell out the thoughts that inspired the organization of the Ndzon-Melen mass, Abega insists that the inspiration is the assembly (*etongan, ekaon*) of the Beti, an ethnic group in Cameroon. In the assembly, there is a particular problem to be discussed, the convocation is generally informal, all present express their views freely and fully, at the end the leader of the community summarizes the points made and announces the proposed solutions, and the assembly acclaims. Then a meal is served by the leader, bringing the ceremony to an end.[14] Drawing on this Beti assembly, Ngumu and Abega created a Cameroonian liturgy that calls for the intensive participation of all present. However, this tradition, or Beti memory, does not explain all the innovations in the Cameroonian mass. It seems unlikely that this alone would provoke such a strongly negative reaction to it as "paganization of the Catholic cult" or the complimentary remark that it is the "best liturgical adaptation realized since Vatican II Council."[15] Other types of assemblies, especially religious festivals, constitute part of this African memory inspiring the Cameroonian eucharist.

In research projects I directed in Congo Brazzaville and Zaire on the theme "Liturgical Assembly," it was generally agreed that traditional assemblies are convoked for various reasons: social, political, economic, and religious, with religious aspects functioning freely in any type of assembly. But specifically religious assemblies often followed a pattern, as shown among the Kongo, for example, where a specifically religious assembly includes a convocation and gathering of the community under the leader, libations to the ancestors (*bakulu*), an invocation of the *bakulu* by the chief, awaiting the reply of the *bakulu* through dreams or revelations made to mediums, and the community reactions to the reply through festive celebration or reconciliation, as the case may be.[16]

In Cameroon, Zaire, East Africa, Ghana, and other areas that have made efforts to adapt and inculturate the liturgy, I feel that it is the festive celebration that constitutes the dominant memory for the eucharist. It may be interesting for non-African observers or Euro-Africans to note how the festival characterizes not only joyful events such as marriage, solemn outings of chiefs, initiation rites, and so on, but also ceremonies such as reconciliations, funerals, ritual purifications to cleanse abominations, and so forth. This emphasis on festival is possible in the ritual removal of abominations or in funeral ceremonies because the individuals involved in the action (i.e., the *dramatis personae*—the criminal or the dead) are being reintegrated into the community. The community never views as negative its life received through ancestors and lived in dynamic interaction with them. Neither death nor evil can terminate this life. Celebration, as such, becomes a "living-out" of the triumph of life over death and over other negative forces.[17] Each member of the community actively participates and tastes, affirms, and contributes to the pervasive presence of this life. Only those formally excluded from the community (criminals beyond reconciliation or those who die evil deaths) experience the darkness of death and remain a constant threat to the life of the community.

It is thus the depth of the African memory—the experience of life as victorious—that has dictated the pattern of the eucharistic celebration as a joyful festival in Africa. The integration of the colorful ceremonies of the annual Odwira Festival into the celebration of Corpus Christi among the Asante in Kumasi, Ghana, tells about this joy. The same joy marks the celebration of the eucharist with fanfare as the *ofala* festival of Christ (yearly outing of the chiefs) in some Igbo parishes in Nigeria. Even in a regular Roman-type celebration such as the Chrism Mass in the Awka diocese (1985) and the Enugu diocese (1989) in Nigeria, there was a predictable reaction of the congregation to the charismatic renewal or healing by prayer hymns such as:

> Are you a winner?
> I am a winner
> in the Lord Jesus!

or

> Higher, higher, higher,
> Higher, Jesus, higher,
> Lower, lower, lower,
> Lower, Satan, lower!

People rose spontaneously to declare themselves winners in the Lord Jesus—to lift high the victorious Jesus and stamp out Satan. The note of the festival is unmistakable! This cannot be celebrated with folded hands, but with abundant gestures: song, clapping, and dance!

When the carefully organized Ndzon-Melen mass in Cameroon begins with song and dance to enthrone the Book of the Gospel from which God's word is addressed to the community, and when this joy reaches a crescendo after the institution narrative, it replicates the African celebration of life. By participating, all present must confirm their appropriation of this life, mediated through the ancestors and experienced in a new kind of way in Jesus the Christ.

Both Charles Nyamiti and Bénézet Bujo have expressed the experience of fullness of life in Jesus the Christ by using the ancestor model. Nyamiti sees

Jesus the Christ as the culmination of the Brother-Ancestorship. For Bujo, Christ is the Proto-Ancestor. Bujo does not situate him on a biological line but places him "on the transcendental level, where he is the one from whom the existential strength and life of the ancestors flow." Thus, "the Proto-Ancestor invites his followers to ritual creativity."[18]

Whether one accepts the ancestor model or not, and whether or not the participants in a lively African eucharist are able to articulate their experience verbally, we cannot fail to note the flow of the ancestral memory into the Christian response. Life as it is encoded in the African ethnic experience by symbols is re-expressed and re-experienced through those symbols, by means of gestural behavior patterns, to project its full experience and expression in the Christ.

In this experience and expression, the role of body as primal symbol must be noted. I shall borrow Thorleif Boman's characterization of the difference between Hebrew and Greek thought patterns to introduce the difference between lively African eucharists and the received Roman liturgy.

> The matter is outlined in bold relief by two characteristic figures: the thinking Socrates and the praying orthodox Jew. When Socrates was seized by a problem, he remained immobile for an interminable period of time in deep thought; when Holy Scripture is read aloud in the synagogue, the orthodox Jew moves his whole body ceaselessly in deep devotion and adoration. . . . Rest, harmony, composure, and self-control—this is the Greek way; movement, life, deep emotion, and power—this is the Hebrew way.[19]

The genius of the Roman liturgy, even after the reforms, from the Missal of Pius V (1570) to the Missal of Paul VI (1969), could still be summed up as being precise and to the point.[20] This austere liturgy does not project the body in the same way that liturgies in Africa have recently attempted to do. For example, the dance or rhythmic swaying accompanied by clapping and strident cries figure prominently in the Ndzon-Melen mass. This is true at the opening of the liturgy, at the offertory, during the Sanctus, and after the Institution Narrative (when the Gloria is sung), and every song is executed with meaningful gestures. The same emphasis on bodily gestures is highlighted in the Zairean liturgy.

On the other hand, certain gestures considered to be excessive (like the dance) were suppressed from the Roman liturgy since the Middle Ages.

Consequently, references to the dance of David and similar references in the Psalms were sublimated. They were interpreted as the ecstatic gestures of the pious Christian soul tending toward cosmic rhythm. Yet Justin the Martyr talked about the liturgical dance of children, Chrysostom and Gregory Nazianzen spoke about the modest dance in the church, and there was the Easter dance of subdeacons in the twelfth century. These were exceptions which failed to survive in Western Christian practice.[21]

In Africa these gestures, which are realized by deploying the body in time and space, are not only expressive of joy, as in festive celebrations, but they also tell how the self is experienced. The self is experienced as a whole, from head to toe, corporeal yet spiritual; it communicates bodily through relationships in a given community in both a visible and invisible manner. The body is thus not the beast of burden to be chastised, nor a prison for the soul, nor the machine for the thinking subject; rather it constitutes the center for the total manifestation of the person in gestures.[22] The body is thus the primal symbol with which the African eucharist expresses the experience of the Christ.

It is this healthy, wholesome experience of the self, bodily, that may have influenced the unanimous decision throughout Africa to reorganize the actions of the Liturgy of the Word. These modifications were introduced in the East African, Zairean, Cameroonian, and Nigerian Igbo celebrations (the Igbo sketch is in a preliminary form). Instead of the received Roman pattern: entrance procession and greeting of the altar and people; penitential rite (from the eleventh century *Confiteor),* nonverbal expressions of humility begun before the seventh century, and the fifth-century litanic *Kyrie Eleison*; collect, readings, homily, and the prayers of the faithful, all with Jewish origins,[23] the Ndzon-Melen liturgy has the following pattern: opening hymn accompanied by dance while the ministers are vesting, entrance procession, enthronement of the Book of the Gospel, which is acclaimed; readings and homily; creed, during which people bring their gifts; prayer, with both individual and community intentions indicating areas where conversion is needed, and supplication; collect.

The organizers of African eucharists insist that the word of God must be heard before supplications for God's mercy are made. In this way, they reason, God's word challenges the assembled community. But they are saying more than that. They are also affirming that the first attitude of God's people before its Father (the divine Parent-Ancestor according to Nyamiti)[24] is not guilt but joy, it is not *apologiae* but song and dance.[25] In this manner the eucharist bears witness to an African optimistic anthropology and sets aside the received Western anthropology, which is more pessimistic.

Three aspects of the Western tradition have failed to attract Africans: 1) the long history of fear and suspicion of the body that formed the environment of the patristic reception of the faith; 2) the subsequent entrenchment of this attitude in Western spirituality by a preference for fleeing the corrupt world (*fuga mundi*) instead of staying in it to transform it; 3) the dominance of the Germanic-Celtic spirit in the Middle Ages that centered on the individual rather than the community and was surcharged with *apologiae.* To be authentic and in tune with the African environment, African liturgies prefer a display of the community before God and an intensification of the relationship with God, who exposes to the community, through his word, the way to conversion or self-transcendence.

It is here that African theologians should incorporate into their praxis the "sharp cutting edge" recommended by Desmond Tutu, who says that it does not suffice to reconcile the "split in the African soul." Rather, he says, African theology should also "speak meaningfully in the face of a plethora of contemporary problems which assail the modern African."[26] The body displayed before God in song and dance, in quiet listening to the double-edged word of God, in self-examination, prayers, and supplications is not an individual body but a social body. This is because ritual action in Africa is always action of the social body (the assembled church). The word that challenges this body is the prophetic word. The action of this body in gestures and words not only replicates the heavenly liturgy but imposes a corresponding obligation on this body to act to change the world. Ritual action and ethical behavior are two sides of the same coin. If, as in an experiment by Vincent Donovan among the Masai, the eucharist may sometimes not be celebrated because the "grass has stopped" (i.e., a family has refused sharing in the brotherhood by refusing to accept the handful of grass being passed from family to family),[27] then, similarly, the celebrating African Christian community cannot remain indifferent to poverty and oppression. Tears must be wiped away so that the optimistic African view of humankind and the universe as it is channeled by the eucharist may be concretely lived out. The present organization of the eucharistic celebration in Africa is a challenge to the celebrating church, and that church must realize the ethical consequences of what it celebrates.

Verbal Gestures in African Eucharistic Celebrations

When I use the phrase *verbal gestures,* I should like to insist that words also involve setting the body in motion in time and space. Since verbal communication in Africa is mainly oral, the spoken word assumes a dynamic character. A bard in the Komo initiation society in Mali has said:

> The word is everything.
> It cuts, flays.
> It models, modulates.
> It perturbs, maddens.
> It heals or kills.
> It amplifies, lowers, according to its force.
> It excites or calms souls.[28]

What is expected of the word of God is shown in the ceremonies surrounding the Book of the Gospel. It is acclaimed, especially in the Ndzon-Melen mass and a draft of the Tanzanian mass; the Tanzanian mass prays God "to open our hearts and ears so that we can listen to the readings and cherish them in our hearts." Each reader receives authorization from the presiding priest in Zairean and Tanzanian liturgies. In this insistence on authorization, we encounter what the Bambara describe as the "immensity of the Word," a word whose "length" encompasses the whole of humanity, the integral word that is the patrimony of the whole of humanity, indeed of divinity itself. Thus, a word that is of this magnitude, as the word of God, is "too large" for the mouth that pronounces it.[29] It is this word, confided to authorized and properly initiated elders of the community, including the presiding priest, that challenges the community to conversion.

Eucharistic prayers composed for eucharistic liturgies in Africa try to capture this dynamism and reverence for the word. This is done in various ways: by adopting prayers arising from the traditional African setting to function in African Christian eucharists, by linking the eucharistic prayer itself to traditional African ancestors through whom life is bestowed, by capitalizing on motifs that preoccupy African life.

It is important to note that these prayers are being composed in a Roman Catholic church that is very sensitive about the composition of new eucharistic prayers. In fact, the Roman church refused immediate permission to episcopal conferences to compose their own eucharistic prayers.[30] However, the compositions in East Africa and Zaire, which draw from African life and religion,[31] indicate that the Roman prayers (the Roman canon and the three new eucharistic prayers officially used in the Roman liturgy since the reform of Paul

VI) are not adequate for the African region. Apart from the Zairean eucharist, which received official approval from the Roman church on April 30, 1988, the rest are either on paper (Igbo-Nigeria) or in use mainly in experimental centers (East Africa). The Gaba Pastoral Institute, Eldoret, Kenya, composed four eucharistic prayers between 1969 and 1973. Masses for various occasions were also composed, and there is a draft Tanzanian rite drawn up at the request of the Tanzanian Episcopal Conference that contains two eucharistic prayers, one explaining African values and the other explaining the relational unity of the Holy Trinity.[32] In general, these prayers maintain the main structures of eucharistic prayers as arranged in historic liturgies: opening praise (or preface), epiclesis, institution narrative, anamnesis, intercessions, and doxology. But each has its own striking characteristics.

The first striking motif of these prayers is the link to the ancestors and to the ancestral tradition. Although other contributors to this book discuss the relationship between Christ and the ancestors, and the particular meaning of the invocation of ancestors in the Zairean rite,[33] I feel the need here to stress their importance. I want to draw attention to the fact that the composers of the liturgies do not feel that falling back on the ancestral tradition deforms the Christian specificity. On the contrary! The gathered community is made to perceive itself as both a prolongation of the ancestral heritage, precisely because of the Christ, and thus a Christian community in communion with other communities. For example, from the opening praise to the institution narrative of the Kenyan, Tanzanian, and Ugandan eucharistic prayers, it is presupposed that the community can praise God *because* of the Christ, and in an environment evocative of the ancestral presence. The Kenyan prayer is a good example.

Based on a Kikuyu Prayer:

Celebrant:
  O Father, Great Elder, we have no words to thank you,
  But with your deep wisdom
  We are sure that you can see
  How we value your glorious gifts.
  O Father, when we look upon your greatness,
  We are confounded with awe.
  O Great Elder,
  Ruler of all things earthly and heavenly,

We are your warriors,
Ready to act in accordance with your will.

Based on a Gala Prayer:

Response:
Listen to us, aged God,
Listen to us, ancient God,
Who has ears.
Look at us, aged God,
Look at us, ancient God,
Who has eyes.
Receive us, aged God,
Receive us, ancient God,
Who has hands.

Based on a Kikuyu Prayer:

Celebrant:
You, the Great Elder,
Who dwells on the shining mountain,
Your blessing allows our homesteads to spread.
Your anger destroys them.
We beseech you,
And in this we are in harmony
With the spirits of our ancestors;
We ask you to send the Spirit of life *(hands outstretched)*
To bless and sanctify our offerings,
That they may become for us the Body and Blood
Of Jesus, our Brother and your Son.

Celebrant:
On the night of his suffering,
He gave thanks for the bread which he held in his hands
This bread he shared among his friends, saying:
All of you, take this, eat this
It is my Body which will be handed over to you.

All:

Amen. We believe that this is truly your body!

God is praised as the "Great Elder" (the Parent-Ancestor of Nyamiti) in a prayer supposed to have been pronounced by the eponymous ancestor of the Kikuyu. The invocation of God (epiclesis) to send God's Spirit to change the elements into the body and blood of Christ is again in solidarity with ancestral spirits. The institution narrative and the anamnetic proclamation that follow should be seen as giving the foundation to the community's eucharistic action. And so, in this Christian community, the memory of Christ provokes the memory of the ancestors (for the Christ is the Proto-Ancestor) and the memory of the ancestors reaches out for the memory of Christ, for it is the dynamic power of the ancestors that leads the Christian community to draw life in full in Christ. The ancestral verbal gestures of these prayers drawn from traditional African setting call for the word of the Lord, the eucharistic words, because the Christian community confesses the death and the resurrection of Jesus as the highest act of thanksgiving.

This ancestral link in African eucharistic prayers should surprise no one. The Roman canon (or what is today called the Roman Eucharistic Prayer I), which is about the most difficult prayer of the historic liturgies to analyze, is incomprehensible apart from its Roman ancestral roots. Scholars have shown how it begins with the fact that the eucharist is a "sacrifice of praise." But Roman religion insists that sacrifices are made *for* certain purposes (such as a votive offering), and the deity is wearied to accept the offering by ceaseless petitions. Thus, the Roman canon includes an offering for certain persons and purposes (*te igitur* to *hanc igitur*) and Roman rhetoric and court language (the frequent use of *digneris,* and the use of *prex* for the whole prayer, which is the term for addressing petitions to the emperor) helps to make God favorably disposed toward the oblation. The institution narrative serves as the chief argument before God. God is petitioned to make the oblation the body and blood of Christ *(quam oblationem)* because of the action and mandate of the Lord before he suffered *(qui pridie)*.[34] Both the Roman Christian and African Christian practices demonstrate how impossible it is for Christian liturgical action to be exercised outside ethnic experience. They project the *same* gospel, but in *different* languages.

Another characteristic of African eucharistic prayers is the very functioning of the word in the community. The word as a powerful gesture belongs to the community. In its exercise, no member of the community is indifferent. This explains the strong responsorial accent of the eucharistic prayers. For example, the whole prayer of the draft Tanzanian mass, from preface through doxology, is cast in the responsorial mold.

Priest:

Lord, God, our heavenly Father, creator of all things,
In your power and love, you command and they came into being.

All:

Praise to you O God, for you are great.

(Theological/christological praise)

Priest:

We praise them all.
We ask you to send your Holy Spirit that he may consecrate these gifts
That they may become the body and blood of your
Beloved Son, Jesus Christ our Lord and Brother.

All:

O holy Father, let it be done so.

(Epiclesis)

Roman sentiments lack this assurance of the communitarian appropriation of the word; they are more inclined toward the presidential security of the word. The Roman eucharistic prayer is a presidential address to God in the name of the community. (It was only in the recently composed masses for children that pastoral reasons impose the responsorial style in the eucharistic prayers). Ethiopic and Coptic *anaphoras* (eucharistic prayer) on African soil, and some other *anaphoras* of the Eastern church, integrate congregational responses. In African eucharistic prayers, verbal gestures, like the gesture of the dance, sets the whole body—the entire community—in motion before God. Thus, both verbal and nonverbal gestures express and realize interaction between the community and God.

The link with the ancestors and the deployment of the whole body of the assembled community in praise of God through verbal gestures are reproductive and nurturing of life. The African eucharistic prayers display a community that praises God for the gift of life.

Priest:
We thank you for giving us life.

All:
We thank you.

Priest:
We thank you for giving us freedom.

All:
We thank you.

(All Africa Eucharistic Prayer)

This is a prayer invoking God to fertilize this life.

Father, send the spirit of life,
The spirit of power and fruitfulness,
With his breath speak your word into these things.
Make them the living body and the life blood
Of Jesus, our brother!
Give us who eat and drink in your presence
Life and power and fruitfulness of the heart and body.
Give us true brotherhood with your Son.

(All Africa Eucharistic Prayer)

The praise is thus an acknowledgment of the source of life and a petition for God's blessing, which is understood as the fertilization of life. Here, the African praise tallies with the Jewish praise: the root meaning of the blessing *(brk)* in Jewish tradition is fecundity or fertilization, referring to progeny and material goods; God is blessed/praised for being the source of this fertilization.[35] It is this recognition of the gift of life prompting the petition for its sustenance and its furtherance that colors the perception of the eucharist as a health-giving food. I have noted that the idea of festival dictates the tone of the whole eucharistic celebration, but the festival meal is not a meal of satiety. It is a ritual meal that communicates the healing power of the divinity who is the source of life.[36]

Celebrant:
> Owner of all things,
> We offer you this cup in memory of your Son.
> We beg you for life,
> For healthy people with no disease.
> May they bear healthy children,
> And also women who suffer because they are barren,
> Open the way by which they may see children.
> Give the good life to our parents and kin who are with you.

> (*Kenyan Eucharistic Prayer:* Prayer
> of Offering and Fruitful Communion
> —based on Meru prayer)

The evocation of life, fertilization, and health makes the eucharistic action dynamic; it is a symbolic action that creates the environment for the realization of its purpose. The *All Africa Eucharistic Prayer* in its acclamation and anamnesis declares, "You, Spirit medicine of life are here!" This environment really transforms the life of the community. The optimism of the symbolic action is anchored on the activity of the Christ who acts as a drug in the body. The fourth century *Euchologion* (prayer) of Serapion Bishop of Thimus of the Egyptian region says "and make all who partake to receive a medicine (literally, drug) of life."[37] The embolism of the Pater Noster of the draft Tanzanian mass sums up the areas to be healed in the community.

> O Lord, King of peace
> Grant us true love
> For mutual understanding within our families
>   in our village and in the whole community.
> Help us to be rid of our constant enemies:
>   magic, fear, witchcraft belief (sorcery),
>   misunderstanding, ignorance, disease and
>   poverty.

Enable us to live in peace and love in familyhood
    and justice, in all our activities, in building
    your kingdom
As we wait in joyful hope for the coming of our
    Savior Jesus Christ.

Conclusion

African eucharistic prayers, like the liturgy of the word, exude the African environment. The land, with its valleys and mountains, rivers and lakes, forests and plains filled with animals, joins in the rhythmic praise of the Creator. African Christian eucharistic communities display and pray for harmony in this universe. The attention drawn to the body in the liturgy portrays a confident acknowledgment of God's gift of life, which is nurtured and made productive. The experience of the power of the word projects the anchoring of the life of the community in the dynamic ancestral memory that is confessed as reaching culmination in the word of God—Jesus the Christ. In the Christian ritual context, it is this prophetic word that transforms the community and generates the power for transforming the world. In Africa the whole Christian liturgical action becomes a gestural display before God of the community confessing its reception of fullness of life in Christ, a community at peace with its ancestral heritage and environment. The African eucharistic community expresses in a different metaphor the experience of the same unique salvation in the Christ that is the faith of the universal church.

Notes

1. John Paul II, address to Nigerian bishops, February 1982.

2. J. D. Y. Peel, *Aladuras: A Religious Movement among the Yoruba* (London, 1968); N. I. Ndiokwere, *Prophecy and Revolution* (London: SPCK, 1981); J. A. Omoyajowo, *Cherubim and Seraphim: The History of an African Independent Church* (New York: NOK, 1982).

3. See my "African Personality and the Christian Liturgy," in *African Christian Studies* 3/2 (1987), pp. 61-74.

4. V. Y. Mudimbe, *The Invention of Africa: Gnosis, Philosophy, and Order of Knowledge* (Bloomington: Indiana University Press, 1988), p. 76; see also pp. 44-48. Other authors who shed some light on these factors include Chinweizu, *The West and the Rest of Us* (London: NOK, 1978); O. Bimwenyi-Kweshi, *Discours Théologique négro-africain* (Paris: Présence Africaine, 1981); A. Ayandele, *The Missionary Impact on Modern Nigeria 1842-1914* (London: Longman, 1966).

5. See E. Uzukwu, "African Personality and the Christian Liturgy," *African Christian Studies* 3 (2, 1987); *La Notion de Personne en Afrique Noire,* Colloques Internationaux de CNRS, no. 544, October 11-17, 1971 (Paris: CNRS, 1981).

6. I have advanced some reasons for the ready acceptance of such a model among the Igbo ethnic group of Nigeria in my *Church and Inculturation* (Obosi: Pacific Press Ltd., 1985). A glance at the publications of the Faculté de Théologie Catholique de Kishasa, especially *Cahiers de Religions Africaines*, shows the Zairean resistance to this model.

7. Mudimbe, 67, 141; Placide Tempels, *Bantu Philosophy* (Paris: Présence Africaine, 1969); E. Evans-Pritchard, *Social Anthropology and Other Essays* (1962); M. Griaule, *Conversations with Ogotemmeli: An Introduction to Dogon Religious Ideas* (London: Oxford University Press, 1965).

8. See O. Rousseau, *The Progress of the Liturgy* (Westminster: The Newman Press, 1951), chapter 7; B. Botte, "La Liturgie: Expression et gardienne de la Foi, Un Témoignage," in *La Liturgie, Expression de la Foi,* Conférences Saint-Serge, XXVe Semaine d'Études Liturgiques, Paris 1978 (Rome: C.L.V., 1979), pp. 69-74.

9. N. Standaert, "L'Histoire d'un Néologisme: La Terme 'inculturation' dans les Documents romains," *Nouvelle Revue Théologique* 110 (4, 1988), pp. 555-570; see also no. 11 of 1989 issue of *Church and Culture* for the same understanding of the Gospel and culture by the Pontifical Council for Culture.

10. See E. E. Uzukwu, *Liturgy: Truly Christian, Truly African* (Eldoret, Kenya, Gaba Publications: Spearhead 74, 1982), esp. pp. 46-47; Uzukwu, "Missiology Today, the African Situation," in *Religion and African Culture I, Inculturation,* ed. E. E. Uzukwu (Enugu, Nigeria: SNAPP Press, 1988), pp. 146-173.

11. See M. Schoffeleers, "Black and African Theology in Southern Africa, a Controversy Re-examined," *Journal of Religion in Africa* XVIII (2, 1988), pp. 99-124.

12. See my brief study of the Coptic and Ethiopic Liturgies in "Blessing and Thanksgiving among the Igbo: Towards a Eucharistia Africaná," unpublished Th.D. dissertation, Toronto, 1978, pp. 142-164. See E. Hammerschmidt, *Studies in Ethiopic Anaphoras* (Berlin: Akademie-Verlag, 1961).

13. The francophone West African Episcopal Commission for Catechesis and Liturgy has done a lot of work in the area of Christian initiation. In Upper Volta, a ritual (More Ritual) of initiation has been produced. See the articles published by R. Ouedraogo in *Le Calao* (official organ of the Episcopal Commission) between 1976 and 1980; see also E. Uzukwu, *Liturgy, Truly Christian,* pp. 48-55; A. Diatta, "Et Si Jésus Christ, Premier-né d'entre les morts, était l'Initié?," *Telema* 57 (1, 1989), pp. 49-72; A. T. Sanon and R. Luneau, *Enraciner L'Évangile: Initiations Africaines et Pédagogie de la Foi* (Paris: Cerf, 1982).

14. See P. Abega, "L'Expérience Liturgique de Ndzon-Melen," *Telema* 16 (4, 1978), pp. 41-50; "Liturgical Adaptation" in *Christianity in Independent Africa,* ed. E. Fasholé-Luke (Indianapolis: Indiana University Press, 1978), pp. 597-605; "La Liturgie Camerounaise" in *Médiations Africaines du Sacré.* Actes du 3e Colloque International, Kinshasa, November, 16-22, 1986, *Cahiers des Religions Africaines* XX-XXI (39-42, 1986-87), pp. 515-522.

15. P. Abega, "La Liturgie Camerounaise," p. 515.

16. Students who participated in the project came from the Central African Republic, Cameroon, Gabon, Congo, Angola, Zaire and were studying at the Grand Séminaire Régional Émile Biayenda in Brazzaville and Grand Séminaire Jean XXIII in Kinshasa. See also my "Inculturation of the Eucharistic Celebration in Africa Today," *African Christian Studies* I (1, 1985), pp. 13-27.

17. E. Mveng, "Spiritualité Africaine et spiritualité chrétienne," in *L'Afrique et ses formes de Vie Spirituelle.* Actes du 2e Colloque International, Kinshasa, November 21-27, 1983, *Cahiers des Reglions Africaines* XVII (1983), pp. 263-279. Mveng, *L'Afrique dans l'Église; Paroles d'un Croyant* (Paris: Éditions L'Harmattan, 1985), chapters I & IV.

18. B. Bujo, "Can Morality be Christian in Africa?" *African Christian Studies* 4 (1, 1988),

p. 23; Bujo, "The Two Sources of Life: The Eucharist and the Cult of Ancestors in Africa," *African Christian Studies* 2 (1986), pp. 67-85; Bujo, "Pour une Éthique Africano-Christocentrique," *Bulletin of African Theology* III, 5 (1981), pp. 41-52. C. Nyamiti, "The Mass as Divine and Ancestral Encounter Between the Living and the Dead," *African Christian Studies* 1 (1, 1985), pp. 28-48; Nyamiti, *Christ as Our Ancestor* (Gweru, Zimbabwe: Mambo Press, 1984). See also G. Muzorewa's review essay of Nyamiti's book in *African Theological Journal* 17 (3, 1988), pp. 255-264.

19. T. Boman, *Hebrew Thought Compared with Greek* (New York: W. W. Norton & Co., 1960), p. 205.

20. See E. Bishop, *Liturgica Historica* (Oxford: Oxford University Press, 1918, 1962 reprint), esp. Part I, Chapter I, "The Genius of the Roman Rite."

21. See L. Gougard, "La Danse dans les Églises," *Revue d'Histoire Écclésiastique* XV (1914), pp. 5-22, 229-245; J.-C. Schmitt, *La Raison des Gestes dans l'Occident Médiéval* (Paris: Gallimard, 1990), pp. 86-96. A detailed treatment of liturgical gestures from the African background is contained in my *Worship as Body Language* (Collegeville, MN: Liturgical Press, forthcoming).

22. For my view on gestures and the liturgy, see my "African Symbols and the Christian Liturgy" presented at the XVIIe Semaine Théologique de Kinshasa, April 2-8, 1989. For the unity of the self and the body, see E. Mveng, *L'Afrique dans l'Église; Paroles d'un Croyant;* N. Tshiamelenge, "L'à Priori Pragmatico-Corporel en Liturgie: Approche philosophico-théologique" in *Médiations africaines du Sacré*, pp. 49-66.

23. See J. A. Jungmann, *The Mass of the Roman Rite* (Westminster, MD: Christian Classics, 1978), p. 258ff; G. Dix, *The Shape of the Liturgy* (London: Dacre Press, 1975), Chapter 3.

24. C. Nyamiti, "The Mass as Divine and Ancestral Encounter," pp. 41.

25. For detailed treatment of the guilt complex in the West, see J. Delumeaux, *Le Péché et la Peur: La Culpabilisation en Occident, XIIe-XVIIIe Siècles* (Paris: Fayard, 1983). For "apologiae," see Jungmann, *The Mass of the Roman Rite,* p. 200; and Jungmann, *Pastoral Liturgy* (New York: Herder & Herder, 1962), p. 62.

26. D. Tutu, "Black Theology and African Theology: Soulmates or Antagonists?" in J. Parratt, ed., *A Reader in African Theology* (London: SPCK, 1987), p. 54.

27. V. Donovan, *Christianity Rediscovered* (Maryknoll, NY: Orbis Books, 1982), pp. 119-128.

28. L. V. Thomas and R. Luneau, *Les Religions d'Afrique noire I* (Paris: Stock and Plus, 1981), p. 28.

29. Thomas and Luneau, p. 28.

30. *Eucharistiae Participationem* (April 27, 1973), no. 5. But the document does see the need for more eucharistic prayers (no. 6), leading to eucharistic prayers of reconciliation (2) and for masses with children (3).

31. Recorded prayers of African religion that could help in appreciating African eucharistic prayers can be found in J. Mbiti, *Prayers of African Religion* (London: SPCK, 1975); C. Gaba, *Scriptures of an African People. Ritual Utterances of the Anlo* (New York: NOK, 1973); A. Gittins, *Heart of Prayer: African, Jewish and Biblical Prayers* (London: Collins, 1985); Thomas and Luneau, *Les Religions d'Afrique noire.* Texts of the Zairean, East African and Igbo eucharistic prayers can be found in French in *À Travers le Monde: Célébrations de l'Eucharistie. Dossier presenté par le Centre de Recherche Théologique Missionnaire* (Paris: Cerf, 1981). Texts in English can be found in *African Ecclesial Review* (1975, no. 4), pp. 343-348 (Zairean prayer); A. Shorter, "Three More Eucharistic Prayers," *African Ecclesiastical Review* 15 (2, 1973), pp. 155-160 (for Kenyan, Ugandan and Tanzanian prayers); Shorter, *African Culture and the Christian Church* (Maryknoll, NY: Orbis, 1974) (for *All Africa Eucharistic Prayer*); E. Uzukwu, "Blessing and Thanksgiving

among the Igbo (Nigeria), Towards an African Eucharistic Prayer," *African Ecclesiastical Review* 22 (1, 1980), pp. 17-22.

32. Masses for various occasions are found in B. Hearne and N. Mijere, eds., *Celebration II* (Spearhead, no. 42), 1976. The composition of the Tanzanian mass under the supervision of A. Shorter was completed in 1977. Father Shorter was kind enough to make available to me the Swahili original; the translation was done for me by Rogath F. Mimary, Spiritan House, Nairobi. I had available only the eucharistic prayer embodying African values.

33. In addition to Nyamiti and Bujo, see the numerous articles of Kabasele Lumbala, such as, "Nouveaux Rites, Foi naissante," in *Lumière et Vie* 159 (1983), pp. 61-73; "L'Inculturation Sacramentelle au Zaire," *Lumen Vitae* XLII (1, 1987), pp. 75-84 (French edition).

34. I analyzed this prayer in my unpublished thesis, "Blessing and Thanksgiving among the Igbo: Towards a Eucharistia Africana," pp. 164-182. The following authors bring out the link between this prayer and the Roman culture: R. A. Keifer, "The Unity of the Roman Canon: An Examination of Its Unique Structure," *Studia Liturgica* XI (1976), pp. 39-58; A. Stuiber, "Die Diptychon-Formel für die Nomina offerentium im römischen messkanon,"in *Ephemerides Liturgicae* LXVIII (1954), pp.127-146.

35. See, for example, A. Murtonen, "The Use and Meaning of the words Lebarek and Berakan in the Old Testament," *Vetus Testamentum* IX (1959), pp. 158-177; J. Scharbert, "Brk, berakhah," in G. J. Botterwech and H. Ringgren, *Theological Dictionary of the Old Testament* II (Grand Rapids, MI: Eerdmans, 1975), pp. 179-308; Uzukwu, *Blessing and Thanksgiving among the Igbo,* pp. 15-30.

36. A. Shorter has argued that the Eucharist is the sacrament of healing—see his *Jesus and the Witchdoctor* (Maryknoll, NY: Orbis Books, 1985) and his "The Eucharist as the Fundamental Sacrament of Christian Healing," *African Christian Studies* I (1, 1985), pp. 49-59.

37. Dix, *The Shape of the Liturgy,* p. 164.

7

SPIRITUALITY IN THE AFRICAN PERSPECTIVE

Patrick A. Kalilombe

In the African context, it would be both misleading and inadequate to discuss theology without dealing with the question of spirituality. The reason is simple. One of the basic characteristics of African culture is its holistic and integrating nature. Thus it would be distorting African theology if it were treated merely as a theoretical enterprise, without taking into account the fact that the ideas and theories being discussed are merely extrapolations from a way of life that consists first and foremost in concrete attitudes, relationships, and practices. African religion is essentially a way of living in the visible sphere in relation with the invisible world. This relationship pervades the whole of life, of individuals as well as of the community—or rather, of individuals in the community.

Spirituality has been described generally as "those attitudes, beliefs and practices which animate peoples' lives and help them to reach out toward the super-sensible realities" (Wakefield 1983:549). It is the relationship between human beings and the invisible, inasmuch as such a relationship derives from a particular vision of the world, and in its turn affects the way of relating to self, to other people, and to the universe as a whole. In this sense, spirituality is not restricted to any one religion, but can be found variously in all religions and cultures. It is determined in the first place by the basic worldview of the persons or people concerned. It is also shaped by their life context, their history, and the various influences that enter a people's life.

This essay starts from the conviction that there exists a particular brand of spirituality that can be called, in a general way, African. In a general way, because on the one hand there should be no pretension to claim that what constitutes such a spirituality is exclusively African, and on the other hand, we are not affirming that all Africans necessarily live this spirituality. For, as a matter of fact, many do not, and those who may be said to do so vary considerably in the measure in which they conform to the rather idealized model that I shall present. These caveats are so evident as to need no further discussion; still, in a study such as this, it is not superfluous to formulate them clearly at the outset. The integrity of the very exercise depends on them. As I proceed to describe what this special African perspective is and how it is both a challenge and a contribution to spirituality in general, the value of the claims would be compromised if they were carelessly overstated. I may, then, just as well start by clarifying the points in these cautions.

How "African" Is African Spirituality?

Does it make scientific sense to speak about an African spirituality? The African continent is so vast and diversified. It consists of such a variety of ethnic groups, each with its own customs, history, and ways of life, that sweeping generalizations about things African are always dangerous and risky. Serious scholars of African traditional religion, such as E. G. Parrinder (1962:10) or J. S. Mbiti (1975b:3) preface their studies with a wise warning against treating religious practices in Africa as if they were uniform in every detail, a temptation that in the past was not often avoided by those who loved to tell exotic tales about Africans. E. Bolaji Idowu himself, as he set out to present his pioneering study of African traditional religion, had to admit "that African traditional religion with reference to the whole of Africa, as a subject of study, is an impossible proposition" (1973:105), but he added the precision "where de-tailed study and thoroughness are concerned." Here, I think, is the crucial point.

Whether or not it is legitimate and meaningful to make some generaliza-tions in this area of religion depends very much on the level at which such generalizations are made. Although there is such a diversity in details, there is, however, an astonishing convergence in African cultures and religion when one considers the deeper, underlying outlook, values, and attitudes. This is what gave courage to D. Zahan to pursue his research into *The Religion, Spirituality, and Thought of Traditional Africa*. He writes:

The diversity of African ethnic groups should not be an obstacle to such an undertaking since the variation in religion has less to do with the ideas themselves than with their expression by means of dissimilar elements linked to the occupations and the flora and fauna of the area. (1979:2)

What I shall attempt to propose here is precisely that complex of spiritual outlook and values that seems to undergird the various expressions of African religion.

There is, however, a more practical problem that has to do with culture change. The African way of life, which is the background against which spirituality needs to be examined, is not something static. Over the centuries, African societies have been in constant transformation, mainly due to interactions with the outside, but also due to changing conditions of life, new needs, development of ideas, and modification of techniques and values. Such changes are often gradual, hardly noticeable except over long periods. But at other times they are sudden, violent, or revolutionary. Such dramatic changes have certainly occurred in the past century due mainly to the exposure of Africa to the powerful modernizing influences of the Western world colonialism, industrialization, new religions, especially Christianity. Because of these new influences, the former traditional ways of life have been modified; they are taking new shapes and configurations. But these changes are not everywhere uniform. While in some areas and for certain groups the former traditional ways of life are still operative to a greater or lesser extent, for other individuals and groups, especially among the younger generations and those in the urban context, the influence of modernity is more profound and revolutionary.

The question then is: Where do you go in order to discover the African culture today? Where is African spirituality to be captured? Is it among those who are still influenced by traditional cultural values and customs? Do we have to discard, as irrelevant or unauthentic, the more complicated modern developments, while attempting to recapture an idealized past state of traditional culture?

This is, indeed, an important question, one that cannot be brushed aside or answered in a simplistic way. If, indeed, spirituality is an aspect of human culture, it can only be discovered authentically where people's actual way of life is going on. And so, African spirituality today should be examined within the complexity of present culture change, and not in some romantic and artificial reconstruction of traditional life that is no more really there. This makes the task much more difficult, because it is not possible to present a coherent cultural picture out of the divergent and fluctuating manifestations of the present process of culture change. But this should not mean that there is no way of discovering a sufficiently identifiable pattern of spirituality or spiritualities in today's Africa.

Even in the midst of the most confused culture revolution, it is possible to isolate some basic trends and orientations that form the deeper underlying foundation against and over which the ongoing transformations are struggling. These are the result of past decisions and customs that have marked the life of a people over a long period; they are also the effects of past and present responses to decisive historical events that people continue to carry along even as they move forward developing new ways of living. At any one moment, a people never exists as a *tabula rasa*. It always carries the baggage of its past as a resource for interpreting and dealing with new experiences. What I seek to investigate here as African spirituality is the sum total of this past configuration of values and orientations together with the new trends resulting from responses to modern experiences. Even if this is not a simple exercise, it is nevertheless quite possible.

Finally, a possible misunderstanding needs to be cleared up. When I discuss African spirituality, I do not intend to imply that each and every African individual or group lives that spirituality in the same way or to the same extent as the ideal form. That is certainly not the case. The model presented here can only be a theoretical extrapolation, logically structured from diverse elements deduced from observations. In real life, individuals and even groups may correspond to fewer or more of those elements, depending on a never-ending variety of configurations to which individual situations and histories give rise. The validity of this extrapolation is tested only by the plausibility of verification as concrete individuals or groups are examined against the ideal model. Some will be found to correspond to a number of elements, while others will demonstrate a different pattern, or even prove to be aberrant in that their way of life follows a totally different model. But this does not necessarily prove the model false. I shall base my reflections mainly on my acquaintance with my own people, the Achewa/Ngoni of Malawi, Central Africa.

Where Do We Look for African Spirituality?

In principle, the answer should be easy. If, as I have said, spirituality is an aspect of the total culture, we look for it by examining the African way of life and following up "those attitudes, beliefs, and practices that animate people's lives and help them to reach out toward super-sensible realities," since this is what we chose as a working description of what spirituality is. For Africans, life is a totality; culture is holistic. What one might isolate as the spiritual dimension is embedded in the whole of the people's way of living. It may be valid to distinguish different aspects, such as the economic, social, or political spheres, or again the individual and community aspects. One may consider occupational and leisure activities as distinguished from one another, or isolate the legal system from that of belief and ritual. But in real life all these are held together and given shape by an underlying spiritual outlook, which is what we would like to discover.

In conformity with my reflections in the introductory discussion, it will be helpful to search from two sides of African life today: first from what comes from the past, and then from what results from more recent influences. The underlying contention is that the shape of African spirituality today is a result of the interaction between these two. And yet the first is certainly the more determinant. I will start from there.

The most obvious place to search for spirituality is in the context of traditional religious practice: in worship, ritual, and prayer. Here the shape of a people's spirituality becomes easier to grasp, for their deepest aspirations are made manifest and their underlying outlook on the world of realities is revealed, not in theories or formulas, but in practical attitudes. Two collections of prayers for African religious life appeared in 1975, one by an African (J. S. Mbiti 1975a) and the other by a European (A. Shorter 1975). These collections are an important indication of African spirituality as it manifests itself through traditional culture. There is need, however, for some caution here. Collections such as these are a personal undertaking whose demonstrative value depends very much on the answer to such obvious questions as: who did the selection? from what sources were the prayers taken? what were the guiding assumptions and preoccupations in that selection, and to what extent do these predetermine the end result?

It can be argued, for example, that the preponderance given to prayers to the Supreme Being ("Most of the prayers are addressed directly and specifically to God . . . A few, not more than 10 percent, are addressed to divinities, spirits, the living dead, and personifications of nature," Mbiti: 3) is mainly due to the fact that the sources from which these prayers were taken had been preoccupied with demonstrating that Africans, contrary to adverse prejudice, did have a clear notion of the Supreme Deity. And so the selection of the recorded prayers was heavily in favor of those addressed to God. In the real life of many of the ethnic groups mentioned, perhaps the proportion of prayers to the other addressees was more than that meager 10 percent. But this is a minor point that does not really affect the revelatory value of these collections.

The Prayers and the Spirituality They Reveal

The first indication is given in the answer to the question: To whom is prayer addressed? (Mbiti: 2-16; Shorter: 8-13). The prayers are made to the Supreme Deity, but also (whatever the relative proportion) to other spiritual realities such as divinities, spirits, the living dead, and personifications of nature. All these can be subsumed under the notion of "the invisible" or "the other-world of spiritual realities." Prayer is based on the view that the world of realities consists of two interrelating spheres, the visible and the invisible, of which the visible is in some ways dependent on the invisible. The project of human living, both individual and communitary, consists mainly in an ongoing interaction between these two spheres. What goes on among the living in the visible sphere cannot be fully accounted for solely from a consideration of the palpable processes of the visible or physically observable realities, for there is a mystical interaction of forces and wills between the two spheres. African traditional spirituality is based firmly on this premise.

There is, thus, a basic cosmology that underlies many of the traditional myths, stories, beliefs, customs, and practices. Mbiti (1975b: 40) represents this cosmology by a sketch:

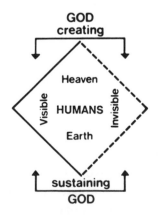

God, or the Supreme Deity, is all-encompassing as creator and sustainer, up above heaven as down below the earth. This omnipresent Reality "in whom we live and move and have our being" is so much taken for granted that the

Supreme Deity often is not mentioned explicitly and is rarely (in many ethnic groups) offered sacrifices and the customary ritual worship: the Supreme Being is above it. Some observers, intrigued by this, have concluded that the Supreme Being is a remote, even "otiose," deity, indifferent to the creation. This is a gross misunderstanding, although we have to admit that taking God's presence for granted in this way does create the danger of doing as if God does not count very much. But then, it is important to understand the significance of this "distance."

It is not absence by any means, for, as it is often repeated, the presence of God is so obvious that you do not have to convince people about it. Rather, it is a special type of presence: a presence that operates concretely through mediation. *God's presence asserts itself through the interaction of heaven and earth, the visible and the invisible.* God is like the paramount chief in the tribe or nation. God's will and authority pervade the whole of life, but in the working-out of events and relationships, the normal processes on the lower levels must be respected; only when these fail or are inadequate is recourse to the higher instances in order. What the family can deal with, for example, should be left to the members and elders of that family. Appeal will be made to the village head or to the chief only if the matter is beyond the competence of the family.

In theological terms, an important assumption is being made—*the absence of a radical dualism.* Good and evil, life and death, love and hatred, justice and injustice, good luck and misfortune—all these are, indeed, the two opposing camps in the drama of the cosmos. But God is not involved on one of the two sides in such a "partisan" way that another agency (Satan or some such) would be on the other side as an equal opponent. On the contrary, God is above this drama and is there to act as the ultimate arbiter. But, of course, God is ultimately the champion of good, life, love, justice, and harmony, so there is always, even in the midst of the worst developments, an underlying optimism that in the long run God will triumph. This, I think, is the real explanation of that kind of optimism that seems to rule traditional life and expresses itself in a kind of "resignation" even when things are really unbearable. Some observers have interpreted this as the effect of belief in determinism or blind fate, and think this is how you can explain the astonishing capacity of African individuals and communities to take in a lot of suffering and pain without apparent bitterness or despair (think only of the long centuries of slavery, colonialism, and now neocolonialism, and the accumulated misfortunes visited on modern Africa). I rather think the explanation is in this cosmology that places God and God's basically good intentions above, below, and in the whole of the world.

Humanity (individuals and community) is at the center of consideration, as the diagram shows. African spirituality is based on this centrality of human beings presently living in the concrete circumstances of life this side of the grave. It consists of their attitudes, beliefs, and practices as they strive to reach out toward the super-sensible realities: God, the spirits, and the invisible forces in the universe. The central concern is how to make sense of this life and ensure that it is meaningful, harmonious, good, and worth living. The outcome of the project of life depends on how successful and beneficial the relationships are between the living and the invisible world.

But for traditional Africans, humanity is first and foremost the *community*. In the first place is the extended family based on blood kinship or on affinity through marriage, and then the clan, the tribe, or the nation. Kinship and affinity create a special kind of bonding within which mutual rights and duties are exercised unconditionally. Individuals acquire their basic identity through these relationships, and they enjoy a feeling of security in life as long as the exchange of these rights and duties is guaranteed. It has often been said that where Descartes said, "I think, therefore, I am" *(cogito ergo sum)*, the African would rather say, "I am related, therefore, we are" *(cognatus ergo sum)* (Pobee: 49). In African spirituality, the value of interdependence through relationships comes high above that of individualism and personal independence. By the same token, the practice of cooperation is more relied upon than competition.

There are positive consequences of this exigence for kinship and community solidarity. Among them is hospitality. Members of the same family or clan exchange hospitality as a matter of course. But it is also extended to outsiders, though here it is first necessary to make sure that the stranger is not an adversary. The bonded kinship community does have its boundaries: they exclude the enemy and the totally unknown incomer who might be a potential danger to the community. Any stranger, therefore, is first required to become known as *bona fide*. Only then is she or he accepted, and becomes an honorary kinsperson.

The community solidarity tends also to create requirements of sharing and redistribution of resources, so that no individual accumulates and hoards resources that become unavailable to others when they need them. Hence, the fear of anyone who surpasses others too obviously in wealth, power, or influence. The underlying fear is that such persons become a public danger and are likely to use their surplus for selfish purposes over against the others. Only those whose role is that of centers of redistribution (such as heads of families or chiefs) have surpluses of any kind. Any breach of this requirement of basic egalitarianism creates jealousies and ill feelings.

There is also a great dread of those who renounce the duties and rights of solidarity: those who are notoriously cruel, quarrelsome, egotistical, unforgiving, or unkind. They attract the suspicion of being witches or eaters-of-human-flesh. The widespread fear of witchcraft, and consequently the frequency of beliefs and accusations about witchcraft and sorcery and practices to counter it, are signs of the central importance of kinship solidarity. M. G. Marwick (1965; and 1970, 1982 ed.) and other scholars have demonstrated that witchcraft and sorcery are really about feelings of a breakdown in family and community sense of solidarity.

The primacy of community and cooperation may be related to the fact that, in general, traditional African life was based on a simple technology with a minimum of "scientific" knowledge of and mastery over the rest of the universe. We should perhaps state it more clearly. The relationship between the human community and the rest of the universe was not conceived of as a project of struggle where human beings would look at the world as an object or an adversary whose nature and working should be investigated and reduced to formulas so as to master and exploit it. Rather, the universe is seen as a common heritage, its diverse components as potential partners in the shared project of existence. There is, therefore, a feeling of mutual dependence among the different parts: human beings, the animal world, vegetation, the elements, the heavenly bodies, the departed as well as the diffuse forces, visible and invisible, that circulate all around.

Success in living depends very much on how well these different parts interact, negotiating carefully and "respectfully" the common resources available to all. There is a certain awe, something like a religious attitude, in this interaction: it is as if the whole universe possessed personality, consciousness, sensitivity, and "soul." Scholars coming from scientific and industrialized cultures are wont to call this attitude "superstition," and they have coined words like "animism," "animatism," "fetishism," or even "idolatry." These words, which attempt to make sense of "strange" peoples' religious attitudes but the point of view of another culture, are, in fact, more confusing than helpful. I would suggest that the key to a better understanding is to appreciate the significance of the relationship between the visible and the invisible.

The Invisible World

The relation between human beings and the rest of the universe is governed by the distinction between the visible and the invisible. The invisible is not just what cannot be perceived by the human senses, but rather what is beyond the range of ordinary perception. This category of ordinary is not identical with the Western one of natural as opposed to supernatural, since these Western categories are based on a particular worldview that is the foundation of modern science. According to this worldview, the universe is conceived of as being regulated by a set of laws of nature (which religious believers grant were laid down by the divine Creator, while atheists and deists deny or simply do not worry about). Events and processes occur in conformity with these laws, and if something happens outside or contrary to these laws, it is deemed super- or preternatural. Believers will call it a miracle, while nonbelievers will tend to be skeptical or assume it is the effect of a hitherto unknown natural law. This universe, which is thus regulated by natural laws, is partly visible and partly invisible.

It is not in accordance with such a worldview that the cultures we are describing here distinguish the visible from the invisible. The background thinking is rather that the whole world of realities—spirits, persons, objects, words, gestures—are bearers of force and efficacy at two levels: the ordinary one that is perceptible and manageable without special knowledge or power (this is what I call visible), and another that is mystical and can be perceived and handled only with a heightened perception and power. And that is what I call invisible. The whole idea of force and efficacy has turned into a confused controversy ever since Placide Tempels came up with the idea of *force vitale* as a central element in what he called Bantu ontology (Tempels 1949: 33-47). Scholars have had ample occasion to criticize and refute various aspects of that theory (see, for example, Maurier 1985: 58-9). The intention here is not to enter again into this discussion, but simply to remark that the idea of interacting forces is an enlightening intuition for a proper understanding of this question of the invisible.

African spirituality is based on the assumption that life is influenced by relationships between human beings and the visible and invisible forces. These relationships are basically ambiguous: they can be beneficial or harmful, life-giving or destructive, good or bad, reinforcing or weakening, auspicious or misfortunate. At any rate, we cannot account for what happens or can happen simply by considering the visible, since the influence of invisible forces cannot be ruled out as a cause of any occurrence—death, illness, fortune or misfortune, success or failure. Hence, the crucial importance for individuals as well as for the community of the knowledge of the invisible and the power of dealing with it.

Specialists of this knowledge of the mystical (diviners, prophets, visionaries, interpreters of omens and dreams), and medicine practitioners who have powers to deal with the visible as well as the invisible are a crucial category in society. The frequent sessions and rituals of divination, ferreting out evil influences and dealing with them, are more than mere cultural practices; they are elements of the people's spirituality. Medicine is a central part of this worldview. A medicine is not, as in the West, simply a substance imbued with natural powers for healing. It is anything that activates the visible and invisible forces and enables human beings to deal with them for good or for ill. Since objects, as well as words and gestures, can be repositories of both visible and invisible forces, they are potential medicines for all sorts of effects. Medicine people know of these forces, more or less, and are capable of using them. The notion and practice of medicines is thus an important aspect of African religion. By the same token, belief in and practice of magic cannot be excluded from the wider ambit of religion, since in various ways the working of the mystical and the unusual is part of religious practice. In Christian parlance, we can put it this way: the miraculous or the preternatural is essentially part of African religious consciousness.

The world of the invisible is indeed quite wide. It includes, first of all, the heavens where God resides. It also includes divinities and nature spirits for those cultures whose worldview reserves a place for them (v.g. in Western Africa, cf. Idowu: 165-73; Mbiti 1975b:65-70). And almost everywhere in Africa the spirits of the dead (especially the dead ancestors) are the central area of the invisible, as I shall demonstrate presently. But other parts of the universe are also potential fields for the invisible: animals, vegetation, and other objects.

Spirits of the Dead

The centrality of the conception of the spirits of the dead follows logically on the fact that African spirituality assumes that the center of consideration is the community of those presently living. This community is seen in terms of kinship and affinity relationships, on which even the wider expressions of neighborhood, clan, tribe, or even nation are modelled. That is why marriage, as the foundation of the family, is so important. As Mbiti has so aptly expressed it:

Marriage is the uniting link in the rhythm of life. All generations are bound together in the act of marriage—past, present and future generations. The past generations are many but they are represented in one's parents; the present generation is represented in one's own life, and future generations begin to come on the stage through childbearing. (Mbiti 1975b:104)

The family and the community thus are not limited to those presently alive: they include members of the past and also future members. This link is seen in real terms as a continuing flow of the same life. The life of the present generation is not a novel creation; it is a carry-over from those who preceded us. Even physically we owe it to them, and we cannot understand who we are or what our exact identity is except by remembering them.

In the same way, the present generation does not have to reinvent the rules or art of successful and harmonious living or take the risk of making fatal mistakes in the process. Its best bet is to interrogate the past and receive the accumulated wisdom of those who have gone ahead. That is why there is much store laid by the traditions of the ancestors, their customs, taboos, instructions, and directives. They know better. As the standard African saying goes, these dead are not dead; they are still around and are part of the families and the community. They understand fully what is going on, share in the preoccupations and projects of the living members, and are intimately interested in what is going on. Thus, those who have preceded us and are now in the spirit world are the models and guides of the present generation. They are also its source of identity. Hence, their importance.

But there is more. Having passed through death, they have become prominent members of the invisible world, whereby they share in mystical powers not ordinarily available to those presently alive. They are nearer to God, the invisible *par excellence,* with whom they are able to communicate and to whom they can present more effectively the needs of those still alive. They are also nearer to the other invisible forces, such as those in the "bush" (animals, vegetation, the landscape, the elements, and other forces of nature), and so are in a position to mobilize them for good or for ill toward the living. (Symbolically the dead are usually buried in the cemetery, outside the village, and actually in the bush!)

In this position of special power, the spirits of the dead are natural guardians of their relatives on earth and can act as mediators with God. This is a position of tremendous power. That is why the living cannot afford to ignore them: the more so as their intervention, although normally beneficial, can also be punitive if the living misbehave or break the basic rules of life (such as the taboos). The living get in touch with the spirits as often as there is need to ask for help or for advice, to seek protection, or simply to show them that they are not forgotten. Recourse to the spirits is most likely at important moments of individual or community life, such as initiations, marriage, birth of children, sickness, installation of chiefs, funerals, and moments of danger (drought, epidemic, war). This contact is made through prayer and invocation, and often accompanied with offerings of foodstuffs or libations. On their part, the spirits get in touch with the living through dreams, apparitions (visions), or ominous occurrences that are usually interpreted by specialists.

Christians will naturally see a strong parallel between this notion of the spirits of the dead and the belief in the communion of saints. But there are important differences. One is the strange dependence of the spirits on the living, for according to a widespread African belief, the spirits of the dead need to be "fed" by the living through rituals of remembrance. In fact, a spirit remains operative and present as a beneficial guardian and mediator only so long as its memory is kept among the living. If its memory has died out or is deliberately obliterated, the dead recede into the hazy but dangerous zone of ghosts, spirits that have lost their link with the living and can only linger around as restless and frustrated beings prone to mischief and harm.

I think this indicates the function of this belief in spirits in the philosophy of the people—both why they are important and how they relate to God, the real invisible. I suggest that the notion of spirits serves as a practical way of handling the problem of transcendence and immanence. As I indicated above, God's transcendence is safeguarded through the respect of God's distance from the living. Contact with God is maintained through the mediation of the spirits. In a way, the spirits render the transcendent immanent, but in such a way that the transcendent becomes "tamed," manageable, and even negotiable. The remembrance of the spirits assures the benefits of care, protection, and involved interest from the invisible. But there remains the possibility of rendering the invisible humanly manageable, since the living have some grip over the spirits. Thus, there is an intrinsic danger if religion is centered too much on the remembrance of the spirits: it tends to lower religious practice to a humanly manageable enterprise. But this should not make us forget the positive advantages of such a spirit-centered religion.

What Is the Content of African Spirituality?

I have attempted to describe the worldview on which African spirituality is based and the various parts of this universe around which this spirituality revolves. Let us now try to see it at work.

A useful way of doing this is to go back to the collections of prayers we examined earlier, to see what is asked for in these prayers. One thing seems to be common in the list of things that make up the object of prayer (Shorter: 14-15; Mbiti 1975a: 16-18). They are things that are basic to the very existence of individuals and the community or to survival, things like children, rain (against drought and famine), abundant food, success in hunting or gathering expeditions, protection or healing from sickness and epidemics, aversion of war or success in it, reconciliation and peace, detection of evil (witchcraft, sorcery, adultery, breaking of taboos, curses) and its defeat. On the one hand, people ask for what they need to survive and live well, and on the other they ask to be protected from evil.

If, as we said, spirituality is the complex of beliefs, attitudes, and practices that animate people's lives and help them to reach out to the supersensible realities, we can see the orientation of this spirituality. It seems to be based on the conviction that the community of the living is involved in a dramatic struggle between life and death, and that the outcome of this struggle depends on how successfully the human community can avail itself of the help of the invisible world. Two elements, then, animate African spirituality: first, the consciousness that individuals and the community are committed to an ever-present struggle against menacing evil if life is to be worth living; and secondly, that in this struggle the decisive key is the availability of assistance from the invisible.

Furthermore, there is the conviction that this struggle is not pursued by individuals alone in isolation, but that it is in and through the community that the fight can be carried on effectively. African spirituality relies on the spirit of community, on cooperation rather than open competition, on sharing and redistribution, rather than on accumulation or individualistic hoarding. This community is conceived of in terms of "family," that is, in terms of kinship and affinity relationships whereby ideally duties and rights are exchanged unconditionally. This type of relationship offers a greater feeling of security at the same time as it builds up a strong sense of identity and belonging. The ideal good life is predicated on the smooth working of all this, and "death" is felt to ensue when these relationships are denied or threatened.

The list of things asked for in prayer also indicates a marking characteristic of people's life in general. Since in Africa there was little advance in technology and in the mastery of nature, most of the time of individuals and communities was taken up in activities of sheer subsistence and survival. The overarching preoccupations were about existing; hence, the importance of family and marriage, children, health and sickness, security and danger of death. Most activities focused on ensuring life and survival in the face of all sorts of menaces and dangers.

There was also the constant struggle to produce sufficient food; hence, the preoccupation with land (a basic commodity that should not be subject to individual possession), with rain, the weather, cultivation, harvesting, storage, and appropriate distribution and consumption of foodstuff. In this struggle for survival, the people were only too conscious of the tremendous odds they were up against: possibilities of drought, famine, failure of crops. Human beings on their own were open to tragic failures, and so they had to rely on the succor coming from "above," from alliance with the invisible. Such failures were a common occurrence. People expected them and had grown accustomed to hardship and suffering: sickness, accidents, misfortunes, even death. It is impressive to observe the calm and courage with which people faced such trials of life, taking them almost in their stride and maintaining a sense of equanimity, even a defiant response in humor and a sane *joie de vivre*. It is as though, faced with constant death, they responded with optimism and a refusal to be broken. Such people are masters in frugality, "poverty of spirit," and simplicity of life. It has been observed how, in the face of tremendous odds, the Africans have developed a spirituality of joy: the song, the dance, the celebration.

There is danger in romanticizing all this and thinking that the African is a naive, childish, and carefree individual, perhaps insensitive to human misery. In actual fact, the general lot of African people's lives was a tragic experience. One also has to admit that this capacity for suffering patiently, without rebellion or desperation, was not the case of everyone. There are sufficient cases of psychological and even physical breakdowns, instances of heart attacks and suicides, to prevent us from painting too rosy a picture. Moreover, it must be admitted that this kind of resignation is basically a weakness: it prevents people from organizing a real struggle for improvement. This failure to be assertive; the too-ready acceptance of events as if they are inevitable; the reluctance to exhibit openly impulses of individualistic ambition, aggressiveness, and self-interested acquisitiveness—all this adds up to a recipe for easy defeat in the face of determined aggression. These traits of African spirituality may help explain why historically it has been easy to enslave and keep in subjection whole groups of African peoples. And yet one must still appreciate the power and beauty of this spirituality of realism and humanity. It calls to mind the kind of sane spirituality proposed by the Book of Proverbs, where the supreme ideal is expressed in these words:

> Remove far from me falsehood and lying;
>> give me neither poverty nor riches;
>> feed me with the food that is needful for me,
> Lest I be full, and deny thee, and say,
> "Who is the Lord?"
>> or lest I be poor, and steal,
>> and profane the name of my God. (Prov. 30: 8-9)

Modern Experience: African Spirituality Put to the Test

The foregoing discussion has attempted to examine the kind of spirituality that one can deduce from African traditional culture. But as I pointed out at the beginning, my interest is not really with such a spirituality extrapolated from a past culture that is no longer there. In the past two centuries or more, Africa has been forced into a rapid and radical culture change, due mainly to its contact with the Western world. The results of this culture change must be taken into account in order to understand the present state of African spirituality.

Evidently such a summary exposition as this does not allow for an extensive and discriminating analysis of this contact with the outside—in the first place with Asia, and then with modern Europe and America. I can only mention its main manifestations insofar as they are of significance for this discussion. Three such manifestations deserve particular attention, namely slave trade, colonialism, and neocolonialism. With these we should include the introduction of new religions: Islam and especially Christianity, since these religions coming from outside have confronted more directly the indigenous religion and spirituality. For the purposes of our discussion, these contacts introduced a different and thus alternative worldview. They also disturbed the balance and coherence of those cultural values on which the people's spirituality was based. And so this spirituality has been put to a severe test.

Slave traffic for the purposes of a foreign economic system provoked, on the surface, a disturbance of family, tribal, and indigenous national security surpassing by far the effects of even the most devastating local wars. It instilled a traumatic sense of insecurity enhanced by the feeling that, while it was a human-made disaster, the usual mechanisms of self-defense and redress were totally inadequate. But even more critical was its radical questioning of the basic understanding of the human person, for here the human being was treated as a thing, an object of mere utilitarian transaction.

Colonialism, on the other hand, inflicted a loss of independence on the native cultures. New norms and customs were imposed on the people in such a way that they had to live and act in conformity with a foreign worldview. It was continually impressed on them that their own culture was not valid: it was primitive, pagan, and retrograde. If they wanted to move forward, then they had to abandon it and adopt the civilized way of life of the West. Clinging to their own traditional culture was going to keep them backward and incapable of functioning successfully in the modern world.

Given the circumstances, the adoption of new ways was not really a matter of choice, for colonialism was an imposition by force. And yet the means of enabling people to adapt to these new ways and function successfully within the new context were in no way equally available to everyone. Modern education and training, unlike traditional methods, reach individuals and communities in a highly selective manner, and the conditions for obtaining them are not totally in the hands of the people themselves, but dependent on the good will of the colonial powers and their successful allies. Success in the modern world is dependent mainly on the individual's own efforts and personal ambition, rather than on community cooperation and sharing. It is a worldview that puts a premium on aggressive and self-interested competition.

The result of colonialism has been that only a relatively few Africans have managed to acquire the tools needed to have access to power, wealth, and success in the modern context. The large majority are still left behind, trying to cope with the new situation as best they can. They struggle to assure a measure of survival with the help of some remnants of the traditional culture that are still familiar to them, and bits and pieces of the new system that they are able to take hold of. But they are at a disadvantage, and end up being at the mercy of those who are more successful. In general the process has been one in which more and more people are becoming poorer and poorer and more and more powerless in face of modern forces. The real tragedy is that traditional culture has been practically discredited. Everyone is fascinated by the power and promise of modern life and secretly hopes somehow some day to become part of it. Even those who have to fall back on traditional culture do so only as a measure of desperation. There is very little else they can do. If it were possible, they would exchange places with those who are making it in the new world.

To begin to appreciate what a severe testing traditional spirituality is undergoing as a result of colonialism, we should consider what is actually taking place, now that colonialism is officially over in most African countries and African societies are now developing into independent, self-governing nations. In the early years of independence, there was much hope and enthusiasm for development and progress. After several decades of sincere efforts, what do we see? A kind of development has surely been taking place in most nations: fantastic urban growth, modern industries, and agricultural projects resulting in higher gross national products (much wealth being produced), better infrastructure (for communication and transport), and social and health services. But why is it that this development has not been sustained? And why have only a relatively few benefited from this wealth, while the majority become poorer each day? How was it that almost immediately internal power struggles started, resulting in tribal and regional wars, oppressive military regimes, corruption, bribery, nepotism, land-grabbing, extortions, exploitative and unfair labor practices, displacement of whole populations (refugees, expulsions, asylum seekers), imprisonments, tortures, and executions? How does all this tally with traditional culture and spirituality?

This question becomes all the more pressing when we consider the present situation of neocolonialism. This is a shorthand designation of the fact, processes, and consequences of the relation between the developed and industrialized nations (the North) and the less developed and poorer nations (the South) to which Africa as a whole belongs. The decisive point in this relationship is that the South is in practice the dependent and servant member. Its economy is basically subsidiary to the North, which explains why the South is less powerful and consequently exploitable and poor. But when you consider the actual situation in the nations of the South, not every individual or group is really powerless or poor. You often see concentrations of power, wealth, and privilege in sections of these poor nations, side by side with extreme poverty and disadvantage. Not that in traditional society there was no poverty, injustice, jealousy, or suffering. There certainly was. But there is a radical difference, nonetheless, a difference not simply of magnitude, but rather of basic structure and orientation—a difference in spirituality.

I submit that the key to a proper understanding of what is going on is to realize that contact with the outside has introduced a new, alternative spirituality based on a worldview quite different from the traditional one and governed by a different set of values and priorities. This new spirituality is humanly more powerful and imposing. It promises attractive, immediate, and palpable results and has the capacity to validate these promises by offering samples of success that are hard to ignore or pass by. Central to this spirituality is the supremacy of the value of acquiring, possessing, multiplying, and enjoying material goods by individuals. This value precedes all others and should not be unnecessarily restricted by other values, such as the consideration of other people's needs and feelings.

Traditional African spirituality (ideally, though perhaps not always in fact) would rather consider as primary the value of good and harmonious human relationships, and esteem that material goods, however desirable, should not take precedence over these. But it is not so with this new spirituality. On the contrary, the pursuit of individual ambition and self-interest through fair competition is a *positive* value. African spirituality incorporates an almost superstitious fear of such open self-interest, unless it can be justified as serving the purposes of the group. There is a lurking suspicion that such a competition is never really fair. The playing down of personal ambition and the strictures induced by the need to consider the interests of the group tend to make the task of achieving success or acquiring personal wealth much more inhibited and less effective. Likewise, the high value placed on cooperation and the sharing of resources puts a brake on the instinct of acquisition and hoarding. The new spirituality releases people from such restrictions and thereby liberates the powerful drives of self-interest and individual acquisitiveness. Those who manage to get the chance can now go ahead and become powerful, rich, and successful without feeling bad about it or being bothered by the obligation to share their good luck with other people.

In all fairness, we should recall that another side of the contact of Africans with the outside has been Christian evangelization, which in some cases preceded colonialism, and in many others came together with it. The Christian message is, by and large, in opposition to what we proposed as the "spirituality" of colonialism. It is centered on love of God (not mammon) and love of neighbor. Although it seeks to promote human development and well-being, at the same time it warns against the danger of riches. It proclaims the sacred value of the human person and yet castigates self-centered individualism by exalting the value of community. In fact, there are many similarities between the values Christianity preaches and those I have pointed out as belonging to African spirituality. There are, of course, radical differences between the two, which it is not my intention to explore here. But the haunting question is this: Has Christian spirituality recognized African spirituality as a potential ally in the struggle against the worst aspects of colonial and neo-colonial infection?

The answer cannot be a simple yes or no. Christianity came to Africa in many shapes and models, and so its encounter with African cultures has not been the same everywhere. Two contrasting attitudes can be distinguished, one of opposition and rejection and another of openness and dialogue. In some cases, Christianity regarded traditional culture and religion with suspicion, even hostility. It was seen as the work of the devil, a backward and pagan way of life that must be destroyed totally if the pure religion of Christ is to be preached successfully to the people. And yet often, after this destruction had been achieved, what was proposed to the people instead was very much like the colonial spirituality. In other cases, Christian evangelists were able to recognize valid and positive elements in the traditional way of life side by side with other negative ones that the gospel would have to destroy, as has been the case with every human culture where the Christian message has been preached. In deciding between the two attitudes, Christians have tended to seek guidance from Holy Scripture. This procedure is not only legitimate, but the only sure way. The problem, however, is that it is not as simple and straightforward as some people would think. It is not simply a question of discovering some isolated texts in the Bible and then coming to this or that conclusion. Rather the whole trend of God's dealing with humanity as revealed in the Scriptures needs to be taken into account. After all, the decisive question is this: In the development and functioning of human cultures and spiritualities, such as the African one, has the God of our Lord Jesus Christ been totally absent? Is it possible that God was at work with the Spirit, inspiring and promoting positive values for the guidance of God's people, even if human sinfulness always tends to put obstacles in front of God's saving work?

Conclusion

When considering African spirituality as we have done, these questions are extremely important. For if it is true that "God did not leave himself without witness" (Acts 14:17), then whatever is true, honorable, just, pure, lovely, and gracious in what God has done among the nations has to be respected and used with gratitude. God loves to "choose what is foolish in the world to shame the wise . . . (God chooses) what is weak in the world to shame the strong . . . what is low and despised in the world, even things that are not, to bring to nothing things that are, so that no human being might boast in the presence of God" (1 Cor. 1:27-29). In our present world, cultures of greed and violence are creating death while people long for peace, security, and joy. It may be that simple spiritualities, based on more human and humane values, like those coming from the weak and poor nations of the world, are the hopeful reserves for humanity's future survival.

References

Idowu, E. Bolaji, *African Traditional Religion: A Definition* (Maryknoll, NY: Orbis Books, 1975).

Marwick, M. G., *Sorcery in its Social Setting* (Manchester University Press, 1965).

Marwick, M.G., ed., *Witchcraft and Sorcery* (Harmondworth: Penguin Books, 1970, 1982).

Maurier, Henri, *Philosophie de l'Afrique noire* (St. Augustin: Anthropos, 1985).

Mbiti, John S., *The Prayers of African Religion* (Maryknoll, NY: Orbis Books, 1975a).

Mbiti, John S., *Introduction to African Religion* (Maryknoll, NY: Orbis Books, 1975b).

Parrinder, E. G., *African Traditional Religion* (London: Sheldon Press, 1962).

Pobee, John S., *Toward an African Theology* (Nashville: Abingdon, 1979).

Shorter, Aylward, *Prayer in the Religious Traditions of Africa* (London: Oxford University Press, 1975).

Tempels, Placide, *La philosophie bantoue* (Paris: Présence Africaine, 1949).

Wakefield, Gordon S., ed., *A Dictionary of Christian Spirituality* (London: SCM Press, 1983).

Zahan, Dominique, *The Religion, Spirituality, and Thought of Traditional Africa* (Chicago and London: University of Chicago Press, 1979).

8

CHRISTIANITY AND LIBERATION IN AFRICA

Jean-Marc Éla

For more than twenty years, priests, theologians, religious communities, and committed lay persons have shared an ardent quest for an African Christianity—a quest that is a genuine challenge to the churches of Africa. In Africa today, experiments are taking place in theology, catechetics, liturgy, and religious life.[1]

Research institutes have been founded to promote these experiments, while John Paul II's trips to Africa have also stimulated local initiatives. A close reading of the documents of the Second Vatican Council, in which the church consecrated legitimate differences in the expression of a common faith, puts an end to the reproduction of models that have not been developed within our own African sociocultural context.[2]

The fact is that we have reached the age of responsibility in our search for a language of faith. As Eboussi has written, "It is time mission Christianities were constructed from within. It is time they took the initiative themselves, seizing control of the processes that have constituted them, so to speak, from without, in order to lead them to their perfection, their reflexive interiority."[3]

The task is obligatory, given the current crisis of African society, where still too often men and women fail to find appropriate responses to their life problems in our churches. What is the place of the gospel in the great religious

Translated from French by Robert R. Barr.

market when Christian institutions feel so helpless in the face of the proliferation of sects? We must ask ourselves about the relevance of Christianity at a time when "Africans are desperately plunging into these movements and associations imported from abroad."[4] This phenomenon coincides with worsening living conditions—the degradation that prevails in those "sectors of life in which the human being is particularly mistreated."[5] The "place" *par excellence* where ancestral religious traditions are being reactivated and numerous spiritual movements are unfolding is incontestably the misery of our people. "Desperate, not knowing where to turn, [our people] sometimes yield at last to the proselytism of sects and mysticisms . . . In their perplexity, persons looking for salvation become easy prey for these propagandists, whose promises are all the more alluring and fascinating as their victims feel such interior confusion."[6]

This concrete, historical irruption of the poor into our midst poses questions for our faith today—and this is a "situation of apocalypse" in which "we can no longer remain silent."[7] We cannot become the inheritors or administrators of a Christianity that simply continues on its way, passing by the victim lying in the ditch (Luke 10:30-32). How can a *credible* Christianity be created while so many factors are tightening a noose around Africa's neck? This is a decisive question.

Irruption of the Poor: Challenge to African Christianity

We in the African churches need to pause for a moment. Let us cease, if need be, activities which pose the danger of being too comfortable and permanent, and rethink evangelization in depth—in terms of the great challenges of Africa today. It is not evident that the problems worrying the clergy are also the problems of women and men whose basic rights are being flouted. In many of our countries, access to drinking water, a balanced diet, health and hygiene, education, or self-determination are, more often than not, luxuries for a self-serving small club. While people wallow in misery, we are centering our reflection and action on religious rites and customs! As the gospel comes face-to-face with African traditions, we must find another way to understand and live our faith. Perhaps we ought to ask ourselves whether the attraction of the sects does not reside precisely in the disappointments suffered by men and women who refuse to identify with Christianity as it is lived in our churches.

There is still great hope that churches will seek emancipation from foreign guardianship so they can come of age.[8] Does this quest identify with that of the poor people of our villages, of the hills, or the slums of African cities? How can there be free expression in our churches unless we take into account the traumatic situation of the starving millions and the perilous condition of the outcasts of our societies? What meaning can faith have in churches that seek to be liberated without sharing the peoples' battles with the forces of oppression assaulting their dignity?

These are frightening questions. They threaten our institutional comforts, our invested privileges, our secure situations, and they threaten established practices and certitudes. But they are inevitable, unless the churches intend to content themselves with criticizing, arousing, and exhorting others without criticizing, examining, or questioning themselves. The churches should renounce preaching the "truth" and begin to criticize themselves and their lack of family spirit, their unwillingness to share, and their lack of active solidarity with persons struggling to break free from misery and oppression.

An experience of faith that holds itself aloof from people seeking to escape marginalization poses a serious risk to the future of Christianity in Africa. By reappropriating the meaning of faith in terms of our culture and standing before God with our own humanity, we must address questions in the name of the gospel. Then the gospel will be an appeal for conversion and demand that we leave our cozy shelters.

On this continent, where one abortive "independence" after another stirs bitter disillusion, the everyday life of millions of men and women begins to appear as a long, drawn-out Calvary. This poses questions for the disciples of the Crucified One of Golgotha. The churches of Africa are beginning to be aware of this. "How long shall we have to wait for a small portion of happiness?" the Zaire bishops' conference asked recently, and observed: "Failure upon failure! In the meantime, shameless exploitation, organized pillage for the profit of foreign countries and their intermediaries—while the mass of the people wallow in misery, at times in artificially created situations."[9]

Few countries of Africa escape this condition. All across the continent, a process of recolonization is under way, declared the Symposium of the Episcopal Conferences of Africa and Madagascar (SECAM) at Accra in 1977. The African bishops, meeting in Yaoundé in 1981, sounded a warning.

Be aware of the prevailing international domination, a domination at once political, economic, social, and cultural . . . Think of the enterprises of the multinational companies. . . . All of these factors weigh upon the African continent. They perpetuate situations of injustice, and create frequently insurmountable obstacles along the path to development, and economic and social progress.[10]

While the effects of dependency continue to multiply and domination returns to haunt us in new guises, "There are situations and systems," declared John Paul II at Nairobi, "within countries, and in relations among states, that are marked by injustice, condemning many persons to hunger, disease, unemployment, ignorance, and the stagnation of their development." It is altogether obvious. Our people's situation cannot be attributed solely to the penetration of our continent by the multinationals, which regard Africa simply as a playground for the superpowers. We must look for internal factors in the dispossession of the African masses. This process continues despite modernization programs and growth efforts, since their benefits are monopolized by an elite in an Africa of ever-worsening economic and social disparities.[11] Along with the injustices perpetrated upon us from without, we now have a parade of miseries resulting from relationships within—between state and people,[12] elite and masses.

We need only recall the trauma that rocks our families and the state of insecurity that reigns in most countries of Africa, which are gradually becoming a "human rights desert." The bishops of Africa are concerned with a *political context in which violence and torture are seen more and more as a standard way of exercising power.* For many leaders, politics has become the way of dictatorship, totalitarianism, and the oppression of the weakest. Freedom of expression and the right to information are nearly or entirely lost to the people. How many countries see their constitutions scoffed at! Then people become the cheap pawns of unbridled powers that bear down with all their weight on minds and bodies.[13] This is *not* the Africa of postcards, safaris, or official visits.

Stripped of its popular traditions, African reality raises its brutal head. The violation of human rights, undernourishment, starvation wages, conflicts, and uncertainty about the future create a society built on a foundation of injustice and domination. The result is deteriorating living conditions that affect the rural and working classes and the middle-class employees, "whose purchasing power crumbles away daily, in the face of the arrogant, abusive security and prosperity of a small minority."[14]

It is interesting to find this view of reality appearing in African theological movements.[15] "Welcome to Africa, the native land of the poor, the weak, the oppressed," acknowledged Engelbert Mveng in an opening address at the first Congress of African and European Theologians in Yaoundé. At its 1977 meeting in Accra, the Pan-African Conference of Third World Theologians made its options very plain. Its Final Document declared that the new challenge to African theology was manifestly "the liberation of our people from a certain cultural captivity." What made the Accra colloquium such a landmark was its admission that oppression is at work not only in our culture, but also in our political and economic structures, and in the mass media used as a tool by the ruling powers. Hence, Accra announced, "African theology must also be *liberation* theology."

These urgent problems of contemporary Africa become the obligatory *locus* of theological research. The women and men who have joined in the struggle for an African Christianity face a fertile challenge: it is no longer enough to pose the questions of faith on the level of culture alone. We must also pay attention to the mechanisms and structures of oppression at work. These realities constitute a challenge to our African "intelligence of the faith." In this regard, among the other forms of oppression we must include the "marginal role reserved to women in the churches."

Faced with this situation, we must act. The Accra Colloquium set forth the extent of the needed transformation. "We have acknowledged that there are many forms of oppression. There is the oppression of Africans by white colonialism, but there is also the oppression of blacks by blacks." Any possibility that our efforts to deliver ourselves must depend on external forces is tantamount to supposing that the commitment of African Christians to liberation is illegitimate or foreign to our tradition. What was actually called for at Accra was Africa's reconciliation with itself. The history of this continent is a history not only of slavery and domination, but of struggle and resistance to oppression. Witness the protest movements that have seared the memory of our people, generation after generation.[16]

The Accra phenomenon was precisely the people's refusal—in the name of faith—to accept a world of injustice and oppression, a refusal based on a new perception of the requirements of the gospel. "We stand against oppression in any form because the Gospel of Jesus Christ demands our participation in the struggle to free people from all kinds of dehumanization." This major imperative was recognized by the bishops of Africa and Madagascar at its Nairobi conference. "It is this human being," the bishops said, "that, according to our faith, Christ has come to save and deliver." And the liberation Christ seeks is "liberation from everything that oppresses the human being. Christ wills total liberation—a liberation that regards the human being in all dimensions of his and her being and existence." This specificity keeps us from avoiding any ambiguity or misunderstanding. It would be unjust to accuse African Christians of betraying their faith or reducing it to ideology merely because they strive to live the gospel in situations of starvation and injustice that contradict the will of God. If we shut Christianity up in the universe of sin, grace, and the sacraments, don't we risk voiding the historical, concrete dimensions of salvation in Jesus Christ?

The bishops have taken pains to apprise us that the liberation at issue "is not only of a spiritual, interior order. It has a direct impact on the individual and collective concrete life of humanity . . . The human being's liberation means decolonization, development, social justice, and respect for imprescriptible rights and basic freedoms." We must deal with this problem if we are to incarnate the faith in Africa.

Toward an Evangelization of Liberation

For persons who discovered Jesus Christ through a theology of the "salvation of souls" and a mission practice that has, by and large, transplanted Christianity from the North, a new day is dawning as we enter the second century of African church history. Now is the time of challenge: *we must renounce the evangelization of Africa in dependency.* After a hundred years of evangelization and colonial trafficking and domination, Africans have become slaves of death and servitude. Matters may even be worse now than they were before African independence. Independence has been a disappointment to us. And the church has seemed to proclaim the gospel in Africa without any deep involvement in our struggle against exploitation.

Seated at the table of the West, the church seems to have thrown us "poor, poor blacks" nothing but crumbs. It has been unwilling to force imperialist countries to look honestly at their African enterprises. In its "compassion for the Negroes," the missionary church has failed to confront the forces that subjugate plantation and factory laborers. What is the stance of the church vis-à-vis societies that exploit, starve, and destroy the peasants of Africa? Anyone honestly examining the situation of the human being on African soil can only be struck by the breadth of oppression that prevails.

Everywhere we turn, the wave of repression is accompanied by economic and political degradation. In some countries repression is directed not only against political militants, students, and intellectuals, but also—in total paranoia—against anyone practicing civil disobedience, or even simply the peasantry. All are reduced to silence. We need to understand that the meaning of our faith is concretely and historically relevant only in the measure that, in

Jesus Christ, it is translated into terms of dangerous forthrightness (cf. Acts 4:20), witness, and martyrdom.

At the moment when our people are seeking to reread the Bible in terms of our actual experience, the challenges of poverty and oppression suddenly provide a *locus* where the church can work to understand itself and its mission. The text drafted for the Sixth Assembly of SECAM included this arresting declaration. "A church is not yet authentically rooted in a people unless it seeks to establish justice amidst that people and perform the works of that justice."

We must reconsider the genesis of the church in Africa. Up until now, we have been inclined to examine the problem of the birth and implanting of the church in terms of Rome as the center of the universe. Hence our insistence on a native clergy and hierarchy. If the church is organized in terms of the society in which it lives, then we cannot ignore the situations of dependency and economic practices imposed on us by the North. We have to evaluate the role of multinational capital in the formation of our society. We have to take account of the exploitation of the peasantry and popular masses as cheap labor that helps an elite prosper.

In all events, salvation in Jesus Christ is liberation from every form of slavery. Therefore, the *church ought to signify this salvation concretely, by creating conditions that liberate human beings and enable them to grow*. The perverse effects of growth without development, the flight from the countryside to the city, prostitution and juvenile delinquency, marginalization and unemployment, nutritional problems and abominable hygienic conditions, injustice and repression, call the church and its mission into question. The most crying outrage to us Africans is what Paul VI called "situations of cultural neocolonialism sometimes as cruel as the old political colonialism." In this context, recalled the Holy Father, "the Church . . . has the duty to proclaim the liberation of millions of human beings, many of whom are her own children—the duty of assisting the birth of this liberation, of giving witness to it, ensuring that it is complete. This is not foreign to evangelization."[17]

The church must adopt the practice of Jesus himself. Jesus did not limit his mission to preaching an inner conversion. His concern was precisely for the liberation of the poor and oppressed (Luke 4:16-21). In Jesus, God is glimpsed in the gesture of shared bread and in the act of the person who rises up and walks. The practice and message of the good news will be translated by acts of liberating people from legalism and ritualism.

In our African context, how are we to implement the practice of the One who is not simply the savior of souls but the hope of the poor and the oppressed, the One who reveals to human beings the genuine name of the God of the exodus (John 17:6)?

The inspiration needed for mission in Africa today and tomorrow is an overriding concern to testify to the gospel message in terms of *incarnation*. It will not be enough for missioners to take account of the values of our culture. It will require as well that they assume the conflicts of our history and, on the basis of these conflicts, strive to reread the symbolic and cultural forms of the African world. Christianity must be lived in terms of the historical and social dynamics of the Africa of our times.

The basic challenge, then, is to conceive and promote modes of presence and action in the perspective of the new creation (Rev. 1:5). What gives meaning and value to our apostolic commitments is whatever contributes to the remaking of the human person and the world in the name of the gospel. Accordingly, we must renounce stagnant, entrenched practices that produce a vacuous Christianity. We must experience a renewal of mission that searches for pertinent answers "to the questions posed by our various historical contexts and the current evolution of our societies."[18]

What should become the center of gravity of our experience of faith and of our celebration of salvation? Our primordial sacrament should be the poor and the oppressed, those disturbing witnesses of God in the warp and woof of our history. African reality imposes on the church a kind of *pedagogy of the discovery of situations of sin and oppression*— situations that rear their heads in contradiction with the project of the salvation and liberation in Jesus Christ. In societies where death is all about us, we are forced to open our eyes to what is happening, in order to be willing to respond to God, in faith, to the questions that come to us from the "Africa of the villages" and the Africa of the slums—from depths where men and women and children are locked up in hellholes of misery and despair. When all is said and done, what we shall have to do is become aware of our kinship with Jesus Christ in humiliation. After all, it is Jesus himself who walks unrecognized today in the African people. Mission today calls for an encounter with a soul-piercing question: "Why do you persecute me?" (Acts 22:7).

This is how far we really must go when we examine the "prisons of Africa," and hear the howls of torture victims. Living the incarnation must surely be more than merely adopting African words and African rhythms to speak of God and celebrate the divine praise. We must "keep in mind Jesus Christ" (cf. 2 Tim. 2:8), the "man of suffering and acquainted with infirmity" (Isa. 53:3). "So marred was his appearance, beyond human semblance, and his form beyond that of mortals," that he was "one from whom others hid their faces, he was despised, and we held him of no account" (Isa. 52:14, 53:3).

Welcome to Africa, Christ's native land! Welcome to that "world disfigured by injustice" described by the Sixth Assembly of SECAM. The eyes of faith reveal to us the Son of Man in the life of black peasants whose production is bought for next to nothing or whose land is seized for the profit of big capital. It is Jesus' labor that is used by the local and multinational companies, for wages not even adequate to feed the uprooted families of the urban centers or factory farms. Jesus is present in the sick who are exploited in a corrupt society where disease itself is a source of profit. Does Jesus never wear the face of the refugee or stranger struggling along the road of an exodus? Isn't Jesus completely in solidarity with the world of the excluded, the world of our next-door neighbors?

Accordingly, the church will have to submit to a critical analysis of itself and its practice and be willing to question itself. As the African reality is stripped naked and set forth for what it actually is, we see its *radical incompatibility with God's plan for the world.* How are we to become men and women whose hands sow hope, without overcoming the sociocultural and material distances that divide us from the poor people of Africa? Haven't we finally arrived at the point where we must put an end to the habits and languages that shut us up in our ecclesiastical ghettos? Are we finally willing to soil our hands and learn to live in solidarity with the vanquished? If conversion to God is inseparable from conversion to the poor, don't we have to rethink mission "from below"—where we find the oppressed? An in-depth evangelization of the African person cannot escape what Bishop Kabanga called the "descent into hell." It is that descent that will enable us to reach our "people who await the Messiah-Savior."

The Bible and Africa

New paths of evangelization open up to Christians wherever they and their churches make an effort to redefine themselves in terms of service to persons stripped of their rights. We must begin mission anew and become traveling companions to individuals and groups who now set out on their exodus. We must look for a new articulation of the Bible with the African situation.

Are the churches of Africa reading the Bible from the situations of captivity in which so many men and women struggle and cry out in our villages and our neighborhoods? As we move from the catechism composed as a tool of the Counter-Reformation to revelation in Jesus Christ, we find a new catechetical route imposed on us by the summons of the gospel: we are obliged to do a rereading of the Bible that renounces any dissimulation of the contradictions of our societies. Until now, our church has read the Bible to people from the lofty "chair of Moses" (Matt. 23:2), without always opening its ears to what is said of God when the starving and the pariahs of the new African states undertake to speak of God. Instead of speaking of God as proprietors of the truth, we must be willing to restore the word to these "least ones," to whom the Father has revealed the mysteries of the Reign (Matt. 11:25; Luke 10:21-22). Plainly, when the Bible is given an African reading, it is capable of liberating, of giving a message of life that has not always been understood in the churches. This has come about because the churches have been little concerned with reinventing catechesis or with building the language of faith on the basis of the concerns of justice, humanization, and liberation.

For the sake of the credibility of the gospel, we must renounce religious discourse pronounced from on high, where it wafts above the byroads of misery and indignity. We must enable our people to find their way of speaking of God precisely where they must face the forces of death in everyday life. Otherwise we shall not be able to give them the gospel's entire wealth of protest, its demands to transform the world. A genuine discussion between Christianity and Africa can help the churches rediscover the authentic face of the God of revelation, the God who hears the cries of the afflicted (Exod. 3:7; Ps. 34:18-19).

God is not neutral. This is the discovery we make when we read the Bible from the viewpoint of the poor. For centuries, the Bible has been helpless to manifest its potential for transformation. The church has always referred to it in its prayer, in its reflection, and in its defense of the faith. But in Africa, particularly, sheer reality has remained untouchable—immunized, as it were, against all change. Truly, how can the coexistence of the Bible and domination be justified? How can a person read the Bible and leave a people in a state of poverty and marginalization? Isn't Christianity, rooted as it is in the Bible, in its very essence liberation?

This is the perception we are led to by a comprehensive rereading of revelation; we read of Jesus Christ, who took the part of the poor and denounced injustices of every shape and kind. Jesus Christ is not that perverse God who might be appealed to by the processes of oppression or the justification of repressive power and situations of injustice. We must meditate on the mystery of Jesus Christ himself, as we behold it in the twofold event of his death and resurrection. This is the basic message of the gospel. As Archbishop Kabanga writes, "Jesus is accused and sentenced because he dares tell the truth.

In his death, he is in solidarity with those society rejects. But for us and the world, Jesus raised becomes a power of liberation—the sign of a new world to come and already beginning to be."[19]

Here we must draw the practical conclusions forced upon us by what German theologian Johannes B. Metz calls the "dangerous, subversive memory" of Jesus Christ. We must take account of our situation that is the result of the joint enterprise of the multinationals, the cozy smugness of the ruling classes, and an all-pervasive corruption. When we view this situation in the light of the central mystery of our faith, that wellspring from which we draw the strength to forge ahead, the first thing we discover is the prophetic character of the poor and the other marginalized groups who, by their very existence within our societies, manifest the nature of sin in its historical structure. It is in situations like these that the gospel reveals to us the "sin of the world" that led Jesus to the cross.

The dynamics of faith have their origin and foundation in the salvation event that reveals the true face of God. The church cannot recall Jesus who was crucified and yet speak of the crucifixion as if it were to take place at the end of time. How is the ecclesial experience of the cross to be embodied? What shape is it to develop here and now? We must renounce any kind of preaching that glosses over the historical lot of human beings. Any temptation to enthusiastically interpret the gospel, as happened in Corinth, must be met with renewed insistence on the central place of the cross (1 Cor. 2:1-5). Preaching the gospel carefully and explicitly to focus on the world in its most ordinary, daily, comprehensive reality can set us ablaze in Africa; it can fire us with a passion for a people whom Christ has taken to his heart. Nothing can blind us to this brutal fact: *Africa today is crucified.* An African theology that rereads the Bible in terms of this fundamental locus will have to be a "theology of the cross."

But Jesus Christ is God in conflict with a world that shrinks from the divine will. In assuming the condition of the people, the Servant battles for the liberation of the human being and the coming of the Reign of God. It is not true that there is no connection between Jesus Christ and the conflicts and struggles we wage for life. The truth is that *the struggles of our people bring the memory of the Crucified One right into our own life and times.* Caught in the structures of a sinful world, the cross holds a "reserve" of critical exigency, of demand for change. This implies a process of opening up to the full potential of human beings anticipated by God. In other words, any reference to the cross in the church implies a quest in history for the nearest match to God's plan.

And so a project of fullness of life for the poor and oppressed is intrinsic to a profession of Jesus crucified. Therefore the will of God "on earth as in heaven" can be accomplished only through the life of the least of God's people.

Christ, then, is not to be looked upon only as the Lord of worship, whose direct, immediate presence we extol at the eucharistic supper. Christ is actually Lord of the world in all its dimensions. The hope of a new world—a world to be built in a perspective of justice and peace, healing and life, and in a word, deliverance from evil—is at the heart of Christ's passion and resurrection. The fundamental task of the church is to proclaim this hope to the Africa of today.

With this understanding, Christians are obliged to undertake, in the name of the cross, a radical critique of our world as it is. This examination must command the options to be taken and the commitments to be made to restore our history to the course desired for it by the Lord of the universe. *There can be no profession of faith without concrete responsibility for persons and for life, and increased militancy.* To "translate" the gospel into transformations of life and society, the churches must begin to believe and celebrate their faith in terms of necessary commitments, wherever the immense wealth and limitless potential of certain countries are exploited. Such exploitation is for the profit of foreigners and local minorities and it overcomes millions of adults and children with hunger, sickness, and idleness. It requires a true effort of imagination to respond to the Risen One's call to a new life based on actual, current situations, so that the goods of the earth will be distributed according to a system less shot through with inequalities. Today wages distributed to workers in Africa are so inadequate that most people are forced into "making do" or corruption, and there are many forms of manipulation and organized distraction to keep the poor in ignorance, resignation, or silence. In order to reach the crucified African and set him and her on the pathways of life, Christians must take account of the whole context in which famine leads to malnutrition and death, while the specter of unemployment hurls the young into the streets, into drugs and prostitution, crime, despair, and suicide. In short, we in the church must take up the Africans' current problems and look at them in the light of the gospel, in order that "hope may germinate" in the center of our reality.

This, without a doubt, is the step intimated to us by the celebration of the "mystery of faith." The Eucharist renders unacceptable a world where one is hungry and another is glutted (cf. 1 Cor. 11:21). The Eucharist is the place where a word of liberation is spoken in memory of Jesus' death (1 Cor. 11:26). It is also the place where the multiplication of the loaves (John 6:1-13; Mark 6:41, 14:22) continues. In a sense, the church is built up around shared bread.

Christ must be recognized as the one who gives to eat to the poor and the starving.[20] In this perspective, the Eucharist is a serious challenge at the heart of the church, an urgent summons to Christians. As an invitation to sharing, it is a call to justice and to the transformation of the current structures of our societies. *The Eucharist itself, given its place in the life of the church, should throb with the dynamism that will enable Christians to resist this world of unjust structures and domination.*

As we attempt to reorganize our communities around new services, there is a need to restore the dignity of the ministry of healing. Questions of health and well-being constitute one of the loci of the revelation of God's design. In Africa, conditions of well-being have been unjustly confiscated by an elite.[21] In view of the intrinsic relationship between health and human advancement, we must add justice and watchfulness (Ezek. 37:1-9) to the list of "new ministries," if we hope to make the word of God credible today. Our engagement of faith and God's revelation imposes this imperative upon all of God's people.

> For Zion's sake I will not be silent,
>> for Jerusalem's sake I will not be quiet,
> Until her vindication shines forth like the dawn
>> and her victory like a burning torch.
>
> Nations shall behold your vindication,
>> and all kings your glory. [Isa. 62:1-2]

In order to accomplish God's basic plan, we need a genuine "pedagogy of seeing" to help us discover the profound reality of our world. Although we may be more comfortable in responding to emergencies or working in Christendom's works of social charity, we must learn to search for the signs of sin and death written on the face of everyday life. We cannot transform our reality "without knowing all the forms of oppression and causes of corruption that vitiate the social order. We must develop, in ourselves and in our faith communities, that 'critical faculty' that will lead us to reflect on the society in which we live . . . This inventory of forms of oppression and causes of corruption will best be made working in a group at the grassroots."[22]

Our small communities constitute a privileged locus to practice our faith. The critical task of an "intelligence of the faith" must be performed at the grassroots, where persons and groups are confronted with factors that keep them in poverty and dependency. We cannot participate in the life of the base communities until we locate and identify the obstacles preventing or slowing down the deliverance of the poor and the liberation of captives.

Our villages and popular neighborhoods today are steeped to the skin in situations of domination and new forms of dependency. They are caught in the grip of multinational companies, which are scarcely philanthropic societies. Here base communities can enable people to discover who it is that is really responsible for poverty. A fact is a fact: *the word of God is heard through questions that commit us to build a society in which nutrition, employment and health, education and a share of happiness are no longer luxuries for a small elite group.* We must return to the grassroots. We must open our ears to Africa, take account of the mute voice of a people—in the street, in the village, in the neighborhood, in places where ordinary folk gather to talk—a voice not necessarily heard in official discourse, or in the media, often part of the machinery of the parties in power.

Couched in this "word from below," the God of life is revealed to those who strive to discover the concrete signs of the presence of the Reign. In this quest, in which the gospel delivers its liberating message, our communities have a responsibility to God to transform conditions of existence. At a moment when the "manipulation of the believable"[23] is rampant in Africa through the proliferation of imported sects and mystiques that threaten to demobilize the poor people of our continent,[24] faith in the risen Jesus reveals a different kind of relationship with God. Now is the time of challenge. Now is the time when the church must organize itself to deal with the basic problems of life. Now is the time when the church must bear witness to the Risen One through forms of expression and commitment where prayer and struggle are in harmony. Then spirituality and everyday life—the confrontation of the Bible with daily questions and an understanding of the faith and its celebration—will promote humankind and fight for justice.

In this way our small communities can become signs of hope to the marginalized and outcast of our societies. Now it will be possible to verify the fact that everyday living cannot be reduced simply to a "pious" or charitable life-style. Rather, we shall discern how faith obliges us to intervene in the sociopolitical and economic domain, where the gospel has exigencies and urgencies in Africa's current context. Instead of resuming our journeys to nowhere, repeating activities that do nothing to upset the mechanisms of mass impoverishment, we should concentrate our attention on alternative experiences, which, by giving the initiative back to the people, may help them escape different forms of dependency and marginalization.

For a long time, Christianity in Africa has devoted itself to the traditional activities of Western Christendom. Today it is time to realize that these activities are part of the context of dependency and exploitation that prevent African development. If there is no viable life in our context, if we cannot suppress inequalities and injustices that engender misery and poverty, then we must work to create groups of men and women who will break with everything that maintains the true causes of underdevelopment.

By moving from "aid" to building centers of political, economic, cultural, and concrete historical decisions—centers internal to a society in need of transformation—the church will create conditions for a development that will also be a liberation. How? By restoring the peoples' power to determine their life and decide their future. Development is not genuine unless it is supported by local initiatives and potential and rooted in a culture.

In becoming ecclesial places where voice and initiative are restored to the ordinary people, our village and neighborhood communities will no longer focus the faith of the laity exclusively on the problems of the clergy. Instead, this focus will be on transforming society. The faith of African Christians must bridge the gap that separates it from everyday life. In order to be integrated into the concrete reality of our people, our faith needs to be translated wherever the poor and exploited, the potential agents of Africa's liberation, are awakening.

Toward a Credible Christianity

In these reflections, I have attempted to identify what is at stake for the faith and the gospel at the current time here in Africa. Those of us who have traditionally enjoyed the invested privileges of the status quo must find the courage to *redefine the purpose of our presence in lands that have changed so extensively since Christianity was implanted here.* We must make the concrete decisions required of us by the Spirit who speaks to us through the urgent needs of our societies. Christianity must try to liberate the gospel from all forms of captivity, including the forces of inertia prevailing in Africa. The world of poverty and exploitation into which we are plunged is a hard test, yet Christianity must bear witness to its truth by its willingness to take up questions judged "indigenous" by a religion of cheap grace.

The test is obligatory. Africans today are striving to reappropriate the meaning of faith, in order to express it in a language that finds its forms in their own culture. But why should the incarnation of the faith be restricted to "cultural loci"? Why should it continue to ignore the popular resistance that constitutes the response of the weak to forces of oppression? What would be the future of a Christianity that would "soar above the scuffle"—staying out of the conflicts from which the future will evolve? Whether it comes from inside or outside of Africa, how can a Christianity that dares not speak the gospel today in terms of real situations of oppression and injustice be credible in the eyes of poor or young people?

Eboussi Boulaga writes:

> Those who have been subjected to Christianity's assaults on their own traditions will never be content with half-measures and half-truths. Christianity will never recover its credibility, at least in the eyes of some. It will suffer from inadaptation to an Africa on the move until such time as the deepest, most radical questions are no longer handled by preterition and evasion. African Christianity will always be suspect as a mere religion of the herd, a theatricalization of the continuing subordination of Africa to the West in the neocolonial context of a shameful, cowardly dependency in all areas—social, political, economic, and scientific.
>
> Hence we must take the measure of the obstacles that an authentic Christianity will have to surmount. It may be that a Christianity to which the African can respond in soul and conscience will be born only from the ashes of so-called middle-class Christianity.[25]

Only a church in solidarity with these men and women around us who have been left "half-dead" (Luke 10:30), stripped by so many mechanisms of pillage and exploitation, can restore all its relevancy to our faith in Jesus Christ in today's Africa. If "the true temple of God is the human being,"[26] then we must review our spirituality, our way of being shepherds, our theology,[27] together with our whole identity as African Christians, in terms of ecclesial commitments whose aim is to liberate human beings in all dimensions of their existence. It is not enough that the "struggle for justice" be included in the official discourse of a certain number of Christians—priests, bishops, or theologians—while the practices and orientations of Christian life as a whole continue to be shaped by the problematic of a Christendom still caught in the subtle machinations of a dominant society. Henceforward *we shall have to dare to live our relationship with God in faith in terms of our experience of solidarity with an Africa that seeks liberation.*

In this perspective, what we need in our churches is a Christianity with "dirty hands"—one that will abandon its ghetto mentality and commit itself to the down-to-earth questions that decide the future of a people. The times in which we live call for a certain *aggiornamento* to the radicalism of the gospel: that we listen to Africans who live in those conditions; that we accept a basic challenge to our experience of faith. What must mobilize us now is a Christianity seeking to redefine itself totally "in relation to the struggles of the people in their resistance to the structures of domination."[28]

What is at stake in this quest for relevance are God and the human person, linked in Jesus Christ in an authentic community of destiny. Inseparable from the Word Incarnate on his cross, the African person should be inseparable from him in his victory over sin and death as well. Nor should the resurrection be a simple event of the past. It should become a reality precisely where millions of human beings are undergoing their passion, in injustice, humiliation, and contempt. Instead of remaining a system swallowed up in routine, the Christian message should be energy to transform the world.

If this comes about, Africans will proclaim the wonders of God with the genius of their own culture—a culture taken on by a Christianity rooted in the life of a people struggling for their liberation. In the dawn of a new day,

> Before your face, an Africa raised from the dead
> Shall tremble with felicity and gladness,
> Shall spread out wide and rustling,
> Manifold and varied, mighty and harmonious and gracious,
> Like the infinite motion of the sea,
> Or like that movement of the forest high and deep
> When the wind comes calling.
> Africa old and new shall dance the dance of jubilation
> To the God of Africa,
> To the one God of the world.[29]

Notes

1. See Monsengwo Pasinya, *Inculturation du message à l'exemple du Zaïre* (Kinshasa: Éd. St. Paul Afrique, 1979).

2. Vatican Council II, Decree on the Church's Missionary Activity *(Ad Gentes),* nos. 15, 22.

3. F. Eboussi Boulaga, *Pour une catholicité africaine* (Paris: Présence Africaine, 1977).

4. Meinrad Hebga, "L'Afrique et ses formes de vie spirituelle," in *Interpellation des movements mystiques* (Paris, 1983), p. 70.

5. *Notre foi en l'homme, image de Dieu,* Declaration of the Permanent Committee of the Bishops of Zaïre, 1981, p. 13.

6. Ibid.

7. See *Notre foi en l'homme,* p. 21.

8. Hebga, *Émancipation d'Églises sous-tutelles* (Paris: Présence Africaine, 1976).

9. *Notre foi en l'homme,* p. 21.

10. See *Justice and Evangelization in Africa,* 9, Congregation for the Evangelization of Peoples.

11. See "L'Afrique des bourgeoisies," *Le Monde diplomatique* (November 1981).

12. For the sucking dry of the peasantry, see my *L'Afrique des villages* (Paris: Karthala, 1982).

13. *Justice and Evangelization in Africa.*

14. Ibid.

15. See various authors, *Libération ou Adaptation? La théologie Africaine s'interroge: Le Colloque d'Accra* (Paris: Harmattan, 1979).

16. As an example, see P. Demuntier, *Masses rurales et luttes politiques au Zaïre* (Paris: Anthropos, 1975). On the same subject, see J. A. Mbembe, "Pratiques culturelles et créativité populaire en Afrique noire hier et aujourd'hui," address delivered at the Institut Catholique de Toulouse, November 29, 1983.

17. See Paul VI, *On Evangelization in the Modern World: Apostolic Exhortation Evangelii Nuntiandi* (Washington, DC: USCC, 1976), no. 30.

18. Declaration of the Bishops of Africa and Madagascar following the Roman Synod of 1974.

19. Kabanga, *Je suis un homme,* 1977.

20. See J. M. van Cangh, *La multiplication des pains et l'eucharistie* (Paris: Cerf, 1975).

21. See my "Luttes pour la santé et Royaume de Dieu dans l'Afrique d'aujourd'hui," in *Bulletin de Théologie Africaine.*

22. See *Justice and Evangelization in Africa,* no. 28.

23. See Michel de Certeau, "L'international des sectes ou la manipulation du croyable," *Le Monde diplomatique* (September 1977).

24. See Eric de Rosny, "Les Églises indépendantes africaines: Fonction sociale et originalité culturelle," *Études* (January 1983), pp. 96-97.

25. F. Eboussi Boulaga, *Christianity without Fetishes: An African Critique and Recapture of Christianity,* trans. Robert R. Barr (Maryknoll, NY: Orbis Books, 1984), p. 56.

26. See P. Nkiere Kena, CICM, "Va, et toi aussi, fais de même," *Africana* (Montreal, 1984).

27. Ibid.

28. See *Libération ou Adaptation? Le Colloque d'Accra.*

29. J. Mbala, in *Des Prêtres noirs s'interrogent* (Paris: Présence Africaine, 1957).

9

IMPOVERISHMENT AND LIBERATION: A THEOLOGICAL APPROACH FOR AFRICA AND THE THIRD WORLD

Engelbert Mveng

My focus is the problems of poverty in the Third World, especially poverty as we experience it in Africa. Our context today is a new experience of enslavement and domination by the powers controlling the world.

The phenomenon of our poverty has been poorly studied, when it has been studied at all. Discourse has centered mainly on underdevelopment, which is a nebulous concept, deliberately set with traps. In accepting the notion of underdevelopment, we condemn ourselves to a state of inferiority, which serves to justify the activity of those who enslave and dominate us. We are inferior beings. We hold a position beneath their level of development, below the normal condition of human beings living in dignity. At any rate, this is the worldview of our oppressors.

This is how sociologists, ethnologists, political scientists—nearly all of them Western—have conjured away the fact of our poverty. The reasons for this feat of legerdemain are manifold (and we examine them below). Among African authors, very few seem to have seen through the smoke screen of "underdevelopment." Albert Tévoédjéré, with his *La pauvreté, richesse des peuples,*[1] must

Translated from French by Robert R. Barr.

be acknowledged as a pioneer and an exception. Still, even his book is essentially only a panoramic reflection on the Third World; it does not inaugurate a critical analysis of the African experience of poverty.

By contrast, Westerners produce an endless and growing literature on the phenomenon of poverty. But these writers are addressing the phenomenon of poverty in their own societies. The works of Lionel Stoleru,[2] Gaston Guel,[3] Eliane Mossé,[4] and Philippe Sassier,[5] to cite but a few French authors, contain long bibliographies, some of them with hundreds of titles. We might also mention the American school, and the numerous publications of the Institute for Research on Poverty, or P. Townsend's research on the British experience (see his *The Concept of Poverty*[6]).

Major newspapers such as *Le Monde* have done periodic surveys of Western poverty. *Le Monde Diplomatique,* in its May 1988 issue, published a series of studies under the general title, "Rich and Poor Across the World" (see pp. 15-22 of that issue). *Le Monde* has published studies on two instances of modern impoverishment: "The Dying Land" (August 28, 1990, apropos of the farm crisis in France), and the case of "Mexico: The Thousand Families," based on the results of a *Le Monde* survey of "The Rich in Poor Countries and the Poor in Rich Countries," covering countries as diverse as Turkey and Germany, Great Britain, India, and Italy.[7]

We readily perceive, through these studies, that poverty in the West is surely an economic, sociological, and cultural phenomenon. But above all, today, it is a political problem—a problem of power, or rather, the problem of a justification of the power of the oppressor over the oppressed, the weak, the needy. This is also Philippe Sassier's theme in his *Du bon usage des pauvres: Histoire d'un thème politique XVIe-XXe siècle (Making Good Use of the Poor: History of a Political Theme from the Sixteenth to the Twentieth Centuries).*[8]

Definitions

Poverty as we experience it today in Africa is indeed a political problem. However, the problem is not identical in Africa and in the West. European approaches present poverty as an internal political problem of the societies and states concerned. The French, in their poverty, have no one to blame but themselves and France. France is regarded as sovereign where its citizens' politics, economics, and living conditions are concerned. Alas, none of this is applicable in today's Africa, either to the citizen or to the state.

The definitions of poverty that are given in these investigations emphasize the following points.

1. Poverty is basically a lack and privation
2. of goods judged to be useful or necessary for the normal life of a human person
3. living in a given society
4. situated in space and in time.

This definition is obviously not very satisfactory. For a considerable number of researchers, "useful or necessary goods" are primarily material goods that correspond to elementary needs (food, drink, clothing, housing) with the stipulation that the satisfaction of these needs must, of course, include not only the individual, but the family, as well.

Finally, it is observed that the want or lack in question must not be restricted to material goods alone. There are other goods—spiritual, moral, cultural, sociological, and so on—the privation of which engenders other types of poverty: spiritual, moral, cultural, and sociological poverty. These kinds of poverty are just as devastating for a human being as is simple material poverty. In the Third World, notably in Africa, they are often inseparable, in the current context, from material poverty. The latter, more often than not, produces misery—the state of absolute indigence in which a human being, deprived of everything, lives in conditions at times inferior to those of an animal.

Anthropological Poverty

When persons are deprived not only of goods and possessions of a material, spiritual, moral, intellectual, cultural, or sociological order, but of everything that makes up the foundation of their being-in-the-world and the specificity of their "ipseity" as individual, society, and history—when persons are bereft of their identity, their dignity, their freedom, their thought, their history, their language, their faith universe, and their basic creativity, deprived of all their rights, their hopes, their ambitions (that is, when they are robbed of their own ways of living and existing)—they sink into a kind of poverty which no longer concerns only exterior or interior goods or possessions but strikes at the very being, essence, and dignity of the human person. It is this poverty that we call anthropological poverty. This is an *indigence of being*, the legacy of centuries of slavery and colonization. It has long since banished us Africans from world history and the world map. The struggle in South Africa, even into the mid-1990s, and the convulsions of a black Africa cornered and desperate, point to our continued exclusion, today as yesterday, from the number of the special little groups who share the power and wealth of our continent. Meanwhile our indigence of being fuels the industries of misery while they forge the chains of our new enslavement. And the chains grow heavier by the day.

Structural Poverty

The poverty of the rich countries and our poverty in the Third World are enormously different. Our poverty is not only many-sided (at once material, spiritual, moral, intellectual, cultural, sociological, and so on); it is above all else *anthropological* and *structural.* It embraces all attempts of people to rationalize their life in space and time. If we accept the word *impoverishment* as denoting either the fact of one's becoming poor (passive meaning), or the act of making someone poor (active meaning), we are obliged to observe that the phenomenon of impoverishment, in black Africa today, is comprehensive, total, and absolute, on the continent, in the states, in the cities as in the countryside.

Thus, the crisis our continent is undergoing becomes a revelation of the chains present everywhere that express our dependency and our servitude. Our rural economy, where the phenomenon of money is linked to production for export, is thus coopted by the industries and consumer needs of the rich countries. Our cities are megalopolises where the structures of sin of the world economy foment social inequalities and where the emptiness of political rhetoric stifles the screams of despair of the poor, the weak, and the oppressed.

In our context, the state incorporates poverty in its structural form. Overwhelmed with debt, strangled by the claws of structural readjustment, prostrate before the International Monetary Fund, on its knees to the captains of cooperation and technological assistance, the black African state is today the most humiliating and shocking incarnation of the debasement of and contempt for black people.

Furthermore, poverty affects both individuals and social groups. With us, it affects, before all else, the state, that symbol of power, independence, and sovereignty. It makes a political vacuum of the state, which in turn wafts above a dark, apocalyptic void: the economic vacuum. Such an abyss can produce nothing. The person who falls in this abyss enters into *anthropological annihilation,* much more frightening than anthropological impoverishment.

Now the problem of human rights appears in its most brutal light. A subjugated state can be neither a state of rights nor a paradise of liberties. Deprived of both political and economic sovereignty, such a state is helpless to ensure the development of its citizens, precisely because of its abuses and its mistakes.

Our states' pretensions to totalitarianism constitute the first of these abuses and mistakes. The African state seeks to monopolize all aspects of its citizens' lives, civic and private alike. For all practical purposes, the state is the only employer. Its aim is to employ and remunerate its entire working population. It monopolizes education, seizes the unions, corners industry, oppressively controls much of business and commerce, and so on. Finally it runs out of steam. Impoverished, reduced to a state of indebtedness, to begging, the state possesses neither means nor powers. And so it delivers itself, bound hand and foot, to the mercy of new colonizers, discovering that impoverishment is an industry of woe in which one forges the chains of one's own bondage.

The Mechanisms of Impoverishment

In their pastoral letter on Cameroon's economic crisis,[9] the Catholic bishops of that country adopted the categories of "structural sin" so familiar to us in the teaching of Pope John Paul II. This is how they seek to identify the internal and external causes of our economic crisis. These categories are certainly valid for an analysis of our kind of poverty. However, a more pragmatic look at our own experience will counsel a more concrete approach. For example, let us take the case of material poverty. How is the mechanism of impoverishment constructed? Here we can identify several cases.

First, *there may be causes and reasons that cannot be laid at the doorstep of the poor themselves.* Material poverty may stem from accidents, natural disasters, disease, and so on. In these cases, poverty is not bound up with the ethical behavior either of the victim or of agents. From a theological viewpoint, a person submits to such poverty; it is neither willed nor desired. It represents, in itself, no evangelical value. An effort to abolish it, on the other hand, will constitute evangelical behavior, for this is how Christ acts when he heals the sick.

Second, *poverty may be a direct consequence of the moral, social, economic, or other behavior of the one who becomes poor.* Such is the case with alcoholics, spendthrifts, irresponsible or vice-ridden persons who end by losing all. Such poverty has neither moral nor religious value. Quite the contrary! Still less may we speak of any evangelical value here. This poverty is a direct consequence of the structures of sin to which we have referred above. Here, the only possible evangelical attitude is a determination to combat these structures and seek to eliminate this type of poverty. This is what God does in forgiving sin: God summons to conversion all who are overwhelmed by physical or moral evils before healing them.

Third, *the causes of impoverishment may be personal, but external to the poor.* They are the result of malice, injustice, or the violence of others (false charges, lies, thefts of all imaginable kinds, attacks with deadly weapons, oppression, "might makes right," and so forth). Thus we are in the presence of the structures of sin and the ravages those structures inflict. This type of poverty has neither moral value, nor spiritual value, nor any other kind. It is simply an evil that must be torn out by the roots.

On this level, it is important to stop to consider the causes and mechanisms of impoverishment more closely. We are actually dealing with a kind of drama, in which principal characters are:

- the agents of impoverishment, incarnations of violence and oppression;
- their victims: the mass of the poor, the weak, the oppressed, and the disinherited, those without voice, without rights, and without power.

Now impoverishment shows its true face. This impoverishment is political, and thereby it corrupts—at their very roots—the interpersonal relations of human being with human being. Human relations become relations between powers: on the one side, the power of domination of the agents of impoverishment; on the other, the "indigence of being" of the victims of impoverishment. It is important to emphasize at once that this kind of impoverishment, which is the effect of structures of sin—the structures of injustice, domination, and exploitation that constitute the law of relationships among human beings in our world—engenders, in practice, all forms of poverty described here. It culminates in the anthropological poverty and political poverty that we have called structural poverty.

The Vicious Circle of Impoverishment

Plainly, the impoverishment of the Third World is a vicious circle—and a hellish one. Given the natural catastrophes that overwhelm Africa (drought, famine, epidemics, AIDS, and so on), impoverishment is cosmic. Nature, which, in our traditions, has been the human being's ally to ensure the victory of life over death, seems to have gone over to the other side, donning the mask and armor of death. The "indigence of being" of which we have spoken appears first of all to be an "indigence of living."

As we have seen, the other forms of indigence (material, spiritual, moral, cultural, social, economic, and so forth) accrue and culminate in an anthropological and political indigence. What makes the circle of impoverishment vicious is not so much finding ourselves simply caught in an impasse; it is the sensation of being lost in the dark labyrinth of despair. The modern mechanisms of impoverishment have this peculiarity, that they keep producing poverty, and thereby render ineffectual any other mechanism that might otherwise have been able to destroy it. That is why the problem of liberation, for the poor, is posed today in terms of the requisite destruction of the world mechanisms of absolute impoverishment.

Perversion of Meaning, Domination, and the Industry of Misery

The concrete order of relationships among persons today is based on a perversion of meaning of political rhetoric. It is a discourse that claims to tell the truth and produces lies, that claims to speak life and produces death, that claims to speak freedom and produces oppression, that claims to speak equality and produces inequalities, that claims to utter justice and produces injustices. I could go on and on. This is the very essence of political discourse in its economic form.

Such discourse produces all of the forms of indigence and mechanisms of impoverishment that I have just enumerated, and then proceeds to call them underdevelopment. What we actually have is a *new discourse of world domination by those who possess force, wealth, and power.* Hiding behind the screen of development versus underdevelopment, these entrepreneurs construct a twin industry of power and misery.

Rebuffing an international society in which the United Nations and the churches cry out day and night the prophetic refrain of human rights, respect for others, and solidarity among the members of an endangered humanity, our industrialists of power and misery forge the soothing, anesthetizing vocabulary of compassion, assistance, and cooperation. They do more than merely offer excuses for themselves and exhortations to us. They actually don the mask of knights of beneficence and stand forth in the front rank of the benefactors of humanity.

These twin factories can run without scruple or impediment. The prime objective of the power factory is to accumulate material goods. After all, wealth constitutes the armament of power. Indeed, it is its absolute weapon. This is why the world's economic order is based on the endless enrichment of some and the endless impoverishment of others. The paradox is that it is by making the poor poorer that the rich become richer. Thus, poverty becomes this industry's indispensable raw material. Poverty is not something to be done away with. On the contrary, poverty is something to be developed. To eliminate poverty would be to exhaust one of the sources of the oppressors' power.

The second objective of the power industry is the production of political poverty and misery, in their many guises. These mechanisms are fearfully effective. The industry of political misery has its headquarters and its panoply of technologies hidden in the recesses of inaccessible bunkers—located "elsewhere." They are guarded by fearsome watchdogs, trained and goaded on by the managers of those structures of sin. And the machines run unendingly, night and day. They turn the immense conveyor belt of the Third World, with its political and economic regimes marching along in a teetering *danse macabre*. They spew out onto the belt ideologies, political systems, governments, heads of state, political crises, economic crises, coups. Then the same machines suck these up and cause them to vanish, spewing forth others instead, a vast tournament of grinning marionettes prancing amidst the din of civil wars, tribal wars, border wars, and the gnashing teeth of starving tribes. The masters of the world watch over this industry with a vigilant and jealous eye. They control the movement of each machine, speeding some up, slowing others down. Thus they have the sensation of holding in their hands the destiny of peoples, and they make and unmake that destiny as they choose.

To fuel these power factories, the masters of the world need raw material. They must empty the Third World of its resources and of any possibility of emerging from its hellish circle of poverty. In particular, they must drug themselves, absorbing the emanations of their nuclear plants, the smoke, the noise, the dazzle of the heaps of death engines that are the outer shell of their power. They need the Third World's gold, oil, and uranium. This is why they have erected their misery factories before the doors of their power factories.

It is the mission of the misery factories to mass produce and perpetuate poverty—that is, misery and wretchedness. These factories suck and empty the veins of the topsoil and subsoil of our countries. They erect structures of alienation that make natives into strangers in their own land. They entrust the control of the resources of the soil and the earth to the world network of the structures of sin. Nothing escapes this systematic, universal commandeering of resources, neither our states nor our human communities nor, least of all, individuals.

Thus it is that the factories of misery spill out over our peoples, thus despoiled, the polluting tides of desires and needs that are not only superfluous, but, often enough, absurd. Wave upon wave, the media unflaggingly distill the flow of dreams and illusions that turn young people's heads, empty the countryside, dislocate families, and dynamite the rock of societies, beliefs, political and economic institutions—in a word, the rock of the age-old certitudes built by our ancestors.

For the consumption of these disabled, helpless peoples, societies, and states, the misery factories grind out ton after ton of recipes of cooperation, technological assistance, and humanitarian aid. And behold, the recipes are discovered to be magical. They prevent the starving from dying, but they make them hungrier by the day; they prevent the poor from dying, but they make them poorer by the day. And so on. Hungrier, poorer, more helpless, they will always need aid, technological assistance, and cooperation. As for our states, these are plunged first into a labyrinth of bilateral conventions, often secret and thus unknown to the people. In these pacts, our states lose practically all political, economic, and military sovereignty. Lacking the means to execute certain conventions, the states are then flung, bound hand and foot, into the iron cage of debt. And the vicious circle is closed.

In a world in which we hear so much of aid, technological assistance, and cooperation, it is scarcely astonishing that not a single instance is to be found of cooperation having brought an underdeveloped country from underdevelopment to modern development. Just the contrary, what do we see in Africa? A political and economic misery greater than that of colonial times. Independence? Who really believes in that? Political regimes are imposed, changed as one changes a shirt. Yesterday, cooperation maintained (that is, imposed) dictators and one-party systems. Today, cooperation imposes its democracy and an artificial, precipitant, multiparty system. To what purpose? In Africa, the people seem neither aware of this nor concerned. They are silent, or agitated, like a flock of animals led to the slaughterhouse. Yesterday, colonization had imposed cash crops: cacao, coffee, cotton, and so on. Today, the erstwhile colonizers do not know what to do with our cash crops. As for other raw material, they name their own prices, and the prices sink ever lower. The crisis in Africa, consequently, is that of states overwhelmed by debts, gagged, without money, without power, without sovereignty. It is that of empty banks, closed businesses, unemployed civil servants, white and blue collar workers thrown out into the street. It is that of peasants in rags hauling their bags of cacao, their bags of coffee, their bags of cotton, looking for someone who will take them in exchange for a little gasoline for their storm lantern, a little soap and salt for their wives, until the next harvest! Finally, it is the despair of youth, on the university campuses, in high schools and boarding schools, right down to the elementary schools, accusing their parents, their directors, their leaders, all of their elders, shouting, brandishing placards with threatening slogans, under the anemic gaze of crowds as helpless as themselves. Such is the visible manifestation in Africa of the structures of sin.

Anthropological Poverty and Evangelical Poverty

A close look at the kinds of poverty and the mechanisms of impoverishment I have just described leads to the conclusion that none of them represents any human or religious value. Quite the opposite. This poverty and these mechanisms are agents of the debasement of people and of the destruction of their dignity as persons and daughters or sons of God. They are anti-evangelical agents, then. By looking more closely, we can better understand the error of those who reproach the gospel for its beatification of poverty. The poor of the Beatitudes are not blessed because they are poor, but because the Reign of God is theirs (Matt. 5:1-12). The Lord has not come to institutionalize and beatify misery, but to deliver us from it. That is what Zechariah sings at the beginning of St. Luke's Gospel (Luke 1:68-79), that is what the Magnificat proclaims (Luke 1:47-55), that is what the charter of the Beatitudes promulgates (Matt. 5:1-12), and that is what the Lord himself reveals in the synagogue at Nazareth, as he inaugurates his public ministry (Luke 4:18-20).

The many situations of manifold poverty that we live and experience in the Third World become a genuine challenge to the gospel. Can the good news of Jesus Christ perchance be for us today the good news of our liberation and our salvation? After all, the good news announced to the poor is that of their liberation and their salvation. One is sometimes surprised at the countless readings proclaimed by certain Western exegetes to decipher the message of the Beatitudes. Whatever be the semantic approaches in the Hebrew or Aramaic vocables *dalim* and *anawim,* or their Greek translations into *penes, ptochos,* and *tapeinos,* we need only observe the praxis of the Lord Jesus in order to appreciate a certain number of evident facts.

1. The crowds that follow Jesus and listen to him are plainly and simply crowds of the poor, the lame, the blind, the halt, the deaf, the mute, and those humble folk who, after listening to the Lord for hours and hours, reach into their pockets and find not so much as a piece of bread or fish to eat!

2. At no moment does the Lord Jesus preach resignation to sin, suffering, wretchedness, sickness, or the like. On the contrary, he has come to set people free, and that is why he works his wonders. His solidarity with

> the poor, the weak, and the oppressed does not consist in sitting down alongside them to bemoan and bewail the cruelty of fate, under the demagogic pretext of identifying with them. Jesus' solidarity with them consists in proclaiming to them the good news of their liberation, as he delivers them from their physical, moral, and spiritual miseries.

Of all of the forms of poverty and impoverishment that we have seen, none is or can be evangelical. Those who preach or teach the neophytes of the Third World the doctrine and spirituality of the evangelical counsels of poverty, consecrated celibacy, and obedience will do very well to know that the poverty of which they speak is elsewhere. It does not lie in the structures of sin that dominate the world, nor in the factories of impoverishment and misery, nor in a return to prehistory, nor in absurdly installing oneself in the bottomless pits of despair and vermin to await the Last Judgment. Evangelical poverty lies in the imitation of Christ, who has freely come to deliver us from sin, from hatred, from death, and from our physical, moral, and spiritual miseries. Evangelical poverty is this great mobilization for the establishment of the Reign of the Beatitudes throughout our world. It is the great battle of the children of light with the children of darkness, the battle waged by the forces of life with those of death, by the powers of love with those of hatred, by the legions of justice with the hordes of injustice. In this great combat of the Beatitudes, behold, the two Reigns rise up one against the other. On one side is the Reign of Heaven, and on the other, the reign of this world. On one side, the Reign of God, and on the other, the reign of the demon. On one side, the Reign of Justice, and on the other, the reign of injustice. On one side, the Reign of Life, and on the other, the reign of death. And it is precisely from the latter reign that one must be freed in order to enter into the Reign of the Beatitudes. One must leave everything to follow Jesus Christ—leave the reign of this world with its structures of sin and its industries of power, wealth, domination, and misery, in order to gain access to the Reign of the evangelical Beatitudes.

The question arises, then, for Third World persons, of how they can win access to evangelical poverty. Decapitated, their feet and hands amputated, enchained and enslaved by the structures of sin of the masters of this world, can they ever be able to follow Jesus Christ who is free, and in his company carry to their siblings the good news of their liberation? *The only answer is that they must first themselves be free.* This is why, in the face of the structures of sin and the factories of impoverishment and misery, the evangelization of the Third World—that is, the proclamation to that world of the good news—demands first and foremost the destruction of the structures of sin and their spawn: the factories of power, misery, and the vicious circle of impoverishment. The political and economic order of the world today is an arrogant challenge thrown in the face of the church. The church can no longer worthily accomplish its mission without a radical reassessment of the political and economic order and the structures of sin that guide the world. It is not enough merely to bring down the Jericho walls that are the structures of sin. The most important thing is to replace them with counter-structures, whose mission is not only to neutralize the effects of the structures of sin but, especially, to mobilize the Christians of the Third World to follow Christ the Liberator and themselves become liberators of their sisters and brothers. In the churches, we must learn, and have no complex about learning it, that the last pages of the history of evangelization in the twentieth century are being turned. It is the Third World, surely, that will provide in the future new pages for a new missiology. It doesn't matter whether the new evangelization is called the "second" or "third" evangelization, as long as it conveys to the Third World the good news of its liberation.

Notes

1. Paris: Éditions Ouvrières, 1978.
2. *Vaincre la Pauvreté dans les pays riches* (Paris: Flammarion, 1974).
3. *Pourquoi la pauvreté quand les produits abondent?* (Paris: Tiers-Monde, 1986).
4. *Les riches et les pauvres* (Paris: Seuil, 1983).
5. *Du bon usage des Pauvres* (Paris: Fayard, 1990).
6. London, 1970.
7. See *Le Monde* (August 28, 1990), pp. 2, 17.
8. Paris: Fayard, 1990.
9. Pentecost, 1990.

10

FEMINIST THEOLOGY IN AN AFRICAN PERSPECTIVE

Mercy Amba Oduyoye

When women do theology that does not differ in substance and style from that done by men, they are hardly ever singled out for condemnation. They are allowed to remain as one of the boys. There have been and there still are many women well versed in the research, teaching, and writing of what—for lack of a better expression—is called classical theology. These women are theologians and, like all theologians, whether they acknowledge it or not, they can only work from their own context and experience, and this is what they have done.

Among Christian women, as among all women, priorities for liberation differ according to whether they belong to the economically poor countries of the Third World or to the Euro-American world. In some countries, priorities differ according to whether women belong to the working class or the leisure class, to the elite or the masses. If they live in South Africa and are black, their priority is certainly the elimination of racism, but that does not mean sexism is condoned, for as Edith Dhlamini put it sharply, South African women are "slaves of slaves."[1]

All this is complicated by the individual woman's situation in life and her attitude toward her own being; it depends on her level of awareness and her aptitude as a person. Among Christian women, there are Marthas and Marys, as well as Priscillas and Sapphiras. What is called "feminist theology," then, is the theology of women and men who acknowledge and subscribe to a conscious application of their experiences in reflections. Some of these persons do describe their theology as feminist, but others might not choose to do so. I am using the word *feminism* because it is language that is now used to communicate globally. I am still struggling with the effect it has on African ears. Does it help or hinder the cause of women in Africa? The term *women's liberation* has already been given a "bad press." Feminism does little better in Africa, but I have chosen to use it as my language here because of its understanding globally.

Since much theology is presented outside the standard theological fields, particularly in literature, I shall include among theologians names that would normally be cited by other disciplines. Theology, too, needs to be consciously interdisciplinary.

I intend to outline issues that engage the attention of African theologians, including both men and women (but mainly the latter), which relate to or highlight women's concerns, lives, and experiences, and which express respect for women's points of view. African men doing theology who focus on various aspects of liberation deal with issues that African women theologians also struggle with. Our context—oppression, poverty and impoverishment, marginalization from the global technological culture, exploitation that results from unjust global trade and economic arrangements—is a significant area for some African theologians, including both men and women. Another common area is the theology of African traditional religion and culture. It is in this area, however, that women's voices often differ from and sometimes even come into conflict with those of men.

Women's spirituality is qualitatively different from that of men because women's experience of socioeconomic realities differs from that of men. Similarly, women's dependence on God tends to be expressed more overtly; hence, their dependence on religious beliefs, practices, and ritual is more intensely demonstrated. When women read the Bible, they often hear what is unheard by men. Thus, women's biblical theology originates at a different depth. The messages transmitted through symbols and songs and prayers and action send vibrations that are received differently by different people; even the movement of processions sends messages. What feminist theologians posit is that their reception of this liturgy and their reaction to it is shaped by their socialization as women and their experience of life. However, it stands to reason that when women express themselves about God, they model themselves on male theology, or else they would have to seek men's approval for what they write.

Western women rightly yearn for a coalition of "strong women around the world." In their search they have turned their attention to Africa's matrilineal (mother-centered) cultures, to African goddesses and market women, and those in the front line of the struggle against apartheid and other imposed structures of oppression in Africa. As academics they have a right to do research. But as women who would be sisters, they have a responsibility to relate to African women in a way that expresses genuine solidarity. On their own, they cannot liberate us. For that reason, I am not pursuing the category of the Western women; rather, I will focus on feminists, whatever their geographical origin.

Focus on Marriage

All feminists cling to the principles of giving and sustaining life, of building community and upholding the dignity of the human person. Their goal is to promote and empower women to live their lives to the full, and they urge men to be more holistic in their perception of community. It is impossible in Africa to talk about marriage and women without talking about issues of family and children. There, women are viewed as procreators and nurturers and men's helpers.

Western women, some African men, and even some African women have interpreted the ceremonies leading up to marriage in Africa in terms of trade. They seek to interpret African wives as persons who have been "sold into marriage" or whose reproductive potential has been purchased by the man they call husband. Feminist voices in Africa insist that these elaborate exchanges of gifts are intended to emphasize the worth of women, to provide community participation and social witness to the coming together of the two persons for the religious duty of procreation; however, this should not be construed as an economic transaction in which a man buys a woman. Of course, if a Western researcher read the writings of Elechi Amadi, she would find that "In ancient Nigeria a wife was regarded as the husband's property. The man paid a certain amount as bride-price, the women became his."[2] However, she would not have interviewed me to learn that my maternal grand-uncle said to my husband, "We are Akan. We do not sell our daughters. If they are unhappy or do not prosper in the marriage we reserve the right to dissolve the marriage." I am not blind to the fact that in both cases the woman has no say, but at least in the latter case she stays in the marriage out of her own volition and not because she "belongs in any sense to her husband's family." In Africa, the meaning of marriage continues to divide feminists.

In Africa, feminism is often associated negatively with women who have "difficulty" relating to men—that is, difficulty in keeping their marriages intact through thick and thin. It is often said that women who talk of liberation are those whose ambitions in marriage have been frustrated. There is a negative connotation attached to women who ask simply to be human; to women with a will and a responsibility; to women who refuse to be objects to be categorized by men as "good" or "bad," "wives" or "harlots," mothers to be placed on pedestals or wives who are no more than instruments of production and reproduction. This is a common viewpoint of African men.

I want to turn now to some crucial aspects of an African woman's life, using as a source three selections from African literature that reflect the aspect of African women's lives that is the touchstone of their existence and determines who they are—motherhood.

On Procreation

Three books, *Anowa* by Ama Ata Aidoo, *A Woman in Her Prime* by Asare Konadu, and *Efuru* by Flora Nwapa,[3] all share the central theme of bearing children. African attitudes to having progeny are very close to those of the Hebrew scriptures. Children are as the Psalmist says they are (Ps. 127 and 128); men become polygamous to have them, and childless widows such as Tamar and Ruth exhaust all the provisions of their culture to fulfill this obligation. Any sexual activity outside the reproductive objective, if it is discovered, receives the same imprecations as were pronounced on it in the Hebrew scriptures. "Increase and multiply, and fill the earth" is a religious duty in the cultures of both African and the Hebrew scriptures. This "command to bear children" also exposes the roots of homophobia around the world. Included in the causes of homophobia, and this is particularly true in the case of lesbians, are the insistence on marriage as the only legitimate sanction of childbirth and the "highjacking" and appropriation of the mystery of birth on the part of men.

For Africans, every newborn baby is an ancestor returned. This belief in reincarnating one's forebears is seen in the principles underlying the naming of newborns. The Yoruba, a large tribal group in West Africa, do not stop with family or genetic resemblances; they give names—Yewande/Yetunde and Babatunde, respectively—that declare that Mother or Father has returned to join the family in this dimension of being. Several names may be given to the child according to how members of both the maternal and paternal families view the birth. However, once the name of a returned ancestor is pronounced, it is likely to become the child's permanent name.

The Asante are more specific, with the returned ancestor coming from the family of the mother. However, the name given is ordinarily from the family of the child's father, either those living or dead. In this way the ancestors of both families are included. The mother brings her ancestors back to the dimension of the living, and the father declares what kind of character he would like the child to have. Whether a patriarchal/patrilineal or matriarchal/matrilineal culture, the duty is the same, and it arises from a religious belief in reincarnation that depends on the procreativity of family members.

As in all human communities, children give a sense of security that goes beyond economic security in old age. A child is someone to relate to throughout life. Children bring prestige or imprecations, depending on how successful one has been at bringing them to adulthood. They provide an avenue for the exercise of our creativity as human beings. A child is a being on whom we stamp our image. So all Africans, women and men alike, want to participate in this creative activity. So far, so good. For Africans there is also a religious factor, that of death. To go to one's rest finally and peacefully, one ought to receive the proper final rites, which involves the participation of children, with one's natural children being the most effective. These rituals are so important that if one has no children, Africans extend the word "children" to include nieces and nephews. The Asante have rituals they perform on corpses of childless persons to ensure that such persons do not return to be born. With this background firmly in mind, I am going to summarize these three literary works.

In *Anowa* by Ama Ata Aidoo, Anowa and her spouse Ako prospered economically but were extremely unhappy because they were childless. It was assumed that Anowa was the responsible partner, and this was confirmed by some diviners. At the end of the drama, when it becomes clear that it was Ako who was at fault, husband and wife both committed suicide. They were victims of a religio-cultural factor with a hold on all Africans, Christians, Muslims, and practitioners of Africa's own primal religion. Note that Aidoo has named the play after the woman.

A Woman in Her Prime by Asare Konadu tells the story of a woman, Pokuwaa, who is more interested in her fertility than in her person. It is her ripeness for reproduction that is underlined in the title. Konadu puts Pokuwaa through all the agencies (mostly religious) that will help her "fulfill" herself and obtain the elusive happiness. Asare Konadu contrives a happy ending, exhibiting in the end the biblical requirement of bearing children by ending the story when Pokuwaa becomes pregnant. As an Akyem (a matrilineal Akan people) he hopes that "It is going to be a girl."

Efuru by Flora Nwapa provides a third way of dealing with the need for progeny. Nwapa names the novel after her female protagonist, Efuru. After going through all that Pokuwaa went through, Efuru had a daughter who died. Efuru's childlessness, economic prosperity, and public acclaim as a "benevolent one" is related to her being a devotee of the goddess Uhamiri. Uhamiri, the Goddess of the Lake, has no children but is the benevolent protector of all who live on her shores. She has deep understanding of the harmony in nature and she honors the interdependence of the whole ecosystem. From a feminist perspective, I would say that a woman should not be seen only as an objective category such as mother or as part of a work force called the "mothering brigade." Men and women should have co-responsibility for life in community and for the survival of the earth.

On Biological Continuity

The African perspective on biological continuity—that you reproduce or die—is anti-feminist. Men have been known to commit suicide when it becomes apparent that the deficiency is on their side. In *The Strong Breed,* Wole Soyinka's main character, Eman, asks the priest, "Then why? Why the wasted years if she had to perish giving birth to my child?"[4] The "she" in the story is Omae, his wife, who had lived twelve years with her father-in-law and had "a brief moment of happiness" with Eman as she gave birth to a son. With the birth of that child, she died, having fulfilled her *raison d'être*. And the priest says "That was as it should be." Such words of religious belief and practice are obstacles to women's development and participation. African feminists ask whose decree this is.

In Ngugi's *The River Between,*[5] Muthoni runs away from her Christian home and returns to her aunt, who had her circumcised according to Gikuyu practice. She then dies because the wound had refused to heal. But, no, they say, that could not be so! Instead, it was the Christian missionaries who deliberately poisoned her, pretending to be saving her life. African anti-feminists would say that if women complain of oppression, they should look to westernization for the cause. They lament, saying that we must live as Africans and remain true to the religio-cultural traditions that are primal to Africa; they say that we must not anger our ancestors by adopting new religions and foreign ways.

I have observed a trend in the works of creative writers in Africa, even among the women, that reinforces the belief that those persons who go against traditions will be punished. An example is *The Bride Price* by Buchi Emecheta.[6]

Womanhood as a Two-Edged Sword

Perceptions of womanhood vary widely. In mother-centered communities, where political, social, and economic status depend on who one's mother is, being a woman is a source of strength. This strength is expected to be used for the well-being of the whole community rather than only for the woman herself. The strength of women in Wole Soyinka's *Ake* is admirable.[7] So is the strength of the market women in West Africa. It is instructive that women's political strength usually lies in their solidarity as women. Viewed together as mothers, their reactions to situations they consider unjust or oppressive to women never fails to send men scuttling around. As mothers, they are to be revered and placated. As daughters, they are to serve their brothers' interests, as wives, their husbands'. As persons, women's self-interest is only honorable when it is located in doing what the community assigns or expects. The ideology is one of "ascribed complementarity" rather than a "negotiated participation."

African women, whether born to matriarchal or patriarchal families, are expected to use what strength they have to protect and not to destroy. But they are to be ready for destruction if that would mean life for the community. Their very imputed strength is turned to weakness. Women continue to observe taboos that place them at a disadvantage in economic, social, and political life. They put their nephews and brothers on thrones that properly belong to them. They submit to anything in order to bear children. They sweat under primitive technology to grow and process food for the lives they have risked so much for. They resist change if change holds a possibility of jeopardizing the calm of the community. Traditionally, women say that all this is as it should be. Feminists today hold a different view. We question the criteria of these assigned roles and we would question their efficiency. I personally feel that fear should be resisted as a means of determining behavior.

Reading *The River Between* gives me the impression that Ngugi is telling all women to "beware of *all* religious manipulations of the humanity of women," while Soyinka's message to African women is that they should resist male manipulation of religion to oppress women. There is no change in relations between men and women if women simply switch roles. In Nigeria, for example, if women simply take over Oro[8] and ask men to lock themselves up, nothing improves. Religion should liberate the human spirit for communication with God, rather than alienate people from each other or manipulate them for the good of others.

African culture has guaranteed the patriarchal takeover of even the most mother-centered structures. It is too easy to lay the blame solely at the feet of westernization. We know that within the African religio-cultural heritage is to be found the seeds of the objectification and marginalization of women. Colonial policies simply helped the process along, and it succeeded to the extent that it was advantageous for African men.

On Purity

Even today the majority of African women are literally rooted to the soil and so to religion. The cycle of nature continues to be the bedrock of Africa's religious intimations. The soil unites all born onto it, and women tend the soil in most of Africa. A rural woman stays in close communion with the elements that bind all things into a unity. She uses all the forces at her disposal to stay in tune with nature. She will not do violence to nature, lest nature do violence to the whole community because of her. She guards all life as if her own depends on doing so. When there is a disaster, she is the first to run to sacrifice herself. In African religion, love of the earth and love of life go together.

The cycle of gestation, birthing, nurturing, and mourning in which women are personally and symbolically involved makes them allies of nature and therefore of religion. Women have become the self-appointed custodians of the primal principles of life, and they are collaborators with the principalities and powers of the unseen world—Orisha,[9] Abosom,[10] and the Nananom,[11] the ancestors. Women stay tuned to their wishes and dictates. They attach themselves to the shrines of gods and goddesses, and when Christianity or Islam arrives, their piety in these religions is unmatched. Women choose to live by faith. This is clearly shown in their experience of widow rites, which women are ready to submit to, difficult though it be, to ensure the proper transition of the spirit of the spouse to the other dimension of being, thus ensuring his membership in the ancestral hosts and subsequent return to this life.

All this is fine and good until we realize that religion is a double-edged sword, a weapon that can alienate as well as liberate. When women's spirituality is exploited by men and by agencies of the community, a process of general exploitation becomes inevitable. In my study of Africa's traditional religion as a source for Christian theology, I do take very seriously side remarks such as "men make God and women worship them."

Male duplicity toward purity leads to similar conclusions, since it is often the measuring rod of patriarchy that divides women into "good" or "loose." Men's duplicity on purity of body and mind is shown dramatically in the way a man guards his wife with his life and yet asks his neighbor's wife for sexual favors; a man would guard his sister's virginity with a knife while insisting on experimenting with his best friend's sister. It is obvious, of course, that all this is a man's game of competition played on the field of women. "When two elephants fight it is the grass that suffers." And often in Africa women are but grass, available for horses to feed on. The demand for a "pure woman" is solely for the benefit of a man. It has nothing to do with any concern for the woman's physical well-being and very little to do with her spiritual health.

Woman Is Life

African men carry none of the life-giving burdens that African women carry. Women with babies on their backs and yam, firewood, and water on their heads is the common image of African women in real life as in art. To the Akan, a woman is a symbol of bountifulness, tenderness, and serenity. She is a symbol of protection, charm, and fidelity in love. What then becomes of the humanity of a man who does not participate in this "woman-beingness"? This is what has led the Akan to the proverb "It is not only a woman who gives birth, a man does also." All parenting is expected to take on the quality of mothering. Living for others is the primary understanding of mothering that is expected of all Akan men and women. Yet women have become the primary custodians, carriers, and practitioners of all *amandze* (that which belongs to the whole nation).[12]

Women abandon themselves to serve others without calculating what is to be gained. That there is no reciprocity does not seem to bother most African women. When such martyrdom results from self-sacrifice consciously undertaken, it should be honored as a religious act of suing for life for others. Women's mothering emanates from the womb and takes no time to calculate gains and losses; it is simply geared toward being the mother of life. I have no argument here, except to add that if this is the case then it stands to reason that the African woman should have a right to share in the management of the community to which she gives without counting the cost. Waiting to react to the action of men is not the position of African feminists. But becoming subjects who determine action in matters that affect women is an important theological issue.

A Feminist Point of View

The most fundamental issues of feminism, as I see it, relate to autonomy—naming ourselves—and integrity, and both have roots in religion. Feminism itself is not a priority among the competing ideologies in Africa, but religion is—in some form or other. Religion remains integral to the various political ideologies that seek to inform our budding nationalism. Understandably, a preoccupation with effective participation in global politico-economic structures often works against the more specific needs of women's development or women's priorities. Nationalism and ethnic survival bear likewise on oppression. The social character of the self in the African worldview seems more entrenched in women than in men, for while women operate always on the principle of persons-in-relation, the African man's autonomy may lead him to independent action that tends to separate him from the unit. Men override culture when it does not suit them, or are conservative when it suits them. African women, especially those who disparage feminist perspectives, tend to be consistently conservative.

The inclination of women to place wholeness above fragmentation often puts them in the category of those who may be sacrificed or negated. Women often suppress their individual interests in the name of the survival of the unit. Socialized not to act boldly, it is anticipated that women will resort to covert action when they no longer feel comfortable under oppression. A woman might resort to lying, but not to murder—the latter would be unwomanly. The expectation that women will learn to make themselves comfortable under oppressive conditions is an admission that women have been placed in an indefensible position. To survive, African women, like their sisters the world over, have devised their own ploys. I feel that such ploys are demeaning and that an open critique of patriarchy by women and men can be salvific.

Some women have preferred to identify with male norms and style rather than attempt self-affirmation as women. And autonomy stretches into authority—power over others. I view female ploys not so much as wantonness but as an indication of determination to hold on to a certain degree of autonomy without disrupting customary expectations. The use of ploys, however, does raise the question of what happens to one's integrity. Wambui wa Karanja describes how "individuals are able to choose the best in each sphere of life (modern and traditional) without feeling a need for a strict logical reconciliation"; she attributes what she judges to be the "relatively favorable position of women" in Lagos with the fact that "inconsistency does not cause mental pain." In her report on patterns of behavior in Lagos, Wambui concluded that one factor that has served to make Lagos a vibrant metropolis is the survival of traditional attitudes and behavior patterns in the modern sector. This pragmatic approach to life keeps urbanized African women observing traditional relationships with men without having to resort to confrontation.

In my perspective (a feminist one), the strategy of coping by ploys and self-abasement to gain the understanding and conversion of men in power proves more and more hazardous in the public sphere, particularly in the field of legislation. But African women today are caught between the strategies of coping and confrontation. Although the inexorable drive in Africa toward patriarchalization of structures and attitudes is obvious, certain types of contemporary feminism do pose a problem for African women. African women want to explore traditional matriarchal values to determine which aspects might be woven into new forms of relations between men and women and a new conception of humanity and relatedness in the human community; they can also indicate methods of attaining and practicing autonomy and life-centeredness. Above all, women need to present mothering as a positive strategy for community life that is to be practiced by all women *and all men.*

Reciprocity and what I call "bifocal ordering," a perspective that reflects a double standard, are age-old principles of relationships in Africa society that in the past mitigated against the essentially patriarchal ethos. Both have come under severe assault as a result of westernization. The situation is aggravated for women as men preach a way of total self-giving, while giving only as much of themselves as they wish to give. Women realize that the reciprocity demanded by culture on other levels does not apply between men and women, and yet women continue to pursue it, helping prevent the total collapse of traditional culture. For them, to abandon woman-beingness is to give in to death, the death of the human. And yet to exhibit humanity is to become vulnerable. Exhibiting humanity is perhaps akin to falling in love, an instinct that works toward the preservation of the human species; however, showing humanity when it is not reciprocated becomes an expensive, oppressive, and alienating venture. I have risked presenting mothering, even to western audiences, as a concept for constructive feminism in Africa because I believe it has merits. I do not speak of motherhood, which is the special privilege of the female. What I am concerned for is the caring stance which I believe both women and men can learn to develop. Being created in God's image, all human beings can learn to love in this way—and thus to give.

The mothering model presupposes that the female is the archetype of the human. This is not a rigid or inflexible model but one that is adaptable to ensure survival. In Akan art, feminine symbols, usually represented by a whorl, are frail but flexible. These symbols embody concepts of continuity, growth, compassion, and peace—in short, vulnerability. But note that this also means that the female is strong enough not to be threatened by flexibility. The whorl in Akan art, as Antubam points out, recurs as the coordinate of the sword of the state, a symbol of power, as well as in the coil of the serpent, a symbol of eternity, and of the changing cycle of life and death.[13]

From my perspective, these feminist principles need to be integrated into societal arrangements to bring about a more holistic view of what it is to be human. For me, the real disease in human relationships is rooted in the perverse patriarchalization of life. The cure I propose is a good dose of woman-inspired wisdom. If, as an Akan proverb puts it, the crab is not to find herself as mother of a bird,[14] then women must advocate and practice feminism. They must work to bring about societal structures conceived and constructed on feminist perspectives. The Akan feminine graces of bountifulness, tenderness, sereneness, which are symbols of protection, of charm, and of faithfulness in love, should be human graces. These religio cultural and socio economic experiences lie behind the theological explorations and reflections of African women. The traditional agenda of systematic theology and the liberation agenda of African theology become feminist theology when they respond to and reflect feminist perspectives.

The Agenda

Theologians and feminists should pay attention to these themes reflected in African literature because many African women and men live these scenes most days of their lives. Such study should take a new look at Christian anthropology. African feminists approach this study from the standpoint of a culture that accords centrality to childbearing and nurturing. Woman-being-ness, quite apart from childbearing and nurturing, is viewed theologically in Africa as a negative factor in religion. This has led African feminist theologians to turn their attention to the whole issue of sexuality and its relation to religion. They feel the need to break the silence on sexuality, a silence that seems to be based on the assumption that human sexuality, in particular in its physical expressions such as menstruation, is not good. Feminists want to integrate sexuality into human spirituality, where it rightly belongs. A diligent analysis of the whole idea of complementarity between the sexes would shed light on the distortion of relations between men and women. From an androcentric point of view, ideas such as autonomy, participation, and power for women are seen as threats because human-beingness is perceived in the image of the male, with the female as a foreigner craving admission.

The lack of ease with words such as *authority, leadership,* or *reciprocity* when applied to women or used by women is also symptomatic of the inability of men and some women to see the possibility of changes in the ordering of the human community so that the worth of a person is based on more than gender. Women should not have a monopoly on the servant role. This is why feminists underline the necessity of highlighting the principle of reciprocity. This is why they affirm there is a necessity for men to understand the idea of sacrifice for the ordering of human society and to learn the arts of sacrifice and mothering. Until this happens, issues of alienation and oppression—physical, moral, and intellectual—will remain on the agenda of feminist theologians. We cannot assign the cross to half of humanity and the resurrection to the other half. Our theology of cross and resurrection must remain together.

When these ideas are filtered through the reflections of women, the outcome is a community approach to human-beingness. In dealing with anthropology from a theological perspective, women emphasize the necessity for self-creation and self-naming and for a liberative theology that stipulates that human beings are the subjects of history, with the Creator intending both women and men to be co-creators. It should also be pointed out that asserting the humanity of the female is a way of resisting the tendency to associate the origin of sin with woman.

The insensibility of men to the demonization of women enables them to shirk responsibility for the ills of human relations and community life. In Africa, men's writing, in theology and in other disciplines, is replete with unthinking illustrations of negative experiences of life with women. In litera-ture, for example, when a person loses a spouse, it is usually a woman whose husband dies so that widowhood rites may be described. Women are held accountable for all the ills of society and yet remain bereft of power to bring about change. What most women do is to protest or react rather than try to bring about something new. This is the result of our current understanding of being human. Feminists must call attention to this and suggest a process and method to bring about changes in our thinking and our perception of who we are as human beings.

The self-understanding of the church is often articulated in language that suggests that the church is a male organization in which women are permitted to participate. Feminist theologians often describe the church in this way to remind the "male" processions that the majority of the people they pass by are women and that ministry should be service in the name of Christ to and by *all* these baptized people. In Africa, feminists seek ways of theologizing a bicameral ordering of African society in all ecclesiologies. Any explanation that focuses solely on complementarity is not acceptable. Women need to apply themselves to serious study to forge a theology of marriage. They should articulate a theology of marriage that will lay to rest the old western missionary issue of polygyny and result in the identification of women as persons through their strength of character and experience and not by evaluating their lives by their marital status as wife.

Sexuality, which was formerly a non-issue in African Christianity, will have to be faced. Hopefully sexuality will come to be identified as an integral part of our understanding of the human body and the human person and not as the *only* significant moral issue. Sexuality will then enter into our understanding of the church, and it will be a reminder of our covenantal relations as sexually distinct beings who do not necessarily have to be identified by the opposite sex in marriage. All of us are persons-in-communion, and our relationships should be devoid of hierarchy or power-seeking. For me, a Christian theology that will be an empowering system of thought for women as well as liberative for Africa will have to re-examine our traditional Christian anthropology and take into consideration both female and feminist approaches to life. When we have learned a bit more about our humanity, perhaps an understanding of what it is God is telling us about divinity will begin to flower.

Bible studies that are scholarly, liberative, *and* empowering for women can be pioneered only by women; our men have other preoccupations. The need to break down the high walls of academia so that lay people may be part of the theological enterprise is already part of the African woman's agenda; this has happened by reflecting on "who does theology for whom and why."

As women biblical scholars emerge, this agenda will be implemented. Faced with the crucial questions of the authenticity and relevance of Christianity in Africa, the church is carefully avoiding "domestic" issues likely to raise conflict within the church. With women visibly on the stage, questions of authority and identity, which are shared with black theology, will be sharpened.

One of the most critical items on the agenda of feminists in Africa—albeit one that is sometimes seemingly less urgent—is the person of God. Who God is, what God does, what is of God and what is not of God—these issues are much more urgent for us than other gender issues highlighted by feminists in other parts of the world. Africans often attribute this limited naming of God to the poverty of the colonial (European) languages used in Africa. Some feminists, of course, have begun to point out that the language about God reflects problems of female-male relations and, therefore, ought to be examined. Meanwhile, African feminists affirm that the fact that maleness is attributed to God does not make God a man, nor does it make men into gods; thus feminists resist all attempts by men to play God in women's lives.

To counterbalance this one-sided view of God as male, some feminist theologians have pointed out that the "source-Being" (God) in some African languages is female, and in others both male and female. Others have turned to research that calls attention to the female divinities of Africa's primal religions with their potential as role models for women and their support to women and men alike. Others use their findings to challenge generalizations about women, for among these female gods are found a variety of ways of being woman. African women theologians need to insist on the oppressive nature of stereotyping, if the creative gifts given by God are to be allowed to bloom.

Conclusion

I have tried to paint the background against which feminists in Africa theologize, and I have focused particularly on our African culture and its continuity through African literature in English. My purpose has been to highlight the fact that the agenda of global feminism as far as global politico-economic interdependence goes is part of the universal feminist agenda; so are issues of science and technology, especially biotechnology. African culture, which tends to insist on continuity where women are concerned, pursues these goals, however, only to the extent that whatever is being continued does *not* empower women. Progress in this area must be a priority on the feminist agenda in Africa. African feminists need to turn to the study of African traditional religion and also Islam, both of which—together with Christianity—seek to place limits on women's culture and being.

Much of what is reported here is from conversations or unpublished papers of conferences and seminars. We women who are doing theology in Africa are just beginning to find our way into print,[15] but when we meet, these are the issues we discuss. It is the members of the Circle of African Women Theologians who will recognize their ideas and hear themselves speaking when this essay becomes available to them.[16]

Notes

1. World Council of Churches consultation on "Sexism in the '70s: Discrimination against Women."

2. Elechi Amadi, *Ethics in Nigerian Culture* (Ibadan, Nigeria: H.E.B., 1982).

3. Ama Ata Aidoo, *Anowa* (London: Longmans, 1970); Flora Nwapa, *Efuru* (London: Heinemann [AWS], 1966); Asare Konadu, *A Woman in Her Prime* (London: Heinemann [AWA], 1967).

4. Wole Soyinka, *The Strong Bread in Three Short Stories* (Oxford: Oxford University Press, 1969).

5. Ngugi Wa Thiong, *The River Between* (London: Heinemann [AWS], 1965).

6. Buchi Emecheta, *The Bride Price* (New York: George Braziller, 1976); *Childhood* (London: Rex Collings, 1981).

7. Wole Soyinka, *Ake-The Years of My Childhood* (London: Rex Collings, 1981).

8. *Oro* is an all-male cult of the Yoruba associated with community discipline. Women are not to be seen in the street during the procession of Oro.

9. *Orisha* is a Yoruba name for divinities that operate at the delegation of God.

10. *Abosom* is the Akan name for these divinities.

11. *Nananom* (Ancestors) are both male and female, but those usually remembered have made significant contributions to their community in their lifetime.

12. The ordinary meaning of amandze is custom or tradition.

13. Kofi Antubam, *Ghana's Heritage of Culture* (Leipzig: Koehler and Amelang, 1963), p. 111.

14. The proverb observes the same phenomena in nature that Jesus observed—thistles do not produce grapes. Given this, why do women not produce human beings who exhibit a mothering attitude toward life?

15. The first published work of these feminist theologians is *The Will To Arise: Women, Tradition and the Church in Africa*, ed. Mercy Amba Oduyoye and Musimbi Kanyoro (Maryknoll, NY: Orbis Books, 1992). See also *Feminist Theology from the Third World: A Reader*, Ursula King, ed. (Maryknoll, NY: Orbis Books and London: SPCK, 1994) with selections by Bette Ekeya, Grace Eneme, Teresa Hinga, Betty Gordinden, and myself.

16. Rabiatu Ammah, Elizabeth Amoah, Rosemary Edet, Bette Ekeya, Musimbi Kanyoro, Bernadette Mbuy Beya, and Teresa Okure. Many of these African women theologians, including others, are contributors to *The Will To Arise*.

11

BLACK THEOLOGY OF LIBERATION

Simon S. Maimela

Black theology can be defined as a conscious and systematic theological reflection on black experience which is characterized by oppression and suffering in white racist societies in North America and South Africa. In other words, black theology, an aspect of a worldwide theological movement known as liberation theology, owes its origin to the unique experience of the people of color, especially of African descent, in white dominated societies where the people's blackness was taken and rationalized by white people as giving them enough reason to subject black people to the life of domination, exploitation, oppression, and humiliation. Hence, in both North America and South Africa, there has been and there exists a conscious or unconscious belief in the superiority of all white people, a superiority which entitles them to a position of political and economic power, dominance, and privilege in relation to black people, who were regarded as inherently inferior and doomed to servitude.

Black theology born out of the situation of black oppression and dehumanization is, therefore, directed against major social evils that the dominant white groups are perpetrating against black humanity. Black theology is characterized by its conscious decision to take a stand for black humanity over against white domination and oppression. This consciously accepted partisanship means that black theology attempts to be a critical reflection on the historical praxis in which the powerful white Christians dominate and oppress the powerless black Christians, on one hand. On the other, black theology represents an articulated form of black resistance to white power structure, hoping thereby to inspire and arm the oppressed blacks in their struggle for the liberating transformation of unjust racist social structures in which they live. In this paper I shall focus my attention mainly on the South African situation and the articulation of black theology.

Racism as a Theological Problem

The diversity of human races and their different cultural manifestations in themselves have not always been and need not be understood as problematic in the church when they are accepted as gifts that the Creator has endowed human beings for their mutual enrichment. This was certainly true in the early church, which was an ethnic and social admixture of different races that reflected the pluralism of the Hellenistic world. This healthy coexistence of different races in the church of Christ in which "there is neither Jew nor Greek, slave nor free, male nor female" (Gal. 3:28), because they are one in Jesus Christ, did not last for long, for many reasons. Among others, one need mention but two important ones. First, the church underwent a major transformation during the Constantinian era, when it reflected a change from being a scarcely tolerated and often persecuted minority missionary movement into an established, official institution with the power to determine life within its members as well as in society. Once the Emperor became a Christian, he began to assert his power on behalf of the church when he opened the entire society for Christianization (Driver 1986:29). In gratitude to Constantine, the church and its religious authorities were taken over and coopted by the ruling class, which expected them to construct a theology whose purpose was to advance and legitimate the cause and interests of the Roman empire (Maimela 1987:134).

Secondly, the collapse of the churches in North Africa and Asia Minor under the assault of Islam transformed the church into "the church of the white nations, of the Christian Occident and Orient" (Gollwitzer 1979:154), with dire consequences for the colored people of the world. With deep insights, Gollwitzer (1979:154) points out that this transformation of the church from its ethnic pluralism into a western, white church offered:

> the white people, endowed with the mobility and activity characteristic of the temperate zones and especially of that peculiar continent of Europe, an unheard of self-confidence which first proved itself in the struggle against Islam and in the crusades, but then reached out over the

entire globe in the age of great discoveries "empowering" the Europeans to regard all non-christian people as destined by God for domination and exploitation. So the coasts of Africa and India were plundered by the Portuguese. The Pope divided up the New World between the Spanish and the Portuguese. The Aztec and Inca peoples were destroyed in a manifold Auschwitz.

The upshot of what is being claimed here is that racial problems have their roots in the Constantinian takeover of the church and its subsequent Christianization of the white nations which, during the modern European colonial period, resulted in a theological self-understanding of the western world that equated Christianity with western culture. Concomitant with this was the belief that those who belonged to western Christianity were superior to non-christians who happened to be the people of color (Gollwitzer 1979:155). Once religious privilege of belonging to the church of Jesus Christ who is Savior and Lord of the universe had been transformed into the political, economic, and social privilege of God's chosen people who happened to be white, it was a matter of time before social structures were created through which white people would enforce white supremacy and thereby subject the people of color to white plunder, domination, exploitation, and oppression. It was during the European colonization of Africa, Asia, and Latin America that a colonial theology was developed to give religious sanction for slavery and socio-political and economic bondage to which people of color have been subjected in racist societies over many centuries up to the present (Gollwitzer 1979:156-157).

Therefore, in order not to speak to you on the problematic nature of racial divisions in general, I want now to focus attention on the South African racial situation, of which I speak as a product and victim, to illustrate how the Constantinian model of a triumphal church and state have worked hand in glove to create the racism from which we are still struggling to liberate ourselves. The problems of racial division were exacerbated by the fact that a white colonial tribe which wields all the political and economic power appropriated for itself the symbol of Israel in a sense that white people in South Africa were specially chosen by God for a mission in the world. Therefore, the whole group of white people *qua* people came to regard themselves as God's chosen race or anointed, called upon to govern and spread western civilization and Christianity even at the cost of fanatical persecutions of those who are regarded as unworthy human beings, the so-called heathens who happened to be the people of color.

Because the Apartheid system of white racial domination has its origin during the British rule in the seventeenth century and was merely perfected by the Afrikaners in 1948, it is important that we discuss the phases of its development.

In the first phase, it was the British imperialists who undergirded their colonial activities by understanding the British people as the elect of God who felt called upon to a mission history of bringing freedom to humanity. This mission was expressed in political and messianic terms whose best representative, Cecil Rhodes, declared that "only one race, 'his own,' was destined to help on God's work and fulfill His purpose in the world . . . and to bring nearer the reign of justice, liberty and peace" because they, as English people qua people, approached God's ideal type (cited by van Jaarsveld 1964:3-4).

Put simply, British imperialism was underpinned by the belief that they were a "new" Israel chosen to fulfill a divine mission, and more importantly that their election was determined by their racial and cultural superiority over those they were destined to rule. Concomitant with this was that the British people had a certain rightness to be elected to dominate the world, to spread the British civilization even at the cost of intolerable persecution of the "heathens" who must be made British at all costs or die at the hands of the anointed ones and with the approval this domesticated British "God" (Maimela 1987:8f, 30, 38). Commenting on the marriage between the throne and altar which enabled such a small island to rule over 500 million people during the height of its power, de Gruchy points out that there existed an inseparable relationship between God, the church, and the British Empire. As a consequence, de Gruchy (1977:45) goes on to say:

> Few, whether Anglicans or Non-conformists, apparently found anything incongruous about the Union Jack coexisting alongside the Cross and Altar, even when tattered and blood-spattered from encounters with the natives . . . in the service of God and Queen.

Of course, de Gruchy's perceptive observations refer to the brutal British rule that managed to bring both the Boers and blacks in South Africa to their knees by repressive forces, believing that the expansion of British imperialism and exploitation of the so-called inferior races were serving divine providential purposes of bringing the gospel and civilization to the "pagans" and uncivilized

Boers. In consequence, the God the British churches talked about was nothing but a fine and loyal "English" God who regarded the Crown and the British people as "his" anointed or chosen race called upon to govern and spread British civilization.

In the second stage, the Afrikaners coopted the Dutch Reformed churches to provide them with spiritual resources to meet the threat of British imperialism and the black majority who, through intermarriage, would dilute their white group identity. In the process an Afrikaner nationalism emerged and the church, wishing to have unquestioning loyalty and authority over the lives of its followers, was just too willing to wed itself to this Afrikaner nationalism. Just as the British had done before, the theology that was propounded by the Dutch Reformed church gave the Afrikaners a theological sense of being a chosen people with a mission, namely, to create a new "white" nation in dark Africa as a beacon of Christian civilization. The Afrikaner leaders became men of calling to fulfill God's will, and this was true from Piet Retief in the nineteenth century in his struggle against the British "Pharaohs" to Dr. Hendrik Verwoerd, the architect of Apartheid policy in the twentieth century in his struggle to prevent the black majority from engulfing his "volk" (van Jaarsveld 1977:17). Believing that part of their mission was to preserve the chosen white race in its pure form and, therefore, that it is against the divine will to be cast into a melting-pot through interracial marriage, a leading Afrikaner, Dr. Mansvelt, in 1892 reminded the white race that, "after their having opened the way for the spread of the Gospel and civilization, I do not believe that Providence has destined (the Afrikaner) to disappear from history without trace and to give it to others" (cited in van Jaarsveld 1977:22).

It is against the background of the Afrikaners' understanding of their divine calling that Apartheid was formulated and carried out. Theology was used to underpin this ideology when it was argued that God has sharply divided human races and the Afrikaner's calling was to help make this goal of the permanent separation of races attainable, thereby preventing the admixture of races which would destroy "western civilization" and the "God-given" identity of the white race. Rationalizing their subjugation and oppression of black people, the Afrikaners argued that they have been placed in Africa by God and commanded:

> to act as the guardian, master and spiritual leader to the black man. To do that the white man has to have at his command the authority needed to uplift, Christianize and evangelize the black man; the purpose is that

the black man who is still a child from the point of view of civilization, shall grow and develop in due course in his own area, with his own language according to his nature and traditions (van Jaarsveld 1977:25).

Carrying out the policies of Apartheid, which were believed to be in accordance with God's will, the Afrikaners could, for a long time, not understand why the entire world faulted them for what they were doing in service of God. Here again, as in the British imperialism, we are confronted with a triumphal white nationalism and triumphal white church—both of which have tried to create God in their own image, a God who is a loyal white-bearded Monarch who is giving "divine" tasks and missions only to white people, while at the same time this God is not bothered about the enormous suffering that the racial policy of Apartheid has brought black people.

Put somewhat differently, the racial divisions that South Africans have suffered over the years are a product of European cultural and religious triumphalism that has given rise to and feeds on the theology of glory, a theology which has to do with the "success motif" of Western Christendom which has forgotten its origin in the crucified Christ, by allowing Christianity to be transformed into a religion of the successful and the mighty who exercise power to determine life both in church and society. This theology of glory has encouraged South African whites to develop an attitude of priding themselves as worthier persons than the people of color by virtue of belonging to Western civilization and by being the elect of God to promote Christianity. Thus, unable to pass judgment on white humanity which has become proud and triumphant because of the alleged superiority of its cultural and educational achievements, the theology of glory has allowed itself to be used as an alibi for the justification of the concrete and unjust suffering of the people of color in a world dominated by whites solely because of their color.

Put somewhat differently, racial divisions have become a theological problem for the people of color simply because racism is not merely a racial prejudice or negative attitude toward a person whose color differs from one's own. Nor is racism merely a vague feeling of racial superiority in relation to other people. Rather racism is a social, political, economic, and cultural system of domination which white people employ to exclude the people of color on the basis of race for the purpose of subjugating them. It creates beliefs and myths about the cultural and biological superiority of the dominant racial group in order to justify the unequal distribution of resources between the dominant and the dominated groups (Boesak 1983:3). It exalts a particular biological characteristic to a universal principle determining what it means to be human. In other words, racial prejudices and stereotypes were developed in South Africa to rationalize the depersonalization and domination of black people; these stereotypes portrayed blacks as inherently inferior. This racial domination and the negation of blacks have their roots in the early history between Africans and colonialists in South Africa, when the former could not compete on equal terms militarily, economically, and scientifically. The Apartheid policy was thus a culmination of a long process of development. The black experience in white-dominated South Africa has been aptly described by Boesak (1976:26) when he writes:

> Blackness is a reality that embraces the totality of black existence. To paraphrase a central message of *The Message of the People of South Africa* (issued by the Theological Commission of the South African Council of churches in 1968): People's blackness dooms them to live the life of a second-class citizens. It determines who their friends may be, whom they can marry, what work they can do and that the work they eventually do is considered inferior to that of white people. Their blackness determines that if they do the same jobs as white people they get paid less. It not only determines what education they can get; it often means that they will get no education at all. . . . It determines where they can get medical treatment, if they are fortunate enough to live in an area where they will not die of malnutrition and neglect before they reach the age of five. It determines their whole life, every single day. . . . To be black in South Africa means to be classified as a "non-white:" a non-person, less than white and, therefore, less than human.

Boesak (1976:57) goes on to say that black experience should be understood as a by-product of white power structure, and notes that:

> The "white power structure," far from being just a term, represents a reality Blacks encounter every day. It represents the economic, political, cultural, religious, and psychological forces which confine the realities of Black existence. Concretely, for Black South Africans the white power structure is manifested in apartheid. . . . The White power structure represents full control of Whites over the instruments of power and over the major resources of the country. It represents an unending spiral of violence inherent in the system of apartheid. It is this structure which

ensures that the future of Black children is as uncertain as the present is for their parents.

Put somewhat differently, in racist societies, the color of one's skin and race become salvation principles, determining whether a person is declared justified or unjustified to enjoy certain economic, political, and cultural rights and privileges. Because color and race are salvation principles, it is not enough to be baptized after confessing Jesus Christ as Lord and Savior. Rather, a person is expected to possess yet another attribute, which in the nature of the case must be reserved only for a select few. Hence, Apartheid was designed and practiced in such a way that the people of color would be continually reminded that they are unworthy persons, regardless of whether or not they are Christians, simply because they do not possess that extra attribute — white skin. The consequence of elevating the genetic factors of race into the criterion of determining the worthy and unworthy, the superior and inferior, has been devastating for the people of color, who were made to feel inadequate. Condemning the negative effects of the apartheid system on the blacks, Archbishop Desmond Tutu (1983:46-47), with deep insight, writes:

Apartheid is intrinsically and irredeemably evil. For my part, its most vicious, indeed, its most blasphemous aspect, is not the great suffering it causes its victims, but that it can make a child of God doubt that he is a child of God. For that alone, it deserves to be condemned as a heresy. Real peace and security will come to our beloved land only when Apartheid has been dismantled.

At the same time, Apartheid system taught whites, regardless of whether or not they are Christians, that they deserve a particular life-style and enormous political and economic privileges are due to them by some natural right: that is, by virtue of their right color.

In the light of this white racial domination and dehumanization of the people of color in South Africa, one would have expected the church and its theologians to be prophetic in its denunciation of white racial prejudices, injustice, and oppression. Regrettably, however, theology in South Africa has largely been done by white middle-class theologians and some privileged black priests who are comfortably situated in the society. The result has been the development of a colonial theology which, wittingly or unwittingly, has taken a preferential option for the powerful in order to serve the socio-economic and political interests of white dominant society. This colonial theology could justifiably be characterized as the enemy of the oppressed black people, for the distinguishing feature of this colonial theology lies in the fact that it taught and continues to teach an authoritarian God who, as the Supreme Ruler of the universe, establishes racial classes in every society. Thus, this God insists that there will always be the rich white people and poor black people in the society, because this colonial and capitalist God accepts poverty as part of the divine will for the underdogs, most particularly for people of color. To ensure that this situation of unequal distribution of material resources remains unchanged, white colonial theology taught and continues to teach that God has established law and order in every society in favor of white folks and demands obedience to the authority of both the church and state (Araya 1987:27-29; Nelson-Pallmeyer 1986:79; Kairos Document 1985:3-7). This attempted theological justification of the glaring unequal distribution of socio-economic and political rights and privileges between different classes in white-dominated societies led the astute politician Napoleon to remark rather perceptively about the ideological function of religion, when he wrote:

> As far as I am concerned, I do not see in religion the mystery of the incarnation but the mystery of social order: it links the idea of inequality to heaven which prevents the right person from being murdered by the poor. How can there be order in the state without religion? Society cannot exist without inequality of fortunes and the inequality of fortunes could not subsist without religion. Whenever a half-starved person is near another who is glutted, it is impossible to reconcile the difference if there is not an authority to say to him: "God wills it so, it is necessary that there be rich and poor in the world, but afterwards in eternity there will be a different distribution" (cited in Carter 1981:37).

The Emergence of Black Theology

It is against this painful background of white racial oppression and dehumanization of the black personhood as well as attempts by colonial theologians to justify white domination and privileges that black theology was born as a theological protest against white inhumanity to black people. It is a theology which aims at reflecting on the black experience under white domination and exploitation in the light of the gospel. It was as blacks began to reread the Bible in the light of their social experience in the so-called Christian country that they discovered there is a fundamental contradiction between what the Bible proclaims and the message their white master taught them. Beginning with their concrete experience of oppression and suffering in a white-dominated society where the Christian faith is being used as an oppressive instrument legitimizing the socio-economic and political interests of white people, black Christians could not help but become suspicious not only about the situation of injustice and oppression under which they suffer but also about white theologies which unashamedly gave tacit support to the privileged status of white people in relation to the people of color. Commenting on the coaptation of theology by white dominant classes to give religious sanction to the socio-political and economic bondage to which the people of color are subject, James Cone (1970:22; also see Allan Boesak 1976:30-36, 107-116), with deep insight, observes:

> White theology has not been involved in the struggle for black liberation. It has been basically a theology of the white oppressors, giving religious sanction to the genocide of Indians and the enslavement of black people. From the very beginning to the present day American white theological thought has been "patriotic," either by defining the theological task independently from black suffering (the liberal northern approach) or by defining Christianity as compatible with racism (the conservative southern approach). In both cases, theology becomes the servant of the state, and that can only mean death to black people.

It is this hermeneutics of suspicion, namely, that in all human societies "anything and everything involving ideas, including theology, is intimately bound up with the existing social situation in at least an unconscious way" (Segundo 1976:8), that has helped black Christians begin the task of unmasking the reality of oppression and the ideological mechanisms that underpin and morally justify the social forces that foster and perpetuate the domination of people of color. According to Segundo (1976:28), one of those mechanisms is the ideology which claims to be color-blind and yet allows white Christians to construct the entire social edifice in which the causes of the oppressed people's suffering is not even mentioned or discussed.

It is against this black experience of being oppressed by white Christians that black Christians began to relate their own experiences of dehumanization to the biblical message of the God of love proclaimed in the Scriptures, asking questions such as: Why did God create me black? Why does God allow white Christians to oppress black people, whom God also loves, simply because of their color? What does God say, and what is God willing to do about this situation of oppression? As they wrestled with these existential questions, it dawned on the believing blacks that the reality of the politics of white domination they see and experience in their lives differed from what they found in the Bible. In the Bible, God is not revealed as a category to be manipulated for the maintenance of the privileged status quo of white domination. Rather God is portrayed there as the liberator God who wages a battle against injustice and human misery in order to establish justice and freedom for the oppressed (Cone 1970:4-5, 8-11, 122-124; also see Araya 1987:27; Boesak 1976:16-25; Maimela 1987:92-97, 106-108, 116-120, 665-73; Mofokeng 1983:24-108, 160-185, 238-263; Mofokeng 1987:5-16).

Black theologians find it significant that the God of the Exodus is portrayed as the God of mercy, who condescended from his or her throne of justice not to any human situation but to the dungeon of slavery in which the oppressed slaves were suffering in order to bring them out and create a new people (Ex. 3:7). The same God continued to express divine concern for the underdogs by calling and sending the Hebrew prophets to denounce injustice and exploitation perpetrated by the powerful against the powerless widows and orphans. God's advocacy for the powerless and oppressed was brought to new heights in the coming of Jesus, in and through whom God chose to be born by poor parents, to live as a poor and oppressed human being who suffered and was crucified as the rejected outcast in order to give the oppressed poor and the downtrodden new life and hope. According to black theologians, the incarnation is the event which clearly demonstrates that the biblical God is the god who takes the side of the oppressed and the defenseless, the outcasts, the excluded, and the despised. Archbishop Tutu puts it eloquently this way:

> In the process of saving the world, of establishing His Kingdom, God, our God demonstrated that He was no neutral God, but a thoroughly biased God who was forever taking the side of the oppressed, of the weak, of the exploited, of the hungry and homeless. Of the refugees, of the scum of society . . . So my dear friends we celebrate, worship and adore God, the biased God, He who is not neutral, the God who always takes sides (cited in Maimela 1986:46).

Agreeing with Archbishop Tutu, black theologians call every theologian to become candid and to put his or her cards on the table and declare on which side of the liberation struggle he or she stands, thereby declaring whose socio-economic and political interests his or her theology is serving. It is for this reason that they challenge the church to take a preferential option for the poor and oppressed in their struggle for liberation. In support of their challenge, they point out that this divine preferential option for the poor and the oppressed is central to the biblical message, running through the pages of both the Old and New Testaments (see Ps. 107:4-6, 113:7, 118:7, 140:12, 146:7-9; Prov. 14:31, 22:22-23; Is. 25:4; Mt. 5:3ff; Lk 1:53, 4:18-19, 6:17, 20-22).

The challenge that black theology poses to the church—that it should take a preferential option for the oppressed and poor black masses, thereby becoming the advocate and defender of the powerless—has invoked great hostility from both conservative and liberal white theologians. They argue that the church cannot take a preferential option for the oppressed because this would mean that God is now portrayed as against the rich and dominant Christians. Bound by the ideology of justification by faith through grace, white theologians resist any meaningful discussion of God in relation to the problems of racial oppression and suffering of the people of color. In their view, such a discussion would necessarily lead to the problem of work righteousness, namely that black oppression and poverty would be sacralized and turned into virtues on the basis of which the oppressed black masses could demand special favor from God. Against this view, white theologians are quick to add that all people, be they white or black, are saved by God's grace and not by good works and, therefore, questions of wealth and poverty, of white oppressor and oppressed blacks, are of little importance to theological discourse.

What is often missed by the critics of black theology is that what is at stake is not whether or not the oppressed are sinners or should be favored by God. Rather black theology of liberation tries to witness to the transcendental and universal love of God, the love which unconditionally accepts the unacceptable, the rejected and humiliated black humanity (Rm. 5:6-8). This divine love demonstrates its historical efficacy by seeking the dominated and marginalized people, especially the people of color in racist societies, simply because they are oppressed and defenseless before the cruel reality of historical structures of injustice that threaten to destroy the life of millions of dehumanized black people.

In order to overcome this threat, black theology argues that it is necessary to portray God as one who assumes the role of an advocate for the cause of the oppressed people regardless of the moral and personal dispositions of the downtrodden people. Rather God chooses to be their advocate simply because the oppressed people need God's defense. Therefore, what is at stake here is not the poor's merit, virtue, or moral worthiness on account of which the oppressed black masses might solicit God's acceptance. It is the justice of God's kingdom which demands that the oppressed people must have life in all its fullness. For that to happen, God, out of love and mercy, assumes the role of being the advocate by making the cause of the defenseless and oppressed people God's own cause. Regarding this divine advocacy for the poor, one of the foremost theologians of the twentieth century who cannot be accused of one-sided partisanship for the poor, Karl Barth, has this to say about God's preferential option for the poor and the underdogs.

> God always takes His stand unconditionally and passionately on this side and on this side alone: against the lofty and on behalf of the lowly; against those who already enjoy right and privilege and on behalf of those who are denied it and deprived of it (cited in Araya 1987:44).

To appreciate the significance of what is being suggested here, it is important to note that wealth and poverty which are consequences of unequal distribution of resources are directly related to that fundamental sin of a breach of fellowship between humans and God (Gn. 3). After this tragic rapture, the Book of Genesis tells us how the consequences of sin began to be incarnated between and among human beings, manifesting themselves through destructive social relationships (Gn. 4). In order to confront and overcome this sinful social condition, God steps in as the God of the oppressed and defenseless. In other words, God's advocacy for the poor and downtrodden should be understood as a precondition for the liberation of both white oppressor and oppressed blacks. God thus assumes the role of an advocate of the underdogs in order to become the liberator of the dominant whites, who must be liberated from the wealth, power, and oppressive tendencies which hold them in bondage, thus preventing them from becoming partners with the oppressed blacks in their struggle against social consequences of sin in order to build up the values of the kingdom of God together and alongside God. In taking the cause of the oppressed black people, God thus declares that the divine self is no longer prepared to put up with the social situation in which black people are oppressed and humiliated simply because they are black (Maimela 1986:44-50; Maimela 1987:96-97, 106-108, 115-120). Consequently, black theologians argue that a just God liberated the people of Israel not only from spiritual sins and guilt but also from oppressive socio-economic and political deprivation in Egypt, God will liberate the oppressed black people not only from their personal sins and guilt but also from historical structures of evil, exploitation, and oppression which have been perpetrated by white power structures.

Thus, drawing their inspiration from a biblical theological vision which portrays God as the liberator of the oppressed and powerless slaves, black theology attempts to provide the struggling black masses with alternative theological models (visions) with which to both resist the extreme demands of white racial oppression and work for the liberation of all people. In so doing, it encourages and empowers the oppressed people, especially the people of color, in South Africa, to become the subjects of their own liberation and creators of just and humane social structures so that freedom, justice, and human rights might become the common property of the majority of the human family.

References

Araya, Victorio, *God of the Poor* (Maryknoll, NY: Orbis Books, 1987).

Boesak, Allan, "He Made Us All, But . . . ," in John De Gruchy and Charles Villa-Vicencio, eds., *Apartheid Is a Heresy* (Grand Rapids, MI: Eerdmans, 1983).

Boesak, Allan, *Farewell to Innocence* (Maryknoll, NY: Orbis Books, 1976).

Carter, Linberg, "Through a Glass Darkly: A History of the Church's Vision of the Poor and Poverty," in *Ecumenical Review* 33 (1981).

Cone, James, 1970, *A Black Theology of Liberation* (Philadelphia: J.B. Lippincott & Co.; reprinted, Maryknoll, NY: Orbis Books, 1990).

De Grucy, John W., "English-Speaking South African and Civil Religion," in *Journal of Theology for Southern Africa* 19 (June 1977).

Driver, John., *Understanding the Atonement for the Mission of the Church* (Scottdale, PA: Herald Press, 1986).

Gollwitzer, Helmut, "Why Black Theology" in Gayraud S. Wilmore and James H. Cone, eds., *Black Theology: A Documentary History, 1966-1979* (Maryknoll, NY: Orbis Books, 1979).

The Kairos Document (Johannesburg: Skotaville Publishers, 1985).

Maimela, Simon S., "Archbishop Desmond Tutu: A Revolutionary Political Priest or a Man of Peace?" in Buti Tlhagale and Itumeleng Mosala, eds., *Hammering Swords into Ploughshares* (Grand Rapids, MI: Eerdmans, 1986).

Maimela, Simon S., *Proclaim Freedom to My People* (Johannesburg: Skotaville Publishers, 1987).

Mofokeng, T. A., *The Crucified among the Crossbearers* (Kampen: Kok, 1983).

Mofokeng, T. A., "A Black Christology: A New Beginning," in *Journal of Black Theology in South Africa* 1 (May 1987).

Nelson-Pallmeyer, Jack, *The Politics of Compassion* (Maryknoll, NY: Orbis Books, 1986).

Segundo, Juan Luis, *The Liberation of Theology* (Maryknoll, NY: Orbis Books, 1976).

Tutu, Desmond, 1983, "Apartheid and Christianity," in John De Gruchy and Charles Villa-Vicencio, eds., *Apartheid Is a Heresy* (Grand Rapids, MI: Eerdmans, 1983).

Van Jaarsveld, F. A., *The Afrikaner's Interpretation of South African History* (Cape Town: Simondium Publishers, 1964).

Van Jaarsveld, F. A., "The Afrikaner's Idea of His Calling and Mission," in *Journal of Theology for Southern Africa* 19 (June 1977).

SELECTED BIBLIOGRAPHY OF AFRICAN THEOLOGY

Appiah-Kubi, Kofi, and Sergio Torres, eds. *African Theology En Route* (Maryknoll, NY: Orbis Books, 1979). Papers from the Pan-African Conference of Third World Theologians (1977) in Accra, Ghana. Significant early work of African theologians.

Bimwenyi, O. *Discours théologique négro-Africain: Problème de fondements* (Paris: Présence Africaine, 1981). Significant; how the African people with their culture and spiritual traditions encounter Christianity (not available in English).

Boesak, Allan A. *Farewell to Innocence: A Socio-Ethical Study of Black Theology and Power* (Maryknoll, NY: Orbis Books, 1976; London: Mowbray, 1977). Relates the black South African experience to liberation movements and theologies worldwide.

Bujo, Bénézet. *African Theology in Its Social Context* (Maryknoll, NY: Orbis Books, 1992). With Jesus identified as "Ancestor," Bujo defines distinctively African roles for the church, clergy, and lay people.

Cabral, Amilcar. *Return to the Source: Selected Speeches of Amilcar Cabral* (New York: Monthly Review Press, 1974) and *Unity and Struggle: Speeches and Writings* (New York: Monthly Review Press, 1979). Early on, Cabral emphasized the importance of African culture and connected political liberation with cultural liberation.

Cone, James H. *A Black Theology of Liberation*, 2nd ed. (Maryknoll, NY: Orbis Books, 1990). First published in 1970, a systematic expression of the meaning of black religion and an indictment of white theology and society.

Cutrufelli, Maria Rosa. *Women of Africa: Roots of Oppression* (London: Zed Press, 1983). The roles and customs of women in traditional African society.

De Gruchy, John, and Charles Villa-Vicencio, eds. *Apartheid Is a Heresy* (Grand Rapids, MI: Eerdmans, 1983). A collection of the liberation struggle against apartheid in South Africa.

Des Prêtres noirs s'interrogent (Black Priests Wonder) (Paris: Présence Africaine, 1956; 2nd ed., Paris: Cerf, 1957). The first explicit manifestation of a distinctively African theology.

Dickson, Kwesi. *Uncompleted Mission: Christianity and Exclusivism* (Maryknoll, NY: Orbis Books, 1991). How Christianity has practiced exclusivism from the Old Testament to Africa today.

Eboussi, Boulaga, F. *Christianity without Fetishes: An African Critique and Recapture of Christianity* (Maryknoll, NY: Orbis Books, 1984). A penetrating analysis of the need for inculturation.

Éla, Jean-Marc. *African Cry* (Maryknoll, NY: Orbis Books, 1986). To become truly African, the church must reject colonial structures with Western culture and symbols.

————. *My Faith as an African* (Maryknoll, NY: Orbis Books; London: Geoffrey Chapman, 1988). A call to care for the impoverished of Africa and to allow them to manifest their faith in an African way.

Fabella, Virginia, and Mercy Oduyoye, eds. *With Passion and Compassion: Third World Women Doing Theology* (Maryknoll, NY: Orbis Books, 1988). The first third of the book contains important essays by African women theologians.

Fanon, Frantz. *The Wretched of the Earth* (New York: Grove Weidenfeld, 1963). An early voice identifying the anthropological poverty that comes from colonialism and the need to revolt—even violently—against it.

Hastings, Adrian. *African Catholicism: Essays in Discovery* (Philadelphia: Trinity Press International; London: SCM Press, 1989).

Hebga, Meinrad, ed. *Personalité africaine et catholicisme* (Paris: Présence Africaine, 1963). An assertion that the African "personality" should be a constitutive element of the Catholic church in Africa (not available in English).

_____. *Émancipation d'églises sous tutelle* (Paris: Présence Africaine, 1976). An early call for African churches to free themselves from western domination (not available in English).

Hickey, Raymond, ed. *Modern Missionary Documents and Africa (Issued by Popes and Roman Synods)* (Dublin: Dominican Publications, 1982). Several significant documents on the church in Africa, including *Africae Terrarum* of Paul VI.

Hopkins, Dwight N. *Black Theology USA and South Africa: Politics, Culture, and Liberation* (Maryknoll, NY: Orbis Books, 1989). An exploration of the relationship between black theology in South Africa and North America.

The Kairos Document: Challenge to the Church (New York: Theology in Global Context Association; Grand Rapids: Eerdmans; London, CIIR, 1986). One of the most significant documents. A theological reflection on the political crisis of apartheid in South Africa.

Kane, Cheikh Hamidou. *Ambiguous Adventure* (London: Heinemann, 1972; New York: Walker & Co., 1963). A novel, the encounter between western Christianity and African culture.

Kretzschmar, Louise. *The Voice of Black Theology in South Africa* (Johannesburg: Ravan Press, 1986). The interrelationship between religion and politics in South Africa.

Maimela, Simon, and Dwight Hopkins, eds. *We Are One Voice: Black Theology in the USA and South Africa* (Johannesburg: Skotaville Publishers, 1989). The commonalities of black theology from two different locations.

Martey, Emmanuel. *African Theology: Inculturation and Liberation* (Maryknoll, NY: Orbis Books, 1993). An excellent overview of African theology, analyzing and comparing the roots of both inculturationists and liberationists. Extensive bibliography.

Mbiti, John. *African Religions and Philosophy* (New York: Doubleday, 1970; Oxford: Oxford University Press, 1990, 2nd ed.). Comprehensive discussion of African traditional religion and philosophy, including divine nature, human nature, values, and so forth.

_____. *New Testament Eschatology in an African Background* (Oxford: Oxford University Press, 1971). Themes of eschatology as they are expressed in African traditional religion.

Milingo, E. *The World in Between: Christian Healing and the Struggle for Spiritual Survival* (Maryknoll, NY: Orbis Books, 1984). The importance of the ministry of healing in the African church.

Mosala, Itumeleng J., and B. Tlhagale, eds. *The Unquestionable Right to Be Free* (Maryknoll, NY: Orbis Books, 1986). Expressions of black theology in South Africa from the Institute of Contextual Theology.

Mulago, Vincent. *Un Visage africain du christianisme* (Paris: Présence Africaine, 1965). An early call for authentic inculturation.

Mveng, Engelbert. *L'Afrique dans l'Église: paroles d'un croyant* (Paris: L'Harmattan, 1985). The importance of inculturation throughout the African church, including spirituality and biblical studies. An early call for an African Council.

Nkrumah, Kwame. *I Speak of Freedom: A Statement of African Ideology* (New York: Frederick A. Praeger, 1961). One of the most significant spokespersons of African cultural and political independence.

Nolan, Albert. *God in South Africa: The Challenge of the Gospel* (Grand Rapids, MI: Eerdmans; London: CIIR, 1988). The challenge of the gospel as good news to the poor and oppressed of South Africa.

Oduyoye, Mercy. *Hearing and Knowing: Theological Reflections on Christianity in Africa* (Maryknoll, NY: Orbis Books, 1986). A prominent African woman theologian reflects on Christianity's need to tap traditional African resources.

_____, and Musimbi Kanyoro, eds. *The Will To Arise: Women, Tradition, and the Church in Africa* (Maryknoll, NY: Orbis Books, 1992). Significant essays by African women on attitudes toward culture, rites of passage, daily life, marriage and widowhood, and the role of women in culture and religion.

Olupona, Jacob K. *African Traditional Religions in Contemporary Society* (New York: Paragon House, 1991). A collection of essays on African traditional religions, with emphasis on those of West Africa, in particular the Yoruba.

Parratt, John, ed. *A Reader in African Christian Theology* (London: SPCK, 1987). Essays on theological method, doctrine, and the role of the church in the world.

Sanneh, Lamin. *Translating the Message: The Missionary Impact on Culture* (Maryknoll, NY: Orbis Books, 1989). A critical comprehensive assessment of the history of Christian missions in Africa.

Schreiter, Robert, ed. *Faces of Jesus in Africa* (Maryknoll, NY: Orbis Books; London: SCM Press, 1991). One of the most important recent books; ten significant essays on christology by well-known African theologians who use different rubrics.

Shorter, Aylward. *Toward a Theology of Inculturation* (Maryknoll, NY: Orbis Books; London: Geoffrey Chapman, 1988). A foundational work on the relationship between inculturation and theology.

_____. *The Church in the African City* (Maryknoll, NY: Orbis Books; London: Geoffrey Chapman, 1991). How the church in Africa is challenged by poverty, urbanization, unemployment, western culture, and AIDS.

Soyinka, Wole. *Myth, Literature and the African World* (Cambridge: Cambridge University Press, 1976). An important book on the role of African culture by one of Africa's leading authors and intellectuals.

Tempels, Placide. *La Philosophie bantoue* (Paris: Présence Africaine, 1948). One of the first publications to stimulate theological debate; a description of African traditional philosophy in terms of ontology, psychology, and ethics.

Villa-Vicencio, Charles, ed. *Theology and Violence: The South African Debate* (Grand Rapids, MI: Eerdmans, 1988). Essays from South Africa presenting the history of the liberation movement and problems of violence and nonviolence.

Wilmore, Gayraud S., and James H. Cone, eds. *Black Theology: A Documentary History, 1966-1979* (Maryknoll, NY: Orbis Books, 1979). The most important statements of black theology.

CONTRIBUTORS

Alphonse Ngindu Mushete, a Catholic theologian from Zaire, teaches at the Faculté de Théologie in Kinshasa, Zaire.

John S. Mbiti, an Anglican theologian from Kenya, is presently director of the Ecumenical Institute at Bossey, Switzerland.

Justin S. Ukpong, CSSp, a Catholic Nigerian theologian, is deputy rector of the Catholic Institute of West Africa in Port Harcourt, Nigeria, where he teaches New Testament and African theology.

Charles Nyamiti, a Catholic theologian from Tanzania, is professor of dogmatic theology at the Catholic Higher Institute of East Africa in Nairobi, Kenya.

François Kabasele Lumbala, a Catholic theologian from Zaire, is professor of liturgy at the Faculté de Théologie in Kanshasa, Zaire.

Elochukwu E. Uzukwu, CSSp, a Catholic theologian from Nigeria, is a member of the faculty at the Spiritan International School of Theology in Enugu, Nigeria.

Patrick-Augustin Kalilombe, M.Afr., a theologian from Malawi, was bishop of the diocese of Lilongwe, Malawi. He is presently director of the Center for Black and White Christian Partnership at Selly Oak Colleges, Birmingham, England.

Jean-Marc Éla, a Catholic theologian from Cameroon, teaches at the University of Yaoundé, Cameroon.

Engelbert Mveng, S.J., theologian, poet, and artist, is director of the Department of History at the University of Yaoundé, Cameroon.

Mercy Amba Oduyoye, a Ghanaian theologian, is currently the deputy secretary general of the World Council of Churches.

Simon Maimela, a Protestant theologian from South Africa, teaches in the Department of Systematic Theology at the University of South Africa, Pretoria.

INDEX